Policing a Safe, Just and Tolerant Society

AN INTERNATIONAL MODEL

Peter Villiers joined the Police Staff College at Bramshill in 1986 and concluded his career there as Head of Human Rights with the publication of this volume. He is now a consultant and adviser both nationally and internationally on policing and other matters. He is the author of a range of publications on policing, ethics, human rights and leadership. He served in the army from 1971 to 1978 in Northern Ireland, Cyprus and Hong Kong and holds degrees from the Universities of Essex and Lancaster.

Dr Robert Adlam read psychology with zoology at Aberdeen University. In 1976 he joined the directing staff at Bramshill Police Staff College, where he spent 25 years developing the current and future leadership of the police service. During his association with Bramshill he published numerous articles on police psychology, leadership and reform. His further qualifications include an MA in management from Lancaster University in 1986, a diploma in facilitation styles and humanistic psychology from Surrey University in 1988, and a Ph.D. in police ethics from Surrey University in 2000. He now heads the independent think tank Ultraviolet.

Robert Adlam and Peter Villiers also edited the acclaimed *Police Leadership in the Twenty-first Century: Philosophy, Doctrine and Developments* (Waterside Press, 2003).

Policing a Safe, Just and Tolerant Society

AN INTERNATIONAL MODEL

Edited by Peter Villiers and Robert Adlam

Published 2004 by
WATERSIDE PRESS
Domum Road
Winchester SO23 9NN
United Kingdom

Telephone: 01962 855567
E-mail: enquiries@watersidepress.co.uk
Online catalogue and bookstore: www.watersidepress.co.uk

ISBN 1 904380 09 3

Catalogue-In-Publication Data: A catalogue record for this book can be obtained from the British Library

Printing and binding: Antony Rowe Ltd, Chippenham

Cover design: Waterside Press

Disclaimer *Policing a Safe, Just and Tolerant Society* is the work of the editors and individual contributors and represents their thoughts alone rather than the viewpoint of the Home Office or any other organization or body, official or otherwise.

Policing a Safe, Just and Tolerant Society

AN INTERNATIONAL MODEL

Edited by

Peter Villiers
Robert Adlam

WATERSIDE PRESS

Dedication

The Police Staff College for England and Wales was set up in 1948 to develop the leadership of the British Police Service. This book is dedicated to those police officers who continue to respect its ideals.

Acknowledgements

We are deeply indebted to the staff of the Department of Law, Criminal Justice Administration and Police Science of the John Jay College of Criminal Justice of the City University of New York for the value of their contribution to this work. We wish to acknowledge the scholarship and professional integrity of all our contributors and their dedication to the unceasing task of improving the quality of policing.

As always, we cannot let this occasion pass without acknowledging the outstanding service we have received from the staff of the National Police Library at Bramshill in Hampshire, who have been consistently diligent, friendly, and immensely helpful.

Finally, we must record our debt of gratitude to our publisher, Bryan Gibson of Waterside Press and his editor, Jane Green. He is a man of vision and enterprise.

Policing a Safe, Just and Tolerant Society

CONTENTS

CHAPTER

Contributors (in alphabetical order)

Sir David Calvert-Smith Q.C. read classics and then law at Cambridge before becoming a barrister and later taking silk. He was Treasury Counsel at the Central Criminal Court (The Old Bailey) for eleven years before becoming Director of Public Prosecutions in 1998. He retired from that position in 2003.

David Canter was Professor of Psychology at the University of Surrey for ten years, where he founded the MSc. course in Investigative Psychology. He is now Professor of Psychology at the University of Liverpool and a police consultant. He is a Fellow of the British Psychological Society and a member of its Forensic Division and a Chartered Forensic Psychologist. He has published 20 books and over 150 papers in learned journals and has lectured around the world on various aspects of scientific psychology. His publication, *Criminal Shadows* (1995), won the Golden Dagger Award for crime non-fiction and its US equivalent an Anthony Award.

Edwin J Delattre is Dean *Emeritus* of Boston University's School of Education, Professor of Education and Resident Scholar in the Center for School Improvement, and Professor of Philosophy in the College of Arts and Sciences. He is an adjunct scholar of the American Enterprise Institute for Public Policy Research in Washington, DC, and President *Emeritus* of St. John's College, Annapolis, MD, and Santa Fe, NM. Dr Delattre has served on the boards of many institutions, professional organizations and government agencies. He is a frequent lecturer at the FBI Academy at Quantico, Virginia, and at police academies and law enforcement seminars and conferences worldwide. Dr Delattre is the author of *Education and the Public Trust* (1988: 2nd edition, 1992) and *Character and Cops: Ethics in Policing* (1989: 4th edition, 2002).

Superintendent Garry Elliott joined the Metropolitan Police Service with a degree in physics in 1974, to which he later added an MBA, and has pursued his career as an operational police officer, force strategic planner and member of the directing staff at Bramshill Police College and currently for the National Police Leadership Centre of the Central Police Training and Development Authority with equal interest and commitment.

William C Heffernan is Professor of Law at John Jay College of Criminal Justice and the Graduate Center, City University of New York. He is also an editor of *Criminal Justice Ethics*. His publications on privacy law have appeared in the *Journal of Criminal Law and Criminology*, the *Georgetown Law Journal*, and the *Wisconsin Law Review* as well as in many other law journals.

John Kleinig is Director of the Institute for Criminal Justice Ethics, Editor of *Criminal Justice Ethics* and Professor of Philosophy in the Department of Law and Police Science at John Jay College of Criminal Justice and in the PhD Programs in Philosophy and Criminal Justice at The Graduate Center, City University, New York. In addition, he is Professorial Fellow in Criminal Justice Ethics in the Centre for Applied Philosophy and Public Ethics at Charles Sturt University, Canberra, Australia. His current projects include books on loyalty and the relations of means and ends in policing, as well as edited collections on jury ethics and correctional ethics. His recent publications include: *The Ethics of Policing* (1996); *Handled with Discretion: Ethical Issues in Police Decision Making* (1996; ed.); *From Social Justice to Criminal Justice: Poverty and the Administration of Criminal Law* (2000; edited with William C. Heffernan); and *Discretion, Community, and Correctional Ethics* (2001; edited with Margaret Leland Smith).

Satish Kumar is the Programme Director of the Schumacher College for Intermediate Technology at Dartington Hall, South Devon and editor of *Resurgence*. His publications include *No Destination* (1992) and *You Are, Therefore I Am* (2002). Satish Kumar lectures and communicates on 'deep ecology' and non-violence throughout the world.

Alasdair MacIntyre began his academic career in the UK and is currently Research Professor of Philosophy, University of Notre Dame, Indiana, USA. Professor MacIntyre is a world-renowned moral philosopher. His many publications include *A Short History of Ethics* (1998) and his more recent books include *After Virtue* (1981), *Three Rival Versions of Moral Enquiry* (1990) and *Dependent Rational Animals* (1999).

The Reverend James McKinney read mathematics at Cambridge University before studying theology and being ordained. He served as Chaplain to the Police Staff College at Bramshill in Hampshire on the appointment of the Bishop of Winchester and has contributed greatly to both its spiritual and educational needs. He is now a parish priest in London.

Seumas Miller is Professor of Social Philosophy and Director of the Centre for Applied Philosophy and Public Ethics (an Australian Research Council funded Special Research Centre) at Charles Sturt University, Canberra, Australia. He is the author of numerous academic articles in professional and applied ethics. These include: *Social Action: A Teleological Account* (CUP, 2001); *Police Ethics* (with John Blackler and Andrew Alexandra, Allen and Unwin, 1997); *Corruption and Anti-Corruption: A Study in Applied Philosophy* (with Peter Roberts and Edward Spence, Prentice Hall, 2004); and *Ethical Issues in Policing: Contemporary Problems and Perspectives* (with John Blackler, Ashgate, 2003).

Milan Pagon is the Dean and Professor of Police Administration and Management at the Faculty of Police and Security Studies, University of Maribor, and Professor of Organizational Behavior at the Faculty of Organizational Sciences, University of Maribor, Slovenia. He received his Sc.D. from the University of Maribor, and his Ph.D. from the University of Arkansas, Fayetteville, USA. His current research interests include police stress, corruption and deviance, and comparative aspects of policing.

Robert Panzarella M.A., Ph.D. (Psychology) is Professor of Police Science at John Jay College of Criminal Justice, New York. He was Bramshill exchange Professor in 1986 and again in 1999. He has provided training and consultation for many police and fire departments. His research and publications have encompassed personnel, managerial and tactical studies of the military, police and fire services. Professor Panzarella now offers his courses online over the Internet, including a virtual seminar on classic works in criminology, legal studies, policing and corrections in the context of the history of ideas.

Neil Richards B.Sc. (Econ), M. Phil., M. Ed., is a Scientific Expert on Police Ethics in the Council of Europe. He was formerly Head of the Police Leadership Faculty, National Police Training, Bramshill, UK where he taught ethics for many years and was instrumental in creating and directing the Chief Police Officers' Development Programme.

Robert R Sullivan is Professor of Criminal Justice at John Jay College of Criminal Justice, New York and a prolific author on political and legal philosophy. He was John Jay exchange scholar at Bramshill, UK in 2003.

Preface Conor Gearty

Slogans are not always wrong merely because they are slogans. In this collection of essays Peter Villiers and Robert Adlam take as their focus the Home Office declaration that its mission is to build 'a safe, just and tolerant society'. Already co-authors of the excellent book *Police Leadership in the Twenty-first Century* (2003), Villiers and Adlam are ideally placed to subject this slogan to critical scrutiny from a policing perspective, which they and their fellow contributors do to great effect in this fine collection of essays.

It is '*a* safe, just and tolerant society' that the book is concerned with—the editors and contributors have rightly taken an international perspective, albeit one rooted in a strong sense of respect for place, for particular history and for local culture. The reader will find in these pages an approach to policing that, though it may originate in critical thinking in Britain and the US, goes far beyond both jurisdictions in its implications and application. Such breadth is especially to be welcomed in this age of increased global co-operation in policing. The police officer, wherever he or she might be in the world, should wear the badge of virtue as well as of authority, and a great strength of this book is that it explains what this means while also showing that it is possible.

The focus of the Home Office mission statement captures the best features of our effort to organize our security as best we can on this small planet of ours, a project all too often subverted by anxieties about soaring crime rates on the one hand and abuse of state power on the other. The just society is one in which, in the policing context, rules are both fairly conceived and (just as important) impartially applied. The tolerant community is a place in which there is to be found a respect for difference, and a recognition that irrelevant distinctions—on grounds of gender, ethnic origin, sexual orientation or religion—should be no bar to leading a successful public life, in the police force as well as in any other sphere. Both ideas are of a piece with the new and powerful commitment to the idea of human rights that has become so evident in the post-Cold War age. The notion of human rights is another way of articulating, and therefore prioritising, our commitment to the dignity of the person. All these phrases can be summed up in the simple claim, that every person matters and needs to be treated properly.

But these are unsettled times. Crucially important is that the Home Office slogan, and therefore this book, is concerned with 'a safe, just *and* tolerant' society. Policing is not about either safety *or* liberty nor about security *or* tolerance. The route to safety is *via* a just and tolerant society. Safety can only be imposed from above in the way that you can silence a screaming child by placing your hand over its mouth: while you do this mayhem spreads from other sources, and anyway sooner or later you have to let go if you are not prepared to deepen your disciplinary efforts to an even harsher degree. That a book of this quality can be assembled by two editors at the heart of innovative thinking on UK policing is welcome evidence that anxieties about the future have not yet destroyed the liberal perspective on policing that is the best guarantor not only of a free but also of a safe society.

Conor Gearty is Professor of Human Rights Law and Rausing Director of the Centre for the Study of Human Rights, London School of Economics.

Introduction

In our earlier book *Police Leadership in the Twenty-first Century* (2003) we argued that policing by consent and democratic leadership fit together and that autocratic leadership has no place in modern policing.

Democratic leadership, however, is a necessary but not sufficient condition for successful policing. The police service of a modernising democracy needs to be sure of its ethos and clear in its social philosophy if it is to assert and retain the operational independence from central or local government direction that is needed for professional excellence. At the same time, a modern police service needs to be able to achieve success in co-operation with other agencies in order to promote and sustain public safety within the context of a just and tolerant society.

In this book, we set out to explore the meanings of safety, justice and tolerance; how their potential clashes may be reconciled; the role of the police in achieving such a reconciliation; and the implications of such a quest for police virtue.

In exploring our theme we have taken an international perspective, and although a number of our contributors are British or American, this is not intended as a British, American or Anglo-American textbook for policing. Rather, it is an international inquiry, in which we have assumed that whilst there is divergence and antagonism in the modern world, there is also convergence, or at least inter-communication. Thus the possibility of an international model of policing which crosses racial, religious, historical and ideological boundaries is not in itself a utopian ideal, although we may be very far from its achievement.

ONE WORLD

Just as there are major differences between societies in the world in which we live, there are also many similarities. Indeed, in the world that we actually see around us, the terms 'modern' and 'traditional' are themselves misleading. Just as there are no purely modern societies, so there are no purely traditional ones either. Modern societies—and this, as we have indicated, includes all societies, although for convenience we may still make value judgements as to degrees of modernity—are subject to pressure, influence and change: and none exists in isolation.

We have taken it as given that the society in question is either an already established democracy, in the broadest sense; or that it is in the process of democratisation; or that whilst formally an absolutist state of some sort, its leaders are subject to democratic pressures. Thus our would-be safe, just and tolerant society is, broadly speaking, inclusive rather than exclusive—whether of goods, ideas or people.

PAST AND PRESENT VIRTUES

The history of any society or institution is in a sense akin to its *curriculum vitae*. In any proper process of evaluation, significant distortions or omissions will be noted and an explanation sought. Any society rests upon the foundations of previous generations and has a responsibility to acknowledge what has led to its development. Thus the values of safety, justice and toleration have an historical context. Anyone who is ignorant of, or ignores, that historical dimension may assume something as a *fait accompli* when in fact it is a potentially fragile achievement that continues to need to be guarded.

For example, let us consider religion. Relationships between Anglicans and Roman Catholics in Britain today are very much better than they were, say, at the time of the Gordon Riots in the late eighteenth century. Britain is now, by and large, a religiously tolerant community in regard to Christianity: and so it may be taken for granted by some that such religious tolerance will continue to exist. (We shall pass over here as too large to discuss in this context, the ongoing relationship between Christianity and Islam as recently analysed by Roger Scruton (2003), in 'a model of elegant lucidity' (*Financial Times*).)

However, the generalisation that Christianity is not, by and large, a source of contemporary political division does not cross the Irish Sea to Ulster, where religious toleration is still something to be striven for—and there are many who oppose it on ideological as well as tribal grounds. Sadly, Northern Ireland has not provided a working illustration of a community that has been able to reconcile safety, justice and tolerance. The Royal Ulster Constabulary bore its share of criticism for the collapse of both law and order in Northern Ireland. Certainly, that force had great difficulty in presenting itself as representative of both sides of the community and capable of maintaining the peace in a fair and acceptable manner in the most recent outbreak of 'The Troubles', from 1969 onwards. The problems faced in Northern Ireland, however, were incapable of resolution by even the most enlightened and rights-conscious police service, acting alone. That is at least part of our reason for stressing the need for a social doctrine towards which the police can contribute, and which they must help to make a reality by means of the politics of accommodation.

To some extent (as we explore in greater depth in our unfolding text) it is possible to contrast the virtues of safety and justice on the one hand with tolerance on the other. Putting it rather too crudely, whilst we can never have too much safety and justice (compulsive risk-takers and extreme libertarians notwithstanding), there may be limits to the virtue of toleration. Tolerance comes under question from several directions.

Our contributor Satish Kumar (*Chapter 1*) would prefer to see a society working towards compassion rather than one which rested at the half-way stage of tolerance. This point of view could be linked to an argument for social justice, although an excessive degree of compulsion in achieving such a state of affairs, would not, in our view at least, be consistent with Kumar's general outlook.

From another perspective, Sir David Calvert-Smith, the former Director of Public Prosecutions, has argued in *Chapter 2*, in our view very properly, that there must be limits to tolerance itself: for no society would wish to tolerate the intolerable.

As the French philosopher André Comte-Sponville (1996) has argued, a democracy needs to defend itself, if necessary by limiting free speech. This author further distinguishes between peaceableness, a virtue he admires, and pacifism, an ideology to which, unlike our own contributor Satish Kumar, he does not subscribe: the use of legitimate force may be both necessary and desirable on occasion in order to combat tyranny.

Tolerance does not necessarily imply relativism. Comte-Sponville argues that one need not 'renounce the love of truth in order to be tolerant… [But] loving truth means recognising that we can never know it absolutely and with utter certainty.' Thus, rather than be dogmatic, we must practise tolerance—other people's right to be wrong: 'Only the potential danger of an attitude, not its own degree of tolerance or intolerance, ought to determine whether one should tolerate it or not.'

Thus, to be tolerant of something does not mean that one approves of it, or is indifferent to it. The real challenge to a tolerant society comes when it is forced to decide whether or not to tolerate something of which it disapproves, and could suppress if it chose to do so. The professionals charged with sustaining a tolerant society, be they social workers, doctors or police officers, must on occasion be required to be tolerant towards people with whose attitudes they might disagree and of whose behaviour they might disapprove, for the sake of the greater good—just as on other occasions they will be required to be intolerant of those whom privately they might admire, at least in some regards. The virtues that this state of mind and capacity for decision-making requires are explored further throughout this volume, and include the capacity to be able to act with impartiality, integrity, reasonableness and the proper use of discretion.

POLICE VIRTUE

Much has been written about virtue in ethical theory, and there has been a revival of academic interest in this area that to some extent may be attributed to the work of Alasdair MacIntyre.

However, police virtue is a relatively underdeveloped area of study—with the significant exception of the work of such pioneers as John Alderson, William Ker Muir and Edwin Delattre. In this book we set out to define police virtue within the context of a safe, just and tolerant society, drawing upon new work by Edwin Delattre (*Chapter 3*), John Kleinig (*Chapter 8*), William Heffernan (*Chapter 7*), Seumas Miller (*Chapter 12*), Milan Pagon (*Chapter 9*) and Alasdair MacIntyre (*Chapter 4*). We have added a chapter ourselves (*Chapter 6*), based on the valuable contribution of James McKinney on the need to clarify both personal and organizational values.

BEST PRACTICE

Best practice is a phrase much used but rarely defined, and the indefatigable Garry Elliott has set out to examine what it means and to explore some of the obstacles to establishing and spreading best practice within the epistemological context of policing (*Chapter 5*). In *Chapter 11*, David Canter has compared the work of the police officer and that of the academic and pointed out how each needs the other, drawing on both new and long-established work on the psychology of prejudice in order to illustrate how the transformation of an organization requires more than good intent—however necessary that may be as an impetus to change.

CONCLUSION

Our conclusion (*Chapter 15*) draws upon all the sources as presented in this volume in presenting a model for a safe, just and tolerant society and eliciting its implications for police leadership and police virtue. We draw attention to the strategic work of two further American scholars who contribute to our text. Both of them are professors at the John Jay College of Criminal Justice in New York that has maintained a long academic exchange programme with the Police Staff College at Bramshill.

Firstly, Robert R Sullivan (*Chapter 13*) argues with his customary dash and élan that Britain is already a safe, just and tolerant society, comparatively speaking, and its police service is already aware, at least at its strategic level, of what needs to be done to make this society both safer and yet more tolerant. Secondly, Robert Panzarella (*Chapter 14*) presents an immensely illuminating and scholarly review of the various models that have influenced policing up to, during and after the creation of the Metropolitan Police by Sir Robert Peel in 1829. He concludes that the police service is now adapting to a new model of public safety policing. This necessitates both active collaboration with other agencies, and the resolution of the conflict between privacy and protection that has engulfed the world's democracies since 11 September 2001. How are we to achieve a society that is both tolerant and safe? That is the key challenge of the twenty-first century, and the quest towards which this book is dedicated.

Peter Villiers and **Robert Adlam**
May 2004

REFERENCES for the *Introduction*

Adlam R and Villiers P (2003), *Police Leadership in the Twenty-first Century: Philosophy, Doctrine and Developments*, Winchester: Waterside Press.

Comte-Sponville A (1996), *A Small Treatise on the Great Virtues: The Uses of Philosophy in Everyday Life*, New York: Henry Holt and Co.

Scruton R (2003), *The West and the Rest: Globalisation and the Terrorist Threat*, London: ISI Books.

A FRESH BREEZE mournfully droned through the wire rigging and angrily dispersed the ragged, low-flying clouds. The troubled waters of the Yellow Sea splashed against the side of the battleship, while a thin, cold, blinding rain fell, and the raw air penetrated to one's very bones. But a group of officers still stood on the after-bridge, watching the silhouettes of the transports slowly disappearing in the rain haze.

On their masts and yard-arms signals were being flown, the last messages and final requests of those who had been our fellow-travellers on the long voyage.

Why is it that at sea a friendly greeting of this kind, expressed merely by a combination of flags, touches one's heart so deeply, and speaks to it even more than salutes, cheers, or music? Why is it that until the signal has been actually hauled down every one looks at it, silently and intently, as if real words, instead of motley-coloured pieces of cloth, were fluttering in the breeze, and becoming wet with rain? Why is it that on the signal being hauled down everyone turns away, quietly moving off to his duty, as if a last handshake had been given, and 'good-bye' had been said for ever?

The Battle of Tsu-Shima

Captain Vladimir Semenoff,
Imperial Russian Navy

John Murray, London (1906)

CHAPTER 1

Tolerance and Beyond: An Alternative View

Satish Kumar (as interviewed by Peter Villiers)

Satish Kumar was born in Rajasthan in India in 1936. At the age of nine he renounced the world and its entanglements and became a Jain monk, dedicating himself to a life of total non-violence, meditation and frugality. Now no longer a monk, he retains his ideals and continues to put them into practice in his daily life, as well as lecturing and communicating on 'deep ecology' and non-violence throughout the world.

Kumar came to England in 1971 and has lived in North Devon since 1979, where he edits the magazine *Resurgence* and founded the Small School in order to educate children to respect both the environment and each other: for here as elsewhere, Kumar believes in putting his ideals into practice. He is the programme director of the Schumacher College at Dartington Hall in South Devon.

I interviewed Kumar in April 2003 in order to find out his views on a safe, just and tolerant society and the religious and philosophical values underpinning his social beliefs. The resulting text is produced with his approval.

Kumar's latest book is entitled *You Are, Therefore I Am* (2002) and I have drawn on this and his autobiography *No Destination* (1992) in the course of transcribing this interview. I have also considered the work of the transformational Indian Police Service (IPS) leader Kiran Bedi on prison reform, to which Kumar introduced me. In this context, it is interesting to note that officers of the IPS, who are selected by open competition from the whole of the Indian population, may be called upon to serve in any state, and in other branches of the public service besides policing.

Kumar's ideas are not 'mainstream', and some would dismiss his views—reluctantly or otherwise—as hopelessly optimistic. One begs to disagree. Hopeless optimism is a contradiction in terms; and the views of this illuminating and persuasive communicator, at home in Devon as on the dusty plains of Rajasthan, deserve sustained attention.

As a Jain, Kumar believes that all life—whether human, animal or plant—is sacred, and that one should live without violence and as harmlessly as possible. He is an admirer and follower of Mahatma Gandhi and shares Gandhi's view of the need to work towards a peaceful, inclusive and compassionate society. Like Gandhi, he takes the long-term view. Peaceful protest, for example, may seem a futile activity if considered for its short-term effects, where the forces of repression in an autocracy or indifference in a representational democracy may appear too powerful for it to be of any effect.

But real change, Kumar believes, may take at least 20 or 30 years of dedicated and selfless struggle in order to be successful; and he points to the success of the civil rights movement in the USA as an example. (One might also consider the collapse of Apartheid in South Africa, which was achieved by peaceful means.) Violent struggle may appeal to some people, but it contradicts the fundamental principle of non-violence to which Kumar is dedicated. It is in any case not likely to be successful in achieving real change, whether because its ostensible aims usually remain unachieved or because of its corrupting effect on its supporters, who are warped by its use: as for example with the IRA, which despite massive bloodshed has failed to achieve a united Ireland.

Kumar also believes, as a Jain, that no one, without exception, is truly and wholly evil and incapable of transformation. Society should work to contain and reform the misguided and dangerous within its ranks: and those most in need of compassion are those who have transgressed furthest. There is therefore a need for both police and prisons, but not as they operate at present. Dialogue is never wasted, and communication is a necessity even when the pessimist would assume that it is least likely to achieve change. (Here the work of Kiran Bedi of the IPS in the transformation of one of India's largest prisons, housing some of its most dangerous convicts, is of positive inspiration.)

Kumar bases his thoughts on policing and police virtue on three axioms:

1. The vast majority of the population does not consist of violent and dangerous law-breakers, but ordinary people going about their ordinary business. The main function of the police should be to support the majority of the population in what it is attempting to achieve, e.g. by directing traffic so as to ensure better access to a popular event, or by facilitating peaceful protest so as to ensure a vibrant democracy. (And at the same time, of course, by discouraging such crimes as pick-pocketing whereby the unlawfully-minded may prey upon the vulnerable.)

   By contrast, however, some police forces tend to regard the public in general with suspicion, and seek to investigate, control or block what they are doing as a matter of course. This is to act as a force rather than a service.

Comment:

i. This is a spontaneous expression of support for the philosophy, doctrine and practice of policing by consent as explored in depth in Adlam and Villiers (2003). Policing by consent (under the title of 'community policing') was practised by John Alderson, a contributor to that volume and far-sighted police reformer, as Chief Constable of Devon and Cornwall.

ii. The 1964 Royal Commission on Policing referred approvingly to the traditional role of the police as 'a friend in need'—although modernising governments seem less clear as to the worth of that aspect of police work, upon which accountants do not place a value. It is in fact of central rather than peripheral value and in logical terms necessary rather than desirable. If the police do not provide a service to those in need, then they are not policing properly—a sentiment recognised by some very hard-nosed police officers of my acquaintance, who refer to themselves, sardonically but approvingly, as the only social service to be open at all times.

2. Kumar's second axiom, as it were, is that the key role of the police, as Peel, Rowan and Mayne recognised long ago, is to deter crime; and police direction should be based on that principle. It is deterrence that should be rewarded, rather than a successful investigation of a crime

that occurs because deterrence has failed. Kumar quotes with approval the custom of ancient China, whereby the doctor was paid if the patient were well. If the patient became sick, however, then it was the doctor's turn to pay. The police are concerned to preserve the social health of the community, and their role is therefore analogous to that of the doctor for the individual patient.

Comment

i. To move a police officer from one district to another because he or she has not made enough arrests, or to close a rural police station because it does not deal with a sufficiently large number of crimes, are on the face of it violations of this principle. Deterrence should be rewarded and not punished, and the performance management culture is conspicuous for its perverse incentives and unintended outcomes. (Adlam and Villiers, 2003, *passim.*)

ii. Kumar believes that the police should trust rather than mistrust the citizenry for whom they provide a service, and we may infer that the police should be trusted in their turn. As Professor Onora O'Neill (2002; 2003) has argued, however, there has been a systematic breakdown of trust in public life. In her 2002 Reith Lectures and elsewhere she offers an extended discussion of the decline of trust in contemporary life, as opposed to the decline of *trustworthiness*: a contrast about which she has some very interesting things to say. The audit explosion that attempted to address and improve trustworthiness has in fact failed to solve the problem of distrust in public life, and instead made professional work less effective—an unintended outcome indeed.

iii. Not surprisingly, Kumar stressed throughout our interview that he believes that the police should be a service rather than a force.

3. In the interest of working towards a safe society, Kumar's third axiom is that the police need to be able to control the violent, the dangerous and the aggressive, and on occasion this may require the exercise of controlled force. However, much more could be done to train the police in the use of effective non-violent skills of pacification and restraint. Like any other skills, these need to be taught, practised and absorbed; and Kumar suggests that as a starting-place, five per cent of the police budget should be devoted to the development of effective non-violent skills of intervention, pacification, restraint and conflict resolution.

A SAFE, JUST AND COMPASSIONATE SOCIETY

Safety

For Kumar, safety is something to be worked towards. Greed, materialism, and the collapse of spiritual values are some of the underlying causes of the unsafeness of society, and those are things that the police cannot rectify alone. However, a police organization which works as a service rather than a force, and which supports the peaceful and socially responsible as well as controlling those who transgress accepted norms, is more likely to promote a safer society, in the long run, than an organization that simply concentrates upon law enforcement.

Justice

As a Jain, Kumar does not believe in absolutes, and so does not set out to achieve a perfectly just society. He is prepared for some disparity in distribution and resources, and does not believe in what the former Soviet Union used to define as 'social' or 'economic' justice—i.e. a society officially dedicated to an equal distribution of property. However, it is impossible to read anything of underlying Indian social philosophy, whether Jain, Hindu or Buddhist, without realising that the Indian ideal is one of balance, moderation and harmony. The fingers of the hand are of different sizes, and yet are able to operate together. The hand would, in fact, be less effective were the fingers of equal size; but at the same time, they cannot be utterly disproportionate if they are to work together. They need to operate in harmony and so do people if they are to co-operate in society. This requires some aspect of harmony and proportion in the distribution of wealth and resources.

As far as criminal justice is concerned, a just society is one in which prisons are centres for the reform of criminal behaviour, which should be carried out with compassion and by non-violent techniques. Crime should certainly not be tolerated but the purpose of arrest, sentencing and incarceration is not punishment but reform.

Compassion

Tolerance, for Kumar, is a half-way house: it may be necessary, but it is not sufficient. A society that exalts tolerance as a primary virtue is in danger of being a passive society. Like the contemporary doctrine of human rights, the doctrine of tolerance does not go far enough. People may benefit from rights, in terms of having a means to rectify a grievance: but what they really need is respect, which must include some recognition of their capacity to contribute as well as to receive. A tolerant society does not transform its citizens. It would be better to build a safe, just and compassionate society, in which people were able to achieve both outer and inner freedom.

IN CONCLUSION: THE VIRTUE AND DIRECTION OF THE POLICE

As a Jain, and therefore an agnostic about both absolutes and 'isms', Kumar believes firstly that everyone is capable of transformation and secondly that it is inappropriate to condemn any institution *in toto*. When I asked him if he believed that the British police were institutionally racist, he was disinclined to talk in such terms. By inference, therefore, one might suggest that the British police should worry less about overall aspirations such as representing the population in ethnic terms, and more about developing and displaying the appropriate individual virtues and social culture of policing amongst the officers whom they do recruit, of any background.

I sense that in many ways, however, it was what Kumar did not say, as much as what he said, that made this interview so interesting; and that he would not eschew criticism if it were an effective means to an end. He was reluctant to criticise and keen to encourage; and I hope that this account conveys a flavour of his style of communicating as well as a précis of what he had to say.

In conclusion, one may infer that Kumar believes that:

- a safe, just and tolerant society is a worthwhile ideal;
- a desirable stage beyond tolerance is compassion;
- the ideal should be worked towards as a long-term goal;
- it must be achieved by non-violent and frugal means; and
- the role of the leader is to inspire, lead by example, and develop his or her followers as leaders in their turn.

The police have a vital role to play in the transformation of existing society, and the means they use are as important as the goals they set out to achieve. They must transform themselves as well as the society of which they are a part. Non-violence is not a doctrine of withdrawal and abnegation, but requires an active, skilled and positive police service to make it work.

REFERENCES for *Chapter 1*

Adlam, R and Villiers, P (2003), *Police Leadership in the Twenty-first Century*, Winchester: Waterside Press.
Kumar, S (1992), *No Destination*, Foxhole, Dartington, Devon: Green Books.
Kumar, S (2002), *You Are, Therefore I Am*, Foxhole, Dartington, Devon: Green Books.
O'Neill, O (2002), *BBC Reith Lectures*, London: BBC Publications.
O'Neill, O (2003), *Autonomy and Trust in Bioethics*, Cambridge: Cambridge University Press.

A note on Kumar's sources of inspiration

Kumar's ideas on inner freedom are influenced by the Indian philosopher Krishnamurti, a centre for the study of whose thought has been established in Bramdean, Hampshire, England (which maintains its own website at www.brockwood.org.uk). The other figures whom Kumar mentioned with admiration in the course of our interview were the Buddha himself; Mahavir, the founder of Jain; Mahatma Gandhi; Martin Luther King; Mother Theresa of Calcutta; and the Dalai Llama. All have distinguished themselves as advocates of non-violence, who have nevertheless worked unceasingly to achieve their cause by peaceful protest and prayer in action, and have inspired others by their example.

CHAPTER 2

Sustaining a Safe, Just and Tolerant Society: the Role of the Crown Prosecution Service

Sir David Calvert-Smith (as interviewed by Peter Villiers)

Sir David Calvert-Smith QC, formerly Director of Public Prosecutions and thus in charge of the Crown Prosecution Service (CPS), was born in London. His father was a lawyer and his parents had met before the Second World War in the course of helping refugee Jews from Nazi Germany to resettle in Great Britain. Educated at Eton, Sir David read classics and then law at Cambridge, at the same time helping youths on probation, before becoming a barrister. He described his legal apprenticeship as not a very professional process, in which almost all depended on the relationship between pupil and master—a process he supplemented by omnivorous reading of famous trials and barristers. He proved highly successful in his profession and was Treasury Counsel at the Central Criminal Court for eleven years, during which he prosecuted in many famous cases, before becoming DPP in 1998. He worked from CPS Headquarters in the City of London—a modern office block surrounded by the temples of both God and Commerce.

Sir David believes that one's first understanding of what is meant by justice is gained in the home, before the family tribunal. One has to believe in the moral authority of the problem-solver, and to feel that one has had a fair hearing, in order to accept the verdict of the court. Criminal justice is part of social justice, and is one of the few unifying forces in a multi-cultural society, in which the state must seek to find the common principles on which all or most people, whatever their racial and religious backgrounds, are agreed.

It is Sir David's view that most people would agree that such crimes as murder, rape, arson and wife-battering are wrong and should be punished, as are aspects of anti-social behaviour which may be less dramatic and less obviously harmful but which should nevertheless be discouraged. In the comparatively rare cases where there is a profound cultural disagreement as to whether something is right or wrong, then a fair hearing must take place; but at the end of the day there is only place for one law and that must be the law of the land.

Perhaps paradoxically, the ordinary person may feel least like a criminal when he or she has committed an offence—for example, driving through a red light—when there was no obvious danger to others and the offender does not deny carrying out the act. Under such circumstances, the concept of justice as fairness may appear to have been violated. This is especially so if the motorist feels that disproportionate attention has been paid to a relatively minor offence, when there are 'real criminals' waiting to be caught.

A safe society is one in which people tend to feel safe. It is a society in which ordinary people do not expect to be robbed, burgled, assaulted or otherwise scarred by crime as a matter of course.

The CPS faces a difficult task in deciding whom to prosecute, and whom not—when *not* to prosecute someone who sounds like a very dangerous person may be a source of great public unease. However, one cannot prosecute without evidence; and it is right to base the reason to prosecute on the realistic prospect of a conviction. Too many prosecutions will result in conviction figures going down, resources being wasted and a decline in public confidence.

It would be possible to base the decision to prosecute simply on the existence of a *prima facie* case, rather than the realistic prospect of a conviction. However, such a policy would make for a much more expensive CPS, and Sir David has not advocated any such lowering of the threshold. Like the experienced police officer, he believes in the use of professional judgement to find and maintain a balance in the use of the powers that the state has conferred upon him, and recognises that no decision will please everyone.

Sir David gives a cautious 'yes' to restorative justice, but doubts its efficacy with hardened criminals, and would not apply it to domestic violence.

He is less optimistic than the Government that it is able to transform society in the interests of this or that goal. Governments do not increase or reduce crime: people do. Governments may, however, have indirect influence and it is right that they should attempt to exert that influence in building a better society. Governments can and should exercise moral leadership and set a moral tone.

Sir David believes that the police must feel fully integrated within the criminal justice system. He has an extensive acquaintance with police officers, often gained in the distressing circumstances of the aftermath of violent and destructive crimes. This has led him to perceive that there is a full spectrum of moral views in the police service, as in society at large; and he respects those officers who have confronted evil at its worst and still managed to retain their faith in the essential goodness of human nature. The belief that a police officer *must* be cynical, hardened, detached and so on, as a result of his or her experiences—and that such hardness is an essential and indeed beneficial acquisition for the occupation of policing—is wrong. There are more possibilities than hardened cynicism and naïve idealism.

Whether or not we prefer a safe, just or tolerant society must be influenced by our own circumstances and position within society. Sir David recognises that someone in his position may have a penchant for justice and tolerance which cannot be felt by the Hobbesian victim of both crime and disorder on the housing estate, who will presumably and rightly put safety first. Nevertheless, in a pluralist democracy that respects both human rights and the rule of law, there is a need to find a balance between the competing needs and values of the populace as a whole.

Sir David recognises tolerance as a virtue, but does not believe that society should tolerate the intolerant if their actions cause harm to others. There are therefore limits to freedom of speech and expression, although it can be extraordinarily difficult to know when to impose them. He is deeply sympathetic to the dilemma of the working constable, who may have to calculate almost instantaneously whether or not vigorous expression is likely to lead to a breach of the peace.

Under such circumstances, the decision made will rest upon the values of the officer concerned; his or her understanding of how the values of society as a whole should be applied in this case; and his or her knowledge of the law. The exercise of professional discretion, therefore, is inescapable.

Sir David puts a case for freedom of expression in the academic context, using the word in its widest sense, as unlikely to lead to a breach of the peace. On this logic, he agreed that some but not all of the speeches that the Reverend Dr Ian Paisley MP, MEP has made over the past 40 years might have led to criminal charges against him had the new laws against inciting religious hatred been in place at the time. To arrest the speaker when surrounded by his fervent supporters might be foreseen to be more likely to lead to a breach of the peace than to allow him or her to continue to speak. As in all such cases, everything would depend upon the circumstances prevailing at the time.

If, on the other hand, a propagandist of racial and religious hatred were only to have committed his or her ideas to a book, rather than to have advocated them on the street, then society would find it more difficult to argue that such a publication should be suppressed as likely to lead to an immediate breach of the peace, although its long-term consequences could be far more damaging.

Sir David has mixed views on the new laws that add an additional dimension to a crime such as assault if it can be shown to be racially or religiously aggravated. On the one hand, it is right that the Government should declare its profound opposition to crime aggravated by prejudice, and the statutory imposition of a longer sentence bolsters that intent and shows moral leadership. On the other hand, the judge already had the discretion to vary the sentence if he or she believed that the crime was aggravated by prejudice, so it could be argued that the new legislation is both unnecessary and limiting.

On balance, Sir David is an interventionist and believes in the expression of moral leadership. It is not hatred *per se* that should be criminalised but the advocacy of policies and actions that are likely to damage others.

Sir David believes that a tolerant society should practise tolerance rather as the word is used in engineering.[1] In other words, a tolerant society is able to absorb stresses and strains. It expands and contracts in order to accommodate change. It does not over-react to temporary phenomena, which are likely to exhaust themselves if left alone. And it relies upon the wise discretion of those it employs in the criminal justice system, including judges, police officers, prison warders, probation service officials and others to see that society's values are reflected in the process of the administration of justice.

At the end of the interview I asked Sir David what we had not covered, and he raised the topic of pre-emptive action. Should society act to prevent the harmful activities of a person who has yet to break the law, and if so, when? The twentieth century tradition, outside wartime, has been not to intervene. However, 11 September 2001 has changed that tradition, as it has changed so

---

1 Tolerance in engineering is the allowable amount of variation in the dimensions of a machine or part (*Shorter Oxford English Dictionary*, 1909 reference): the term is also used in coinage. Medical terminology includes a definition of tolerance as the ability to withstand the deleterious effects of a drug, with the implication that exposure increases tolerance.

much else, and the British state has now incarcerated a number of aliens without trial, because of their terrorist potential and its inability to extradite them.

The practice of prevention could be extended. For example, increasing genetic knowledge may give the state the ability to predict who is likely to carry out acts of violent aggression; and there is a moral argument for saying that those acts should be prevented. However, such a policy would go against a right which is not to be found in the European Convention On Human Rights, but which is a right nevertheless: the right to carry out a crime, and to be caught and punished for it.

CHAPTER 3

Justice, Safety and the Limits to the Tolerable

Edwin J Delattre

In several venues during the summer of 2003, I taught sessions on ethics in policing for nearly 200 police executives from western democracies. About two hours into one of the sessions, a participant raised his hand and said, 'Professor Delattre, I wonder if you know that you are contradicting what all the other professors in this programme have taught us throughout the past several days?' I replied that I was unaware of it and asked him what they had said that I was contradicting. 'All of them,' he answered, 'have told us that as police leaders, we should make the values of our departments conform to the values of the communities we serve. You're saying something very different.' I replied that if that was what the other professors had been saying, I was very glad to be contradicting them.

OATHS OF OFFICE AND THE PUBLIC TRUST

I had been explaining the tradition that calls upon all who bear positions of public trust to live up to higher intellectual and moral standards than are required of other citizens and residents. In giving authority and powers that the rest of us do not have to public servants, we gain a reciprocal right to hold them accountable to fulfil their duties wisely, competently and honourably. In addition, my lecture had focused on the gravity of oaths of office for police and other public servants who, in effect, put themselves on the line as collateral for the trustworthiness of their oath. I had explained further the danger in requiring new recruits to policing to take an oath of duty without their understanding what they are promising to do. Trivialising oaths and promises is no way to draw the practitioners in any walk of life, including policing, toward integrity and competence in the fulfilment of duty.

I had asked how many police from the United States in the session, when they took the oath to uphold and defend the United States Constitution, had known what they were promising to uphold and defend. I had asked as well how many knew whether new recruits to their agencies were familiar with the contents of the Constitution, including its Preamble. To both questions, the answer was, not many; and the same was generally true with similar questions of police from other countries.

In enumerating the moral, political and social ideals identified in the Preamble to the United States Constitution as the reasons for its ordainment and establishment by the people (forming a more perfect union, establishing justice, ensuring domestic tranquillity, providing for the common defence, promoting the general welfare and securing the blessings of liberty 'to ourselves and our posterity'), I had explained that an oath taken to act for the sake of these ideals is not conditional. The Constitution is not advice one accepts or rejects from time to time, not inert shelf paper, but rather the ultimate law of the land and, as such, a fundamental boundary to the domain of legitimate discretion in policing. The Constitution is subject to change by amendment and by judicial construal, but it is not vulnerable to rapid alteration by popular whim, fashion or values. The oath of fidelity to the Constitution transcends local preferences, tastes, passions and values; and a police officer cannot rightly betray it simply because some element or other of the Constitution, such as the inseparability of justice from the right of each person to due process and the presumption of innocence, happens to become unpopular with some or all of the residents of a police jurisdiction.

The police oath of fidelity to the rule of law and the sovereignty of the people as expressed in legislation by their representatives remains binding irrespective of all possible subjection of police and law enforcement officers to political or public pressure to ignore it and despite all shifting fashions in values that, if indulged, might jeopardise both justice and the public safety. Indeed, the oath should serve as a reminder that the security of the rights of the public depends on the refusal of police to draw their mission and ideals directly from the passions, values or factional interests of the public.

These conditions of good policing are by no means unique to the United States. In Canada, the Royal Canadian Mounted Police (RCMP) oath of office is:

> I ... solemnly swear that I will faithfully, diligently, and impartially execute and perform the duties required of me as a member of the Royal Canadian Mounted Police, and will well and truly obey and perform all lawful orders and instructions I receive as such, without fear, favour or affection of or toward any person. So help me God.

The RCMP requires its members, as a matter of duty,

> to respect the rights of all persons; to maintain the integrity of law, law enforcement, and the administration of justice; to perform ... duties promptly, impartially, and diligently, in accordance with the law and without abusing the member's authority; to avoid any actual, apparent, or potential conflict of interests; to ensure that any improper or unlawful conduct of any member is not concealed or permitted to continue; to be incorruptible ... ; to act at all times in a courteous, respectful, and honourable manner; and to maintain the honour of the force and its principles and purposes.

As with law enforcement and police oaths and duties in the United States, the oath and duties of the RCMP are not merely conditional or situational. Their status does not depend on what the 'values of the community' may happen, at any time, to be. They are binding on police above and beyond popular opinion and prejudice, fashion in values, and the ebb and flow of circumstance, just as is the obligation of fidelity among police in Canada to the Canadian Charter of Rights and Freedoms.

The RCMP statement of 'Commitment to Our Communities' similarly transcends the happenstance of values among the public within the agency's jurisdiction:

> The employees of the RCMP are committed to our communities through: unbiased and respectful treatment of all individuals, accountability, mutual problem solving, cultural sensitivity, enhancement of public safety, partnerships and consultation, open and honest communication, effective and efficient use of resources, and quality and timely service.

Furthermore, the tradition that police and others in positions of public trust are obligated to live up to higher standards than are required of the general public rightly commands widespread respect and assent in democratic nations now. The Calgary (Alberta, Canada) Police Commission observes, 'Frequently, Canadian courts have acknowledged that police officers are held to a higher standard of conduct than other citizens.' [1]

POPULAR VALUES AND HUMAN NATURE

The 'values of a community', however zealously they may be held, or however inconstant and transient they may be, do not ensure high enough ethical ground, high enough standards, for the conduct of policing. No public served by the police, no region of police jurisdiction, is, in the words of Alexander Hamilton, a 'happy empire of perfect wisdom and perfect virtue'.[2] Many jurisdictions are not communities at all, but only geographical areas, little unified by any thread of shared ideals woven through the general public. There is never a guarantee that the prejudices of any portion of the public, let alone the prejudices of the majority, in any area or community will be compatible with either justice for all or the general safety. Every jurisdiction of any size contains people of shockingly different and conflicting values, from devoted parents and law-abiding citizens to shrewd, manipulative, and violent predators; from benign and altruistic adults to practising paedophiles and rapists; from the fair-minded and responsibly respectful and tolerant to the remorselessly bigoted and cowardly; and from those who want to cooperate with and rely on police to those who would prefer, for reasons of self-interest, to corrupt them. Police have to deal with many people who are as vociferous in asserting their rights as they are in denying their duties.

Popular opinion, human passions, factional interests, and fashionable values can be and frequently are fickle, unwise, unjust, and unreasonable, and sometimes perverse and cruel. The values of cowardice, wantonness and selfishness are as visible, whether in academic institutions or on mean streets, as those of courage, self-control and fairness toward others. In all of the hundreds of jurisdictions where I have worked on the streets with police during the past 30 years, some members of the public commit both legal and illegal acts against others that are completely in accord with their own values and desires and yet are also morally disgraceful and intolerable. Establishing justice and securing the public safety depends on a measure of civic virtue among at least some members of the public, although sufficient measure cannot always be found, and on the refusal of police to let policy and practice be driven downward by widespread public indifference to the common good.

Such facts of human nature and society led James Madison to ask, 'What is government itself but the greatest of all reflections on human nature?'[3] He continued,

> If men were angels, no government would be necessary. If angels were to govern men, neither internal nor external controls on government would be necessary. In framing a government which is to be administered by men over men, the great difficulty lies in this: You must first enable the government to control the governed; and in the next place, oblige it to control itself.

Madison wrote in the tradition of those who understand that the achievement of justice is the most fundamental purpose of government, and governments which deserve the authority and powers they possess accordingly exist, not to grant human rights, but rather to secure them. He therefore went on to warn, 'It is of great importance in a republic, not only to guard the society against the oppression of its rulers; but to guard one part of the society against the injustice of the other part.'[4] No police department can safeguard the public from factions within it, from predatory individuals, or from governmental misconduct simply by making its values 'conform to the values of the community', whatever they may happen to be.

Alexander Hamilton knew equally well that government could not be responsibly established simply to conform to whatever values might happen at any time to dominate any portion of a society. 'Why,' he asked, 'has government been instituted at all?' His succinct reply: 'Because the passions of men will not conform to the dictates of reason and justice without constraint.'[5]

POLICING, THE RULE OF LAW AND SELF-GOVERNANCE

Instead of making their standards 'conform to the values of their communities,' police should, through sustained engagement in their communities, aspire to live up to the high standards of judgment, duty, and conduct that follow from the Constitutional and legal foundations of their own authority. In practice, the most effective forms of policing, including community policing and 'broken windows'[6] policing, are matters of leading, not merely following or reacting. They succeed when police earn and come to possess—by their exemplary conduct and by the consistency of their words, policies and deeds with the rule of law and the ideals of integrity, service and concern for public safety—the trust and cooperation of a significant portion of the public.

Often, police need to teach citizens and other residents how to work together to improve social conditions and how to cooperate with police to solve persistent problems. In so doing, police can sometimes lead and also reinforce the public in creating and implementing informal social controls that prevent disorder, limit intolerable behaviour and reduce vulnerability to crime. Many achievements in modern policing confirm these facts, although even the best and most thorough efforts on the part of police do not always succeed.

As I have noted elsewhere, in the tradition of community-oriented, problem-solving and 'broken windows' policing, the San Diego, California, Police Department has implemented the City Heights Neighborhood Alliance. In City Heights, 60,000 residents are estranged from one another by 'language barriers, cultural differences, lack of knowledge of community resources' and by the fear of discovery among the high percentage of the population who are illegal aliens. In the alliance, a team of officers works with community organizers 'to solve drug related crimes in a partnership with community residents' and 'to provide residents with the knowledge and skills to solve their own problems related to quality of life.'[7]

In practice, police try to generate levels of mutual trust sufficient for residents to cooperate and intervene for the sake of the common good, they help the public to make common cause and mobilise efforts to control vandalism, graffiti, litter, prostitution, loitering, drug dealing and the great host of problems that arise from these forms of crime and disorder. Three central elements of community and broken-windows policing apply: neighbourhood cooperation, shared learning and social control of disreputable and dangerous behaviour. In this work, sometimes succeeding against all odds, police draw law-abiding residents into the arts of self-governance and self-reliance; they enable the public to engage in and understand participatory democracy by acquiring a voice that goes beyond voting and serving on juries; they encourage both youths and adults to respect the rule of law and decent public behaviour; they help to illuminate and bring the values of civility to life in and for the public; and by patient teaching and listening, they help residents to overcome the grinding fear that attaches to ignorance and helplessness.[8]

ETHICAL POLICING AND PUBLIC RECIPROCITY

Nothing guarantees, however, that the public will always respond positively or fairly to ethical and competent policing. Earning and deserving the trust and confidence of the public are not guarantees of acquiring, possessing or keeping them. In an 'Explanatory Memorandum' to the European Code of Police Ethics,[9] the Council of Europe asserts,

> People within democracies have organized their states to secure maximum freedom for themselves within the rule of law. Likewise, the criminal justice systems have been developed with the purpose of providing individual liberty and security ... In general, the public consent to and, indeed, welcome the exercise of legitimate authority by the police so long as the police are seen to carry out their tasks toward worthwhile, democratic ends in an ethically acceptable manner.

Then, with remarkably unconsidered self-assurance, the council concludes,

> In turn, when they fulfill these conditions, police have every right to expect that the public will trust them to carry out their responsibilities, and support and cooperate with them in their activities when doing so.

In this conclusion, the council is flatly wrong. Police should be taught that they have the right to hold the public accountable, as long as they themselves operate within the standards that legitimise their authority. Only when police conduct is legitimate do they deserve the trust and cooperation of the public. Police need to learn from the beginning that when they act otherwise, they ought to be (and at best, will be) held accountable. Police should not, however, be taught that they may confidently expect the public to behave well toward them and that they can safely rely on reciprocation of honourable conduct, let alone that they have a right to such expectations.

The maximisation of liberty and freedom within the rule of law, Constitutional guarantees of freedom of speech and thought, legally entitle the members of the public to harbour whatever prejudices they wish against the police or anybody else. Liberty in contemporary democracies includes the right to hold stupid and biased opinions and to speak with cruel intent. Citizens may be indifferent to the sacrifices and decency of others and persist in irrational hatred and contempt. They may believe that every apparently benign action of government has a hidden agenda in lust for power and suspect that if police are not overtly corrupt and brutal, they are nonetheless covertly so. The people have a right to be forever ungrateful to those in uniform who go in harm's way for the sake of strangers. Where the weight of public opinion, the stigma of moral disapprobation, the preponderance of peer pressure and individual feelings of shame do not militate against unjustified attitudes and indefensible prejudices among the people, the police cannot safely expect fairness and reciprocity or well-deserved gratitude.

In Germany and other European countries, authors of conspiracy theories accuse the United States Government of perpetrating the terrorist atrocities of 9 September 2001 at the World Trade Center in New York and the Pentagon in Northern Virginia in order to provide a rationale for mounting war in Afghanistan and Iraq. When such conspiracy theories, drawn from boundless distrust of the United States, yield best-selling books and videos, police should infer that no idea, however foolish or vicious, is beyond promotion by profiteers and acceptance by the gullible.[10] Exactly the same point holds for Iraq where clan patriarchs 'dismiss reports that Americans had given $30 million and safe passage out of Iraq to the informant who turned in Saddam Hussein's sons' by saying, 'I assure you that never happened. The American soldiers brought out a camera and gave him the money in front of witnesses, and then they took him toward the Turkish border. Near the border they killed him and buried him in a valley. They wanted the money for their own families.'[11] Precisely because there has never been an idea so bad or a prejudice so irrational that it could find no one to espouse it, or a lie so obvious that it could find no one to believe it, police may hope for the best from the public, but they should always expect less and prepare for the worst.

For the most part, police officers who become good at their jobs learn in the course of their daily work which resident members of the public they can safely trust and how far and in what respects; whom they can protect and manage effectively as informants by one permissible means or another; who will lie when they believe they can get away with it; who would willingly corrupt or harm the police and so forth. Sound instruction, introduction to the streets by senior and special assignment officers and conscientious front line supervision cultivate the discriminating judgment police need to safeguard the public and to defend themselves. Newcomers to policing certainly do not deserve to be taught false generalisations about their having 'a right to expect that the public will trust and cooperate with them.'

In training police officers to prepare for and respond properly to public demonstrations and protests, for instance, instructors and supervisors should emphasise that the individuals in a large crowd of demonstrators have many different agendas. Some demonstrators want to bring attention to a cause, an injustice perhaps, in peaceful and orderly ways. Others are determined to commit illegal acts and impose as much disruption on the general public as they can. Some want to be arrested because they see arrest as evidence of commitment. Others want to be arrested only when the television cameras are running, because they care most about personal celebrity. Some protesters will do everything they can to provoke police into overreaction on camera. Some care more about their own rights than they do about the rights and safety of others. Some participants in protests do not care about anything, including the ostensible purpose of the demonstration, except the chance to be abusive and assert their power with relative impunity. And there is always the possibility, even if remote, that terrorists may be lurking in the crowd, armed to commit mass murder.

Police cannot, therefore, take for granted good faith or moral restraint or a sense of reciprocity among protesters. Neither can they afford to be drawn into any form of misconduct, including the use of excessive force, by the tactics of protesters who goad them. Wise police leaders accordingly meet in advance with the leaders of prospective protests to try to establish a sense of limits and terms of cooperation to prevent the worst consequences of the multiple agendas of those who show up to protest. Police leaders teach their personnel that they must not sink to the level of antagonistic, foul-mouthed protesters, and they carefully rehearse the limits to legitimate police discretion. While they urge their personnel to do all they can to avoid turning policing into 'us versus them' confrontation, they also explain that it is neither just nor prudent for police to ignore clear threats to the safety of protesters or police by waiting to act until somebody gets hurt. Justice and safety sometimes call for preventive rather than reactive measures, and the use of reasonable force is, after all, reasonable. The best police instructors I know teach the wisdom expressed by experienced street cops in the adage, 'You have to give people room to do what you want them to do'. They do not teach that if cops do their jobs well in dealing with public protests and demonstrations, they can count on the demonstrators to behave cooperatively and in good faith and on the media to report the events fairly.[12]

It is no more wise, honest or prudent to teach police that they can count on cooperation, reciprocity and fairness than it is to teach children that if they tell the truth and keep their promises, others will respond in kind. As Immanuel Kant and other philosophers have wisely observed, these lessons tend to generate cynicism. Children who are taught them later learn the hard way that they are not true. They tend to conclude that their teachers were either fools or liars. Temptations toward cynicism abound in policing without adding foolish teaching and silly pronouncements. It remains up to police to decide for themselves whether the public whose rights and safety they are sworn to secure are worthy of their service and sacrifices.

Even where there is widespread goodwill toward police, police services should not confidently rely on the public and their political representatives to provide funding sufficient to fulfil the police mission in justice and public safety. In the United States, many of the 50 states and major cities, facing large budget deficits in recent years, have dramatically reduced funding for police departments.

Reductions in personnel in police departments, corrections institutions and prosecutors' offices have led to double digit increases in such crimes as burglaries, car thefts and shoplifting in Seattle, Washington and other urban areas. Criminals are learning that they can commit non-violent property crimes with relative impunity. In Portland, Oregon and its surrounding Multnomah County, 'state officials declared on 1 March 2003 that they would no longer pay for public defenders except for the most violent offenders.' As a consequence, suspects in lesser crimes who are caught red-handed but cannot afford a lawyer are allowed to go free without penalty. Furthermore, where reduced police budgets lead to shortages of police, many of the gains in quality of life through broken windows and community policing cannot be sustained, except by reducing the geographical domains where police concentrate their assets.[13] These are facts of life in policing, and they are nowhere new. We cannot provide any benefit to policing, police or the public by glossing them over or teaching police that the seriousness of their mission will always safeguard their agencies from bad political decisions, mistaken legislation, severe, if unintended, consequences of misguided policy strategies or adverse but unpredictable economic and social shifts. Hard won gains in public safety may be squandered or lost, no matter how diligently police work to maintain them.

In sum, trustworthy policing is a necessary condition of confidence and cooperation from the general public, as distinguished from that segment of the public that benefits from autocratic and corrupt policing; but it is not a sufficient condition. The ethical police officer, as a living exemplar of respect for and commitment to duty and sacrifice for the sake of justice and the public safety, no matter the adversity of circumstance, is an irreplaceable leader, a teacher whose example illuminates a way of life far superior to the widespread moral decadence in modern society. Sadly, great teachers and their lessons do not always prevail.

Many other pronouncements in the European Code of Police Ethics and the Explanatory Memorandum that accompanies it are either doubtful or false. Limits of space prevent me from addressing all of those here; but among the more serious is the assertion that in using minimum necessary force, police must 'shoot to wound' and 'not wound more than is strictly necessary ...'[14]

In my experience, when the use of potentially deadly force is justified in relatively close confrontation, police should shoot at maximum body mass to stop the perpetrator without delay from doing grievous harm to anyone else, including police. The use of that level of force is intended to render the perpetrator immediately harmless. In the nearly chaotic situations I have witnessed where police legally used battering rams to gain access to residences of armed and dangerous suspects, no one could reasonably or justifiably or credibly have instructed the police, 'Well, if you have to shoot, shoot to wound.'

Comparably troublesome are pronouncements in the code about the 'lawfulness of police actions'; they are too confused, and too reliant on the European Convention On Human Rights, to advance competence, legitimacy and morality in policing. Article II (3) of the code says, 'Police actions must always be conducted in accordance with the national law and international standards accepted by the country.'[15] This 'acceptance' qualification exempts police who commit torture and murder in tyrannical regimes that spurn all human rights.

Article IV.4 (31) says,

> Police staff shall as a rule enjoy the same civil and political rights as other citizens. Restrictions of these rights may only be made when they are necessary for the exercise of the functions of the police in a democratic society, in accordance with the law, and in conformity with the European Convention On Human Rights.[16]

Unfortunately, in this and other matters, 'conformity to the European Convention' is an unreliable guide to policy and practice in policing, for reasons identified by Roger Scruton.[17] He wrote that the purpose of the European Convention On Human Rights was to establish an objective, philosophical test of the validity of legislation, and one that could be used to strike down oppressive laws as illegitimate. In practice, however, the Convention has proved vague and contradictory, and also insensitive to the very different social expectations and historical conditions of the people of our continent.

Article V.1 (38) of the code says, 'Police must always verify the lawfulness of their intended actions'; and the commentary adds, 'It follows from Article 3, that the lawfulness test is not limited to national law, but includes international human rights standards.'[18] Police frequently have to act very quickly to safeguard the public and themselves. They cannot possibly always verify in advance the lawfulness of what they do in emergencies; they must rely on their best judgment at the time and depend on investigative follow-up to assess the justifiability of their conduct. Accordingly, trustworthy police departments conduct conscientious and thorough investigations whenever police have used deadly force; and they sometimes ask other law enforcement agencies to investigate as well.

It is surely true that any nation, no matter how thorough its commitment to constitutional democracy and the rule of law, can enact laws that are foolish, discriminatory, unjust or unconstitutional. International bodies are not infallible either; and they are often less competent than individual nations to address questions of justice and public safety and insufficiently resolute or powerful to safeguard anyone.

Faults in a nation's laws are frequently subtle. Reasonable people of goodwill within a nation can disagree about a law's justice or constitutionality and about the adequacy of logical and historical argumentation in judicial construal. It is not the responsibility of police to settle such questions or to intrude on the sovereignty of the people by usurping the duties of the legislative or judicial branches of government. Certainly, police should be held accountable for enforcing laws unjustly; but in a nation dedicated to the security of the rights of the public, police have no right in their establishment of policy to intrude on the separation of powers and the checks and balances within the government itself. Police officers in genuine constitutional republics and democracies who live up to their oath of office satisfy the requirements of lawfulness, even though they are sometimes required by law to enforce laws that are odious to them. As citizens, they may join public efforts to change those laws.

THE TWO EDGES OF TOLERATION

In the 30 years that I have worked with police, I have witnessed improvements in policing and elevation of standards in recruitment, training, supervision, internal affairs investigations, forensics, efficient and effective application of resources, leadership, cooperation with the public and the media, and overall accountability. I have also seen the recurrence of difficulties in policing that cannot be entirely eliminated in any large institution because they are sown in human nature, including corruption for profit, brutality, and dishonest testimony that deprives suspects of their rights. During these years, I have watched as well the deterioration of public education, the rise of urban gangs and related criminal conspiracies, the lowering of societal expectations for public behaviour and other downward trends that make policing more difficult and demanding and, in some cases, futile.

My reflections on my experience convince me that tolerance and intolerance have two edges: the edge that cuts in favour of the security of individual rights, the fulfilment of duty and the common good; and the edge that cuts against them. Intolerance of unjust discrimination against individuals on any grounds, including: colour, sex, age, nationality or creed; intolerance of slavery, involuntary servitude, torture, deprivation of due process and other barbarous affronts to human dignity; and intolerance of arbitrary intrusions by government into individual liberty are all essential to civilisation itself. Toleration of religious, political and intellectual differences and disagreements is likewise integral to respect for individuals, the moral status of individual conscience and quality of life.

In such matters, however, the language of toleration is not always adequate. We speak of tolerating religious freedom, political dissent or intellectual independence, but that way of speaking can be misleading, since toleration normally implies or suggests disapproval. We do not disapprove of these forms of liberty in themselves, and we do not always disapprove of specific considered and conscientious judgments with which we disagree; sometimes we find the grounds on which others disagree with us instructive and admirable, especially where discourse remains civil in matters of great complexity and importance. In such cases, it is more accurate to say we respect another person's conscience, religious faith, political acumen or intellectual conscientiousness, or we respect the way the person thinks and lives, even though we do not share their beliefs or conclusions in every respect.

These forms of tolerance, intolerance and respect mark civilised life; but they have limits. Respect for political liberty and religious freedom does not oblige us to tolerate in silence expressions of political zealotry or religious fanaticism. Respect for freedom of the press and intolerance of certain forms of censorship do not oblige either the police or the public to assent to the false generalisation of the media that 'the public has a right to know'. We have no obligation to tolerate the purchase and use of school textbooks that whitewash the history of any religion, political regime or system or that use special pleading to condemn a religion or nation. We have no obligation to allow any publisher, teacher or school administrator to impose intellectual dishonesty or logical fallacies on students of any age. Academic freedom does not oblige us to tolerate intellectual incompetence or dissemination of propaganda in the classroom or to treat as irrelevant to academic qualification intemperance and irrationality in public speech.

We have no obligation stemming from considerations of diversity to tolerate any style of life that endangers others or violates their right to equal initial consideration; neither are we obliged to indulge or tolerate, in the name of religious freedom or cultural diversity, the practices of any group, including any minority immigrant group, which denies justice and safety to its most helpless members.

Duties of respect, tolerance, and intolerance cannot decently be ignored; neither can they honourably be shuffled into ambiguity, as with various Protocols in the European Convention On Human Rights. The First Protocol, Article 2, says,

> No person shall be denied the right to education. In the exercise of any functions which it assumes in relation to education and to teaching, the State shall respect the

right of parents to ensure such education and teaching in accordance with their own religious and philosophical convictions.'[19]

What do these two statements taken together imply for the duties of the state with respect to girls whose parents, as a matter of religious or philosophical conviction, deny them the opportunity for any education but the most rudimentary training? Is the state to allow female children to be victimised by the convictions, however fanatical or bigoted, of their parents? These are not questions to be treated at leisure in the abstract; they are questions about real children, the quality of whose lives is now in the balance.

The best moral guide in questions of justice and duty is the Golden Rule—Do unto others as you would have them do unto you, and do not do unto others as you would not have done to yourself. A kindred guide for identifying our duty is the Categorical Imperative of duty formulated by Immanuel Kant as, 'Act so as to treat humanity, whether in your own person or the person of another, always as an end in itself, and never as a means merely.' Act toward everyone with equal initial consideration; do not use others as mere means or reduce them to mere obstacles to your own gratification; and don't abandon the helpless.

Parents may unilaterally deprive their children of all sorts of things and deserve no criticism or interference. In my judgment, parents deserve respect and praise for depriving children of unsupervised hours in front of the television, a diet of unhealthy foods or the chance to attend a bad and dangerous school. But when parents, because of their religious or other beliefs, unilaterally deprive a child of educational opportunity itself, destructively deprive the child of equal consideration and treatment, they subject the child to flagrant injustice. No appeal to religious or philosophical conviction or to the will of God can change the injustice the child suffers or the consequences she will face for the rest of her life. Such injustice violates the Golden Rule and the status of girls and women as ends in themselves. I infer that a duty of justice requires our refusal to tolerate such treatment.

The edge of tolerance and intolerance that cuts most obviously and deeply against the ideals of liberty and justice is the refusal to be judgmental. Patterns of tasteless, provocative, loud, intrusive, nasty, crude, obscene and morally base speech, graffiti, dress, and behaviour corrupt the public spaces in which we live. Cheating, plagiarism and other forms of dishonesty undermine the purposes of education. And yet, many among us prefer to tolerate such things in silence.

A society that loses the distinction between liberty and licence risks its own destruction. A culture that tolerates in silence foul and loutish public habits, corruption and deceit without any effort toward informal social control by stigma, tacitly endorses the falsehood that rights entail no duties. Schools, police departments, businesses, media outlets, neighbourhoods, regions and nations where cowardice, dogma or popular values prevent outspoken refusal to tolerate flagrantly excessive and deficient behaviour bury the differences between having a right and acting rightly. In so doing, they abandon the hope that youths will form the good character to which moral restraint, reciprocity and fairness are weighty considerations.

Self-control against temptations to profit by deceit is essential to trustworthiness in any context. Tolerance of cheating in schools and universities debases the workforce of the future, including prospective applicant pools for policing.

Manners, it has long been said, are minor morals. Good manners are properly understood as expressions of respect for others. Leaving manners untended is an invitation to moral decline as surely as leaving broken windows untended is an invitation to criminal incursion and predation. Toleration of the corruption of the public spaces frequented by the young shatters the prospect of their seeing the Golden Rule applied and learning to live by it.

Police remain duty bound to live up to higher intellectual and moral standards than the general public; but good policing and law enforcement can never fully substitute for civic virtue in the people. The widespread collapse of the virtue of being responsibly tolerant into the vice of being persistently non-judgmental takes justice and safety down with it.

REFERENCES for *Chapter 3*

1 'Calgary Police Commission Review of Police Officer Codes of Conduct,' 2000 January 28, Calgary Police Commission Media Release, No. 200-01, p. 1.

2 Alexander Hamilton, James Madison and John Jay, in *The Federalist*, No. 6, ed. Jacob E. Cooke (Middletown, Connecticut: Wesleyan University Press, 1961), p. 35.

3 Hamilton, Madison, and Jay, No. 51, p. 349.

4 Ibid., p. 351.

5 Hamilton, Madison, and Jay, No. 15, p. 96.

6 James Q. Wilson and George L. Kelling, 'Broken Windows: The Police and Neighborhood Safety,' *Atlantic Monthly*, March 1982.

7 Recheal Stewart-Brown, '"Mind Your Own Business" is Bad Advice,' in *Community Policing Exchange* (Washington, DC: Community Policing Consortium, November/December 2000), p. 1.

8 Edwin J. Delattre, *Character and Cops: Ethics in Policing* (Washington, DC: AEI Press, 2002, fourth edition), pp. 314-318.

9 Council of Europe, Committee of Ministers, *The European Code of Police Ethics: Recommendation (2001) 10 Adopted by the Committee of Ministers of the Council of Europe on 19 September 2001 and Explanatory Memorandum,* Article I (1), p. 8. Accessed at <http://www.coe.int>.

10 Ian Johnson, 'Conspiracy Theories about Sept. 11 Get Hearing in Germany: Distrust of US Fuels Stories about Source of Attacks; Videos, Hot-Selling Books,' *The Wall Street Journal,* September 29, 2003, pp. A1, A12.

11 John Tierney, 'Iraqi Family Ties Complicate American Efforts for Change,' *The New York Times*, September 28, 2003, pp. 1, 13.

12 Edwin J. Delattre, 'Protesters and Police Have Role Next Summer,' *Newsday*, June 27, 2003, p. A42.

13 Fox Butterfield, 'As Budgets Shrink, Cities See Impact on Criminal Justice,' *The New York Times,* June 7, 2003, pp. A1, A11.

14 Council of Europe, Committee of Ministers, *The European Code of Police Ethics,* Article V (37), p. 32.

15 Council of Europe, Committee of Ministers, *The European Code of Police Ethics*, Article II (3), p. 18.

16 Council of Europe, Committee of Ministers, *The European Code of Police Ethics,* Article IV.4 (31), pp. 28, 29.

17 Roger Scruton, 'A Kantian Approach to Policing,' in *Police Leadership in the Twenty-first Century,* eds. Robert Adlam and Peter Villiers (Winchester: Waterside Press, 2003), p. 84.

18 Council of Europe, Committee of Ministers, *The European Code of Police Ethics,* Article V.1 (38), p. 32.

19 Council of Europe, *The European Convention On Human Rights Rome 4 November 1950 and its Five Protocols,* Protocol I, Article 2. Accessed at <http://www.hri-org/docs/ECHR50.html#P1>.

CHAPTER 4

Social Structures and their Threats to Moral Agency

Alasdair MacIntyre

Professor Alasdair MacIntyre is the author of *A Short History of Ethics* and other works of moral philosophy which have achieved worldwide recognition. This chapter was adapted from the annual lecture that Professor MacIntyre delivered at the Royal Institute of Philosophy on 24 February 1999 and has been reproduced with kind permission of both the author and the institute. We believe that it is of especial relevance to police virtue, and have added a commentary on its application in that context.

THE CASE OF 'J'

Imagine first the case of 'J' (who might be *Jemand,* 'anybody'). 'J' used to inhabit a social order, or rather an area within a social order, where socially approved roles were unusually well defined. Responsibilities were allocated to each such role and each sphere of role-structured activity was clearly demarcated. These allocations and demarcations were embodied in and partly constituted by the expectations that others had learned to have of those who occupied each such role. For those who occupied those roles to disappoint such expectations by failing to discharge their assigned responsibilities was to invite severe disapproval and other sanctions. To refuse to find one's place within the hierarchies of approved roles, or to have been refused a place, because judged unfit for any such role, was to be classified as socially deviant and irresponsible.

The key moral concepts that education had inculcated into 'J' were those of duty and responsibility. His fundamental moral beliefs were that each of us owes it to others to perform our assigned duties and to discharge our assigned responsibilities. A good human being performs those duties, discharges those responsibilities and does not trespass into areas that are not his or her concern.

A philosopher who comes across the likes of 'J' will understand his attitudes as cultural parodies. They are in part of Plato (conceiving of justice as requiring 'that each do his own work and not meddle with many things' *Republic* 433a) and in part of Kant (doing one's duty just because it is one's duty and not for the sake of any further end). These are authors who had influenced J's schoolteachers. A sociologist will entertain the suspicion that in certain types of social order it may be only in the form of parodies that some types of concept can continue to find expression. But for the moment let us put this thought on one side and return to 'J'.

'J', like everyone else, occupied a number of roles. He was a father; the treasurer of his sports club; and in wartime had been a non-commissioned officer. Afterwards he spent his working career in the service of the railways, rising to a position in which he was responsible for scheduling passenger and freight trains, monitoring their drivers' performance and coping with breakdowns.

Early in that career he had been mildly curious about what 'his' trains carried: commuters or vacationers, pig iron or cattle? But he was instructed firmly by his superiors to take *no* interest in such questions, but to attend *only* to what belonged to his role, so as not to be irresponsibly distracted. Hence he acquired the habit of taking no cognisance of what his trains carried. This habit endured through a later period, when the freight consisted in munitions and the passengers were Jews on their way to extermination camps. When still later 'J' was questioned about this, he said sincerely:

> I did not know. It was not for someone in my position to know. I did my duty. I did not fail in my responsibilities. You cannot charge me with moral failure.

Was 'J''s defence adequate?

MORAL AGENCY

To many people the answer will be obvious and that answer is, 'No'. Their answer presupposes a widely shared conception of moral agency. On this view, to be a moral agent is to be justifiably held responsible. Responsible for what? For one's actions, certainly, but for one's actions in at least three respects:

- firstly, moral agents so conceived are justifiably and uncontroversially held responsible for what they did intend by their actions;
- secondly, they may be justifiably held responsible for incidental aspects of those actions of which they should have been aware; and
- thirdly, they may be justifiably held responsible for at least some of the reasonably predictable effects of their actions.

It is in spelling out the second and third of these points that we encounter complexities. Consider two examples. Intentionally in my role as examiner I award the prize to the competitor with the highest marks, incidentally awarding the prize to the most arrogant competitor, and having reasonable grounds for predicting that the effect of the award will be to make him or her even more objectionable. But in this case it is my responsibility, because of my role, to ignore these latter considerations.

Contrast a second example. I intentionally return a handgun to its owner, as my role in the lost property office requires, incidentally and, as it happens, knowingly returning it to someone dangerously paranoid, and having reasonable grounds for predicting that in consequence someone innocent will be harmed. In this case, because I am aware of these latter aspects of my action, I am justifiably held responsible for them. Moreover, even if I had not known what I did, I might, at least in certain circumstances, be justifiably held responsible for not having found out what I should have found out.

What the first example makes clear is that we may sometimes be able to rebut charges that we were responsible for not taking cognisance of certain facts by citing a role that required us not to take account of them. What the second example makes clear is that sometimes we are justifiably held responsible for not having made ourselves aware of certain facts about our actions, whatever the requirements of our role may have been.

How is the one type of case to be discriminated from the other? It is part of the responsibility of moral agents, on this view of moral agency:

- to know how to discriminate between such cases at the level of practice; and
- to give reasons for so discriminating in the light of the best standards available.

One reason, although only one, why children, the mentally retarded and those suffering from some kinds of brain damage are denied the status of moral agent, or at least of fully-fledged moral agent, is that they are unable to do this. And, if we hold 'J' responsible for knowing what he was doing, whatever the requirements of his role might have been, we are ascribing to him just such a power of reasonable discrimination. Yet we are entitled to hold 'J' responsible only if the best standards available to him would have warranted him in making those reasonable discriminations that we judge that he ought to have made.

So what were the best standards available to 'J'? Here a second remark is to the point. 'J' had been taught that the unquestionably best standards were in fact the standards defining and governing the role requirements of his social order. His habits of mind and action had been formed in a culture in which the truth of this claim was generally taken for granted. Those whose expectations were that 'J' would do what his role required, and who held him accountable, shared his view that the established standards were unquestionably the best. So, if we condemn 'J', we are treating him as justifiably responsible, not only for his actions and for his knowledge of them, and not only also for his practical reasoning, but in addition for having failed to question the hitherto unquestioned. We are taking the view that responsible deliberation requires that on occasion one puts established standards in question, whatever verdict about them one may arrive at in the end.

Moral agents are on this view justifiably held responsible for the standards governing the reasoning from which their actions flow and they have to understand themselves as thus responsible. When 'J' attempted to rebut the accusations advanced against him by saying that he had discharged all his responsibilities, he laid himself open to the questions of:

- what reason he had for taking his socially assigned responsibilities to be his only responsibilities; and
- what reason he had for continuing to believe that the established standards governing his deliberations were the best standards.

By having failed to ask, let alone to answer these questions, 'J''s defence of his deliberate setting of limits to his knowledge also fails. Or rather, it fails provided that we are justified in ascribing to 'J' the full powers of moral agency. But is it possible that we are not so justified?

It is a widely held doctrine that human beings share equally in a capacity to be able to transcend in thought the limitations of established normative and evaluative standards. Yet questions arise. Firstly, one cannot be a moral agent without understanding oneself as a moral agent at the level of one's everyday practice. Secondly, one cannot exercise the powers of a moral agent unless one is able to understand oneself as justifiably held responsible in virtue of one's ability to exercise those powers. But how human beings are able to understand themselves depends in key part upon, and is always in some ways limited by, the nature of the social and cultural order they inhabit. The third question, therefore, is this: Are there or might there be types of social structure that would prevent those who inhabited them from understanding themselves as moral agents? Or, if this seems to envisage too extreme a state of affairs, are there or might there be types of social structure that seriously threaten the possibility of understanding oneself as a moral agent and so of acting as a moral agent?

What is it to understand oneself as a moral agent?

What is it to understand oneself as a moral agent at the level of everyday practice? Three characteristics of such self-understanding are relevant.

Firstly, I have to understand myself as, and to present myself to others as, someone with an identity *other* than the identities of role and office that I assume in each of the roles that I occupy. I have to understand myself as someone who brings to each role qualities of mind and character that belong to me *qua* individual and not *qua* role-player. It is a mistake to think of the relationship of individuals to roles as being the same as or closely similar to that of stage actors to the dramatic parts that they play. For although the lives of individuals are constituted in large part by the various roles that they play, they are generally able to reflect upon their role-playing in ways that are not dictated by those same roles. It is in *how* they play out their roles that individuals exhibit their individual character. What more there is to individuals than their role-playing also includes the continuities of each individual's history, as he or she moves from role to role, from one sphere of social activity to another. My awareness and understanding of myself as an individual is partly constituted by the various acknowledgments of that individuality by others—and my ability to respond to those others as individuals and not just as role-players.

This mutual acknowledgment of our individuality characterises some of our social relationships rather than others and some of our social relationships more markedly than others. And central among such acknowledgments are those judgments in which we evaluate individuals as individuals, in respect of their virtues and the goodness of their lives. But initially such judgments are generally governed by socially established standards—just as much as our judgments about individuals as role-players. We all begin unquestioningly with the unquestioned.

Secondly, moral agents have to understand themselves as rational individuals with confidence in their powers of judgement. Rationally justifiable confidence is necessary, because the critical response of the moral agent has to be distinguished from, and to present itself to others as distinguished from, mindless deviance and revolt. So moral agents have to be entitled to confidence in their own moral judgments, when they are of the form, *'Even although it is almost universally agreed in this social order that in these circumstances someone in my role should act thus, I judge that I should act otherwise.'*

What entitles someone to confidence in such judgments? We are always liable to error in making particular moral judgments. We may:

- go beyond the evidence;
- rely upon some unsubstantiated generalisation;
- be over-influenced by our liking and disliking of particular individuals;
- project onto a situation some unrecognised fantasy; or
- exhibit either insensitivity to suffering, or sentimentality about it.

Our intellectual errors are often rooted in moral errors. We need, therefore, to have tested systematically our capacity for moral deliberation and judgment in this and that type of situation by subjecting our arguments and judgments to the critical scrutiny of reliable others, of co-workers, family or friends.

Such others, of course, are not always reliable and some may influence us in ways that strengthen the propensity to error. So to have confidence in our deliberations and judgments we need social relationships of a certain kind. We need forms of social association in and through which our deliberations and practical judgments are subjected to extended and systematic critical questioning that will teach us how to make judgments in which both we and others may have confidence.

This is not all. Moral agents also have to understand themselves as accountable to at least two sets of individuals and groups:

- those with whom they have engaged together in critically informed deliberation; *and*
- those whose hitherto unquestioning reliance on the established standards of the social order they challenge by their deliberation and their action.

To the former they owe an account of why they take it that their reasons for action have been able to withstand the strongest criticisms so far directed against them. To the latter they owe an account of why their reasons for challenging the established standards are good reasons. In giving such accounts they are inviting those who have hitherto accepted the established standards also to engage with them in critical deliberative conversation. And in understanding themselves and those others as accountable they understand themselves and those others as moral agents.

Accountability to particular others, participation in critical practical enquiry and acknowledgment of the individuality both of others and of oneself are all, then, marks of the social relationships and mode of self-understanding that characterise the moral agent. Strip away those social relationships and that mode of self-understanding and what would be left would be a seriously diminished type of agency, one unable to transcend the limitations imposed by its own social and cultural order. Moral agency thus does seem to require a particular kind of social setting.

There must therefore be a place in any social order for the reflective critical questioning of standards hitherto taken for granted—at the point at which they dictate everyday practice. The necessary presupposition of such questioning is some more or less shared conception of what it is to be a good human being. That conception focuses upon those qualities which individuals possess or fail to possess *qua* individuals, independently of their roles. Those qualities include the capacity to stand back from and reconsider their engagement with the role they occupy. And we may remind ourselves that just this capacity to stand back was what 'J' lacked.

Qualities as virtues: Integrity and constancy

Those qualities mentioned above are the virtues. In different times and places the catalogue of the virtues is not always the same; and particular virtues are sometimes understood differently. But there is a core notion of the virtues as qualities of human beings. Central to it, there is an acknowledgment of two virtues, without which the others cannot be possessed. To those virtues I give their traditional names of 'integrity' and 'constancy'.

To have integrity is to refuse to be, to have educated oneself so that one is no longer able to be, one kind of person in one social context, while quite another in other contexts. It is to have set inflexible limits to one's adaptability to the roles that one may be called upon to play.[1]

Constancy, like integrity, sets limits to flexibility of character. Integrity requires of those who possess it that they exhibit the same moral character in different social contexts. Constancy requires that those who possess it pursue the same goods through extended periods of time, not allowing the requirements of changing social contexts to distract them from their commitments or to redirect them.

So individuals with these two virtues will learn not only how to occupy some determinate set of roles within their social order, but also how to think of their goods and of their character independently of the requirements of those roles. They will be inhabitants of two moral systems:

- that of the established social order with its assignment of roles and responsibilities; and
- that developed within those milieux in which that assignment has been put to the question.

The degree to which these two systems are at odds with each other varies in different social and cultural orders. Inhabitants of those two systems where the requirements are incompatible will be forced either to think their way through a series of more or less painful choices or to find some strategy for evading these choices.

The thinking that is needed is the practical thinking in everyday life of certain kinds of family and household, of workplace, school and church, and of a variety of kinds of local community. What their flourishing will always be apt to generate is tension, which may develop into conflict between the requirements of the established social and moral order and the attitudes of those educated in those social settings that make the exercise of the powers of moral agency

[1] Please see the discussion of integrity and the practice of deception as an integral part of policing, which follows Professor MacIntyre's text in the special note on p. 54.

possible. So to be a moral agent is to have the potentiality for living and acting in a state of tension or, if need be, conflict between two moral points of view. And this is never simply or mainly a tension or a conflict between points of view at the level of abstract and general theory. It is always primarily a tension or a conflict between socially embodied points of view, between modes of practice.

The history of moral philosophy has usually been written—except for those historians influenced by Augustine, Marx or Nietzsche—in such a way as to disguise this fact. Why does this matter? It is because it is from these tensions and conflicts, when and in so far as they are present, that morality gets an important part of its content. There are of course social and cultural orders in which tension, let alone conflict, between such rival moral systems has not yet been generated to any significant degree. But, whenever it has been so generated, it defines an area in which at least some moral agents find themselves with particular responsibilities to discharge. Consider how this might be so with regard to truthfulness, considered as one essential constituent of the human good.

The issue of truthfulness

Both Aquinas and Kant hold that it is wrong to tell a lie in any circumstance whatsoever. But one could refrain from lying throughout one's life without having done what is required to achieve the good of truthfulness. For truthfulness requires of us that, when it is of peculiar importance that rational agents should understand some particular aspect of their lives so that they are neither misled nor deceived, it is a responsibility of those who are truthful to disclose what is relevant to such understanding.

Conflicts about whose responsibility it is to know about what are therefore among those that in particular circumstances, especially the circumstances of distinctively modern societies, provide content for moral uncertainty. *Always ask about any social and cultural order what it needs its inhabitants not to know* has become an indispensable sociological maxim. *Always ask about your own social and cultural order what it needs you and others not to know* has become an indispensable moral maxim.

The established norms and values with which we may be invited to enter into conflict will commonly be to some large degree our own norms and values, those by which we have hitherto been guided. So that initially at least that conflict will be within each of us. This is not only a matter of incompatibility between two sets of practically embodied norms and values. It is also a matter of a certain resistance to critical questioning that claims about the limitations and errors of the standpoint of the established order are apt to evoke. We may in some cases be misled about the nature and degree of such resistance, if we are naive in our identification of the norms and values of the established order.

There are types of social order, including our own, in which those norms themselves not only legitimate but also encourage questioning, criticism and protest. The set of approved social roles includes such roles as those of the Indignant Protester and the Angry Young Person and the activities of criticism and protest are themselves governed by prescribed routines. We need, then, to draw a line between conflict that is internal to and in no way a threat to an established order, and conflict that is more radical. Radical conflict genuinely raises the question of whether established roles and routines can or cannot be justified in the light of the best account we have of the human good. It is conflict of this latter kind that social orders may need to contain or suppress, if they are to continue functioning as they have done.

REVIEW

Where then has the argument taken us? We began with the case of 'J'. He asserted that he could not be justifiably held responsible for his part in making the massacre of Jews possible, because he did not know what or whom his trains were carrying. It was not his responsibility to know this, given his social role and the standards defining the responsibilities of anyone occupying that role. To this it was replied that moral agents should scrutinise their actions and the standards on which they are based. Therefore 'J' was responsible for his lack of knowledge and so indirectly for his participation in massacring Jews. What then might have prevented 'J', even though a psychologically normal individual, from exercising the powers of moral agency?

How we answered this question depended upon an identification of three types of precondition for the exercise of the powers of moral agency.

Firstly, the powers of moral agency can only be exercised by those who understand themselves as moral agents, and, that is to say, by those who understand their moral identity as to some degree distinct from and independent of their social roles. To understand oneself thus is to understand that one's goodness as a human being—the answer that by one's whole way of life one gives to the question *'How is it best for a human being in my circumstances to live?—* is not to be equated with one's goodness at being and doing what this or that role requires.

Secondly, the powers of moral agency can only be exercised by those who are able to justify rational confidence in their judgments about the goodness and badness of human beings. This ability requires participation in social relationships and in types of activity in which one's reflective judgments emerge from systematic dialogue with others and are subject to critical scrutiny by others. Without milieux within which such relationships and activities are effectively sustained, the possibility of the exercise of the powers of moral agency will be undermined. Those who participate in the relationships and activities of such milieux will always find themselves in potential conflict with, and often in actual conflict with, the requirements of established role structures and therefore with those who uphold those requirements. Conflict may help to define what the virtues require in this or that particular situation.

Thirdly, it is only in and through such milieux that moral agents become able to understand themselves as accountable to others in respect of the human virtues and not just in respect of their role-performances. So all three preconditions can be satisfied only within social orders in which there exist spheres of activity which sustain the relevant kind of understanding of the self, the relevant kind of critical discourse and reflection, and the relevant kind of accountability.

Are there types of social structure that preclude the existence of such milieux, so that the very possibility of the exercise of the powers of moral agency might be threatened? The type of structure that I shall use as an example is very different in some respects from that inhabited by 'J'. But it is worth beginning with a more extreme case.

THE STRUCTURES OF COMPARTMENTALISATION

In the 1970s I was a minor participant in a study of the moral dimensions of decision-making in the American electric power industry. One incidental discovery in the course of that study was that power company executives tended to answer what were substantially the same questions somewhat differently, depending on whether they took themselves to be responding *qua* power company executive or *qua* parent and head of household or *qua* concerned citizen. That is to say, their attitudes varied with their social roles and they seemed quite unaware of this. I take this to be a mild example of a peculiarly modern phenomenon that I will call 'compartmentalisation'.

Compartmentalisation goes beyond that differentiation of roles and institutional structures that characterises every social order. Within each sphere of activity or compartment, its own norms dictate which kinds of consideration are to be treated as relevant to decision-making and which are to be excluded. So in the power company case, executives were unable even to entertain, as a serious policy alternative, reduction in the overall levels of power consumption, so long as they thought and spoke from within their sphere of activity as power company executives. But they did not suffer from the same inability when thinking and speaking as consumers or concerned citizens.

Individuals move between spheres of activity, exchanging one role for another and one set of standards for their practical reasoning for another. They thus become to some important extent dissolved into their various roles, maybe playing one part in the life of the family, quite another in the workplace, yet a third as a member of a sports club and a fourth as a military reservist.

Within each sphere such individuals conform to the requirements imposed on their role within that sphere. There is no milieu available to them in which they are able, together with others, to step back from those roles and those requirements and to scrutinise themselves and the structure of their society from some external standpoint.

The ethics of deception

Consider the different forms that the ethics of deception may take in different spheres, and the different answers given to such questions as, *'Who is justified in deceiving whom and about what?'* and, *'Who has the authority to object to deception?'* A first example is that of a business corporation whose chief executive officer decides to exaggerate the progress made by the corporation's scientists on a research project, with the aims both of not losing customers to rivals and of bolstering share prices. Here the scientists have no right to lie to or otherwise deceive the chief executive officer—not to do so is a condition of their continuing employment—and they likewise have no right to speak out. The only grounds on which objection to such deception can be based, if it is to be heard, is that in the longer run deception will fail to maximise corporate profits. (A former chairman of the Securities Exchange Commission explained his decision to endow a chair in business ethics at Harvard University by claiming that in the long run ethics pays.)

Contrast with this the situation of those same scientists when publishing their data in professional journals. In this context no end external to scientific enquiry is allowed to justify deception. The falsification of data warrants their exposure by other scientists and their consequent expulsion from the scientific community. So the individual who recurrently moves between the spheres of corporate activity and of independent scientific enquiry exchanges one ethics of deception for another, often without any consciousness of so doing.

That same individual will of course also move into yet other contexts with their own ethics of deception. For example, take the kind of social occasion in which relative strangers meet, drink in hand, anxious to make a favourable impression on prestigious people and equally anxious to avoid garrulous and insistent bores. Here deception, including lying, is generally a sanctioned aspect of the work of self-presentation—without it I might not be able to make myself sufficiently interesting—and I may defend myself from aggressive conversational intrusions by further lies. Each of these three ethics of deception needs further elaboration. But that elaboration would only strengthen the grounds for concluding that the norms of deception are specific to social context and that to move from one role in one sphere of activity to another role in another sphere is to move from one context-based moral standpoint to another.

Attitudes to death

We encounter a similar range of differences in contemporary attitudes to death. Contrast the attitudes to death exhibited within the sphere of family life by:

- those mourning the death of a child in a car accident;
- the executives of the corporation that manufactured the car; and
- the lawyers who urge the family to sue the driver of the car.

For family members the death is a unique loss for which nothing can compensate. For the corporate executives it contributes to an annual death rate that is an acceptable trade-off for the benefits of automobile sales to their industry and to society. For the lawyers it has a precise financial value calculable on the basis of recent jury awards. And it is only possible to adopt the attitudes dictated by any of these three perspectives by temporarily excluding those of the other two.

So those who move from extending their condolences at the graveside, to a meeting of automobile company executives re-evaluating their production goals, to the offices of a law firm, will find the same death evaluated in ways that are not only different, but to some degree incompatible.[2] But compartmentalisation involves more than this in two respects:

---

[2] I have treated this a little more fully in: 'Some Enlightenment Projects Reconsidered' in R. Kearney and M. Dooley (eds) (1998), *Questioning Ethics: Contemporary Debates in Philosophy*, London: Routledge, pp. 255–6.

- the degree to which each sphere of activity is insulated from others, so that considerations that would carry weight in some other sphere are deprived of it in this; and
- the absence of any accessible sphere of activity in which practically effective reasoning might be used to evaluate the norms and values of each particular sphere from some external point of view.

Insulation is provided by the prescribed standard responses to the introduction into the conversations within some particular sphere of considerations that are by its norms at best irrelevant, at worst distracting. So, if in a policy meeting of the Midwestern power executives one of them had proposed attempting to bring about an overall reduction in power consumption, or if at a social gathering someone were to insist that the standards of truthfulness required in scientific reports should also apply to party gossip, their remarks might be treated as a joke or ignored. But, if such a speaker persisted, they would find themselves deprived at least temporarily of their status in that sphere of activity: treated, that is, as a source of background noise rather than a participant.

The effects of insulation are reinforced by the absence from everyday life of milieux in the home, the workplace and elsewhere in which such agents might engage in extended critical reflection with others about, for example:

- what conflicts the virtue of truthfulness requires us to engage in that time and place; and
- just how its requirements are at odds with the established ethics of deception in that sphere of activity; or
- the significance of death.

The divided self

Such milieux would provide agents with what they otherwise lack, an understanding of themselves as having a substantive identity independent of their roles and as having responsibilities that do not derive from those roles. Such an understanding overcomes the divisions within the self imposed by compartmentalisation and sets the scene for types of conflict that compartmentalisation effectively suppresses.

This divided self has to be characterised negatively, by what it lacks. It is not only without any standpoint from which it can pass critical judgment on the standards governing its various roles, but it must also lack those virtues of integrity and constancy that are prerequisites for exercising the powers of moral agency. It cannot have integrity, just because its allegiance to this or that set of standards is always temporary and context-bound and it cannot have the constancy that is expressed in an unwavering directedness, since it recurrently changes direction as it moves from sphere to sphere. Indeed its conception of virtue will generally be one of excellence in role-performance rather than of excellence as a human being and hence what is judged excellent in one role-governed context may be very different from and even sometimes incompatible with what is judged excellent in others. (This context-bound use of the concept of virtue parodies older conceptions and uses, and in so doing may remind us of

'J'— whose uses of moral concepts were also parodies. But for the moment let us put this resemblance to 'J' on one side.)

Lacking such standards, and without also an awareness that it lacks them, there is nothing about the self thus divided that is liable to generate conflict with what are taken to be the requirements of morality within the established order. In so far as that self recognises and aspires to conform to what it takes to be moral requirements within each particular sphere of activity, it will be a morality from which the elements of potential and actual conflict are missing, a diminished morality that matches its diminished powers of agency.

It must therefore seem that so far as individuals approach the condition of this divided self, they can no longer be justifiably held responsible for their actions in anything like the ways in which moral agents are held responsible. Here, it seems, there is indeed a type of social structure that warrants for those who inhabit it a plea of gravely diminished responsibility. And we may be tempted therefore to turn immediately to the question of whether the earlier twentieth century society that 'J' inhabited sufficiently resembled later forms of compartmentalised social and cultural order for us to enter a similar plea on J's behalf. But this would be a mistake. For we need first to consider some further dimensions of this divided self.

It is, I shall argue, a self that is to a significant degree responsible for its own divisions. It is indeed to be characterised negatively in terms of lacks or absences, but these lacks or absences are, so I will suggest, the expression of refusals, active refusals by that self. Two aspects are relevant:

- Firstly, the self can never be dissolved nor dissolve itself *entirely* into the distinctive roles that it plays in each compartmentalised sphere of activity. The self has another virtue: adaptability, flexibility, knowing chameleon-like how to take on the colour of this or that social background. And it exhibits this virtue in managing its transitions from one role to another, so that it appears, so far as possible, to be dissolved into its roles. But this appearance is, when well-managed, a dramatic feat, an expression of the actor as well as of the roles enacted.
- Secondly, the individual *qua* individual appears not only in managing the transitions from one role to another, but also, as I suggested earlier, in the role-playing itself. There are some roles that may seem purely mechanical, since the individual who plays the role can always be replaced by a machine: where there was once a ticket-seller, there is now a ticket-machine. But the ticket-seller always faced choices that machines never confront: *how* to play the role—cheerfully or sullenly, carelessly or conscientiously, efficiently or inefficiently? For all roles, the way in which they are enacted presupposes not only an answer to a question posed to and by the role-player: 'How is it best for me to play this role?'—but also to such further questions: 'By what standards am I to judge what is best?' and 'Should I continue to play this role in this way?'

It is the inescapability of such questions that suggests that practical reasoning that is adequate for doing what a particular role requires will itself generate reasons for acting beyond those requirements and even sometimes against those requirements. To resist asking such questions, to insist upon terminating one's practical reasoning whenever it directs one beyond one's role requires a peculiar kind of self-discipline. To be able to restrict one's practical reasoning to what will enable one to discharge the responsibilities of one's socially approved roles is to have imposed on one's thinking a set of artificial restrictions. It is to have arbitrarily closed one's mind to certain possibilities of action and, although others may provide one with motives for effecting such a closure, it is only with one's own active co-operation that the habits of mind can be developed which make such closure possible.

What is true of practical reasoning generally holds with special force of those periods during which, but for avoidance strategies, one might find that one had committed oneself to incompatible judgments. The divided self of a compartmentalised social order, in order not to have to confront incompatible attitudes to, say, truthfulness or death has to have developed habits of mind that enable it not to attend to what it would have to recognise as its own incoherences. And to learn how to focus one's attention in this way once again requires one's active co-operation.

I conclude that what I earlier characterised as lacks or absences of the divided selves of a compartmentalised social order are better described as active refusals and denials. The divided self is complicit with others in bringing about its own divided states and so can be justly regarded as their co-creator. It and those others can justifiably be called to account for what they have jointly made of themselves. They may indeed inhabit a type of social and cultural order whose structures to some large degree inhibit the exercise of the powers of moral agency. But they share in responsibility for having made themselves into the kind of diminished agent that they are. Their responsibility is that of co-conspirators, engaged together in a conspiracy that functions so that they can lead blamelessly compliant lives, able plausibly to plead lack of knowledge of as well as lack of control over outcomes for which they might otherwise be held jointly responsible. Their lack of knowledge and their lack of control are often enough real, an inescapable outcome of the structuring of roles and responsibilities in a compartmentalised social order. But they are, so I have argued, responsible and accountable for making it the case that they do not know and that they lack certain powers. They are not passive victims. To have understood this enables us to return to the case of 'J'.

Once more the case of 'J'

I take the social structures of compartmentalisation, although peculiar to the late twentieth century, to be more generally instructive. They provide us with a case at the extremes. This is a case in which, after compartmentalisation has progressed beyond a certain point, many agents exhibit no awareness of responsibilities beyond those assigned to them by their roles in each particular sphere of activity; while in their practical reasoning they admit as premises only those considerations sanctioned in each context by the norms defining and governing those roles. Their lives express the social and cultural order that they inhabit in such a way that they have become unable to recognise, let alone to transcend its limitations. They do not have the resources that would enable them to move to an independent standpoint.

Both their resemblances to and their differences from 'J' and those like him are worth remarking. Both 'J' and those who inhabit a compartmentalised society accept unquestioningly structures that give definition to their lives by prescribing a range of roles that they are to occupy and a range of responsibilities attached to each. And it is not only what they are to do in each type of social context that is prescribed.

What kind of practical reasoning it is for each of them to undertake, *qua* enactor of this or that role, what it is the responsibility of each to know, and what is not a matter for their concern or knowledge are also prescribed. And in so far as both are deprived of participation in milieux in which in the company of others they might have elaborated a standpoint external to their role-structured activities, they have become unable to pass judgment on the limitations of their judgments. These are the resemblances, but there are also striking differences.

'J' and those like him exhibited an awareness of their situation that is absent from those who inhabit a compartmentalised society. 'J' judged that this way of life was the best way of life for him and for others. It is true that he did not and perhaps could not open up this judgment to any extended reflective scrutiny. But he made it and was capable of making it proudly and defiantly. Judgments about compartmentalisation and its effects upon the lives of those subject to it are necessarily third-person judgments delivered from some standpoint that has escaped those effects. 'J' was able to deliver judgment on the organization of his social life in the first person. What kind of difference does this signify?

At least this: that, if those who inhabit a compartmentalised social order can be held responsible as co-authors of their social and moral situation, then the case for imputing such responsibility to 'J' and those like him must be even stronger. 'J' actively chose not to move beyond the boundaries imposed by established role-definitions. He had made himself into what the roles said that he was. By so doing he had assented to doing, reasoning and knowing only as the standards governing his roles prescribed. And in so assenting he had excluded the possibility of moral conflict, for truthfulness as a virtue was itself defined for 'J' by the context-bound standards governing his role-performances, so that much that truthfulness requires had become invisible.

I argued earlier that, 'Always ask about your social and cultural order what it needs you and others not to know' has become in the modern world an indispensable moral maxim. 'J', like those subject to the limitations of a compartmentalised social order, had co-operated in making it impossible to acknowledge the authority of this maxim. But his refusal of such knowledge made him too responsible, in co-operation with others, for not knowing what he did not know. So 'J''s later defence of his earlier actions failed.

It has been my assumption that when 'J' defended himself by denying that he had had the relevant knowledge, he was sincere. Some commentators have insisted that 'J' and those like him must have had that knowledge and that therefore they were guilty, thus implying that if they had not had that knowledge, then they would have been innocent. I have contended by contrast that, even if 'J' and those like him did not have that knowledge, they remained guilty and that their guilt was not merely individual guilt, but, in a sense that I hope has been made clear, the guilt of a whole social and cultural order.

EDITORIAL COMMENTARY

The systematic use of deception

It may be a temptation for some of the critics of the police service—and indeed, for persons who might be called its qualified admirers—to equate the police officer *qua* police officer with the person who lacks moral integrity, and who as 'J' is the subject of Professor MacIntyre's article.

The police officer, after all, belongs to a culture that by and large does not practise, or even attempt to encourage, the habit of systematic moral questioning. The critic might also argue that police officers cannot be moral persons in the full sense, in that they practise deception as an integral part of their daily lives. Here we are referring not only to the systematic and sustained deception that is the working life of the officer who goes deep 'undercover', but also to the everyday practice of some element of deception by all police officers who have concealed their identity, their profession or their values for the sake of 'the job.' Everyday deception is an essential part of policing. The decisions on which it is based are not the result of a careful exercise in applied ethics, but resemble more the outcome of a conscious desire not to reflect on deeper issues which Professor MacIntyre describes as choosing not to be a moral agent in the full sense, and which he condemns nonetheless as a moral choice.

However, there are other factors to consider. Because someone—let us call him 'P'—decides to be a police officer, then he assumes that certain other moral issues have already been decided for him in advance, as it were, and that he has no need to wrestle with them. In the broadest sense, these are some of the fundamental axioms that *P* does not challenge:

- Police work is a necessary and honourable occupation. In order for it to be successful, means must sometimes be used which in other circumstances would be regarded as morally reprehensible, such as a whole range of techniques that show less than a full respect for the dignity of the person.[3] In this case, we are referring to the systematic and indeed 'institutional' use of deception: but it is only one means that may come under moral scrutiny.
- The decision as to when to use a means such as deception on an official and systematic basis will be made by a senior officer of considerable experience, in whose judgement the subordinate officer is right to consider that it is valid to place his or her trust.
- That senior officer will have made his or her assessment of the need to use the means or technique in question on the basis, at least in part, of the possession of information which has been necessarily protected, and the further dissemination of which is necessarily restricted, on the 'need to know' principle.
- It is right that the 'need to know' principle should be used to exclude rather than include. It is *not* a valid criterion, under contemporary security

[3] These issues were explored in some depth in our previous volume, Adlam R and Villiers P (2003), *Police Leadership in the Twenty-first Century*, Winchester: Waterside Press. See especially Miller and Palmer's essay, 'Authority, Leadership and Character'.

doctrine, that the 'need to know' principle should be breached purely in the interests of the moral development and capacity for autonomous decision-making of those who will be required to take action on the basis of confidential information which may not have been shared with them. Indeed, it is conventionally regarded as one of the duties and obligations of rank, if not its privilege, that the senior officer is required to exercise a more profound moral judgement than the junior, in that the former must make moral judgements on the other's behalf. The subordinate cannot be allowed to see the full 'picture', as it were, and must therefore trust his or her superior's judgement without full possession of the salient facts. Where moral development and security clash, security wins.

- The subordinate is entitled to be able to form a general impression of the overall character or virtue of the superior and his or her capacity for wise decision-making. The subordinate is also entitled, at least under an ethically-principled decision-making process, to be given a realistic idea of the risks involved in a particular enterprise, and the degree of support that will be provided both during and after the operation in question, before deciding to put their life or welfare at stake.
- Those requirements do not oblige the senior officer to put information at risk by sharing everything known with the members of the team, including those who will be taking the risks on his or her behalf: and nor would they expect this. For they are in a position to recognise that the senior officer who betrays information may wittingly or unwittingly reveal its source, to whom there is a duty both ethical and legal to protect it; and if they were a source, they would also wish to be protected.
- Therefore, in broad terms, the capacity for moral decision-making of the subordinate officer is necessarily restricted.

As we begin to describe, or rather to hint at, the inescapable reality of police work, we are far from reaching the conclusion that it is a morality-free zone, or that the police officer is incapable of acting as a moral agent in the full sense. What we do begin to see, however, is a complex moral battlefield with few clear landmarks or reliably marked minefields. Moreover, as in the unreconstructed view of the First World War, there is at least a suspicion that the generals are comfortably ensconced in their chateaux, whilst the poor, bloody foot soldiers endure as best they can in their trenches, shelters and shell-scrapes.

The usefulness of professional ethics

> In law and in journalism, in government and in the social sciences, deception is taken for granted when it is felt to be excusable by those who tell the lies and who tend also to make the rules ...
>
> There is little help to be found in the codes and writings on professional ethics... Existing codes say little about when deception is and is not justified. (Bok, 1978)[1]

Is deception forbidden under any of the recognised codes of conduct governing proper police behaviour? We have found no example that it is. There is no mention of deception as such, for example, in the 1992 *Code of Ethics for the Police*, as cited in

Villiers (1997a, Chapter 4) although the need to respect confidentiality of information is recorded.

The *European Code of Conduct for the Police*, published in September 2001, is intended as an authoritative guide for police conduct throughout the jurisdiction of the Council of Europe. However, there is no reference to deception in the code—although it would be possible to infer the widespread and systematic practice of unnecessary deception to be unethical. The possibility of inference, however, is not the same as firm and positive guidance; and the wording of this code is in any case open to interpretation. Consider, for example, paragraph 14—the closest that the code comes to considering deception: '14. The police and its personnel in uniform shall normally be easily recognisable'.

The failure to provide an absolute rule in this area is understandable. Let us suppose that a high-minded state legislature decided that its police force should not carry out any acts of deception at all, and forbad their use. Firstly, we would suggest that such a prohibition would be an impossible undertaking, since there would be occasions when people would deceive themselves with little or no assistance by the police—who would nevertheless benefit. Secondly, the ruling itself would soon be challenged on grounds that an ethicist would describe as teleological. (Suppose, for example, the police failed to prevent a loss of life because of a failure to carry out a suitable and proportionate deception.) Nevertheless, we feel that article 14 is too broadly phrased.

The importance of human rights jurisprudence

Whilst human rights doctrine is not a substitute for the development of professional ethics, it is of relevance. It has provided a new generation of British police officers[4] with a language at least quasi-ethical in its terms, which they would not otherwise have acquired; and it has enabled them to reflect upon and clarify the concept of proportionality.

The right to a fair trial

The European Court of Human Rights (ECHR) has not provided a set of clear and explicit rules on the use of deception in the gathering and use of evidence. Nor, indeed, has it set out to provide such guidance on the use of deception by the police in general, although its views in this area can be inferred in some judgements as one of the reluctant acceptance of necessity in the struggle against crime.

In its judgement on *Doorson v. The Netherlands*, the ECHR stated:

> The admissibility of evidence is primarily a matter for regulation by national law and as a general rule it is for the national courts to assess the evidence before them. The Court's task under the Convention is not to give a ruling as to whether statements of witnesses were properly admitted as evidence, but rather to ascertain whether the proceedings as a whole, including the way in which evidence was taken, were fair.

This judgement has been re-emphasised and developed in later judgements. Consider *Allan v. The United Kingdom*, Application Number 48539/99, judgement dated 5 November 2002, which refers to the disguised interrogation of a prisoner by

[4] The United Kingdom passed the Human Rights Act 1998 and it came into force for the state as a whole in October 2000.

a police informer whilst in police custody, amongst other matters—the prisoner claiming violations of Articles 6, 8 and 13. The Court stated:

> It is not the role of the Court to determine, as a matter of principle, whether particular types of evidence—for example, unlawfully obtained evidence—may be admissible, or indeed, whether the applicant was guilty or not. The question that must be answered is whether the proceedings as a whole, including the way in which the evidence was obtained, were fair ...
>
> As regards the privilege against self-incrimination or the right to silence, the Court has reiterated that these are generally recognised international standards that lie at the heart of a fair procedure ...
>
> [In this case] the information gained by the use of H [the informant] in this way may be regarded as having been obtained in defiance of the will of the applicant and its use at trial impinged on the applicant's right to silence and privilege against self-incrimination. Accordingly, there has been in this respect a violation of Article 6, Paragraph I of the Convention.

The right to privacy

Evidence obtained by deception may be judged to have made for an unfair trial, be excluded during the trial, or be excluded *ab initio*, so that the trial may never begin. However, the European Convention On Human Rights contains other rights besides that to a fair trial, including the right to respect for one's personal and family life—commonly known as the right to privacy. The right to privacy is not an absolute right, and a public authority is entitled to breach that right under certain circumstances such as the need to prevent crime (which has been taken to include the need to investigate crime once it has taken place).

There will be occasions when deception is used but privacy is not invaded. In general, however, the use of deception and the invasion of privacy would appear to be associated. If a public authority such as the police sets out to breach the right to privacy, it must ensure that its efforts are based in law, necessary and proportionate, and that it can account retrospectively for the decisions and actions surrounding the breach.

We would suggest that the practical application of reasoning based on the need to respect and uphold fundamental rights and freedoms such as enshrined in the European Convention On Human Rights, is likely to improve the quality of police decision-making and to render it more liable to withstand ethical scrutiny. Moreover, the need for the police to take into account principles as well as laws serves to reinforce their fundamental identity as moral agents.

Professor MacIntyre argues that moral agents need to build up a justified confidence in their moral judgement, which cannot be achieved alone. They need, in effect, to be part of a network that helps them to challenge their moral judgements.

> [To] have confidence in our deliberations and judgements we need social relationships of a certain kind. We need forms of social association in and through which our deliberations and practical judgements are subjected to extended and systematic critical questioning that will teach us how to make judgements in which both we and others may have confidence.

Does the police service as currently organized provide such a set of relationships? We would regretfully suggest that it does not, but that human rights jurisprudence does, or rather can, help the police towards moral discussion in moral language.

Finally, we return to 'J'. He was an official in a highly authoritarian state, under the grip of tyranny, in which the rights of ordinary citizens were systematically abused by that state and its officials. To provide a defence against the abuse of state power by state officials was the primary reason for the declaration of the European Convention On Human Rights in 1951, and its provision of a legal framework to enforce those rights.

REFERENCES for *Chapter 4*

Adlam, R and Villiers, P (2003), *Police Leadership in the 21st Century: Philosophy, Doctrine and Developments,* Winchester: Waterside Press. With an introduction by former Deputy Assistant Commissioner John Grieve of the Metropolitan Police.
Bok, S (1978), *Lying: Moral Choice in Public and Private Life,* Sussex: The Harvester Press.
Bok, S (1986), *Secrets: On the Ethics of Concealment and Revelation,* Oxford: Oxford University Press.
Villiers, P (1997a), 'A Short History of Police Ethics', in *Better Police Ethics,* London: Kogan Page.
Villiers, P (1997b), *Better Police Ethics,* London: Kogan Page.

Special note

1 Sissela Bok began her penetrating and thoughtful examination of lying when teaching ethics and decision-making in medicine at the Harvard Medical School, and her first book conveys the excitement of voyaging into virtually uncharted waters. Perhaps surprisingly, she makes little explicit mention of deception in policing: but her general view is clear. Deception as lying is seldom if ever properly justified, and in most cases unnecessary, as an alternative means of achieving the same end could be found.

Bok refers to the use of unmarked cars by traffic police as an example of police deception (1978)—in this case *supressio veri* rather than *suggestio falsi*, but still an area where Sir David Calvert-Smith, for example, saw a potential sense of grievance on the part of the motorist, who might dispute the justice of such a policy (see *Chapter* 2.)

We would comment upon her example as follows:

i. The undeclared traffic police officer is unlikely to be causing the crime against which he or she may take action. The offences of speeding, careless driving and so on will be going on whether or not they are observed by a police officer, in disguise or otherwise.
ii. This is not, therefore, a police activity which raises the contentious issues of provocation or entrapment, but that of law enforcement by appropriate means.
iii. One of the most common arguments put forward by apprehended motorists and others is that the police are enforcing the traffic laws because they are easy to enforce, and should instead be chasing 'real' criminals. The counters to this argument are easy to develop and the topic as a whole has more to do with fairness than deception.
iv. Unless obliged to issue a 'fixed penalty' ticket by law (and then only for certain types of offences), the traffic police officer has considerable discretion in how to deal with the erring motorist. Officers may seek, for example, to rectify motorists' behaviour or caution them as to its consequences, rather than to enforce the law by instituting criminal justice proceedings.
v. The proper and improper use of discretion and its consequences for police direction and control are perhaps of greater moral consequence than the use of unmarked police cars. There are other police examples of the use of deception, however, such as in the invasion of privacy and private and family life, where we are on highly contentious moral ground.

CHAPTER 5

Flocking with a Purpose! Learning Faster than the Criminals

Garry Elliott

The sustaining of a safe, just and tolerant society requires more than the simple identification of 'best practice' within its police service, for best practice may not easily be either identified or shared. The issue is to be able to share the inspiration that leads to success in the complex world of policing today, in which there may be a high degree of uncertainty about both objectives and outcomes. Paradoxically, a police service may learn faster if its culture is less constrained by the need to demonstrate the achievement of pre-set 'targets', and relies more upon the identification and sharing of tacit knowledge.

A wise man knows everything but a successful man knows everyone.

Ask a group of police officers about the barriers to forces sharing good practice and you can be sure that somewhere in the top five reasons you will find the 'Not Invented Here' syndrome: which is the belief that unless something was developed locally it cannot be of any use. Leaders stand accused of letting local pride, parochialism, complacency or even arrogance get in the way of their learning from the experience of colleagues elsewhere. However, despite the frequency with which this charge is made, the quotation at the head of this essay may suggest a flaw in the prosecution's case.

It is possible to read into the quotation a message about a successful man, like a lottery winner, attracting friends, or maybe something about gaining advancement through patronage. However, there is another reading that suggests that someone could be successful because of the way they gain knowledge.

Consider the first reaction of most police leaders faced with a problem or task they have not experienced before (and don't know how to tackle). Many will fall back on their networks—contacts with whom they used to work or whom they have trusted in the past. The initial approach is not to invent something new but to learn from others. Eventually what is learned may be developed or adjusted into something new. This example suggests that given the right circumstances, the desire to share good practice is as strong in leaders in the police service as anywhere. The barriers interfering with the spread of ideas around the police service are perhaps less about the unwillingness of leaders to seek help, and more about deeply rooted roles and structures—and the history of the police.

Historically the police service has been slow to share and accept good practice. This apparent reluctance is now being strongly challenged by a doctrine emphasising the value of recognising and sharing experience. However, if this doctrine is to be successful, it needs to take more account of the complexity involved. The rest of this essay will explore this complexity and suggest approaches that leaders may need to adopt if sharing good practice is significantly to improve performance.

Why the fuss about good practice now?

For most of the 170 years of the modern police service's existence there has not been an imperative to share practice as it relates to operational policing. Chief constables saw merit in being seen to belong to the local community and this would often mean differences of uniform, equipment and processes between forces. Any pressures about performance related to specific incidents (e.g. for an arrest following a murder or being seen to suppress disorder). It follows that views about good and bad police performance were highly subjective. History and traditions were prized and there was no business imperative to drive change.

The last ten years have seen a major turnaround in this position. Interest in the value of sharing good practice started with studies by Her Majesty's Inspectorate of Constabulary (see, for example, HMIC 1995); gained momentum with Best Value Reviews; and has culminated in the Police Reform Programme. The White Paper setting out the ideas of the Programme noted, 'Successful innovation [in the police service] has been slow to spread ... This results in the wide variation in performance' (Home Office, 2001). It went on to describe the then new Police Standards Unit whose role would be to 'identify the most successful approaches and spread them to BCUs [Basic Command Units] with poorer performance'. The paper, of course, then went on to describe the sticks which would accompany the carrots associated with the spread of good practice.

Coupled with this Government imperative, the need for the police service to learn has never been more intense. Nowhere is this clearer than in the implications of the rapid advancement of technology. This has brought opportunities for better communication, evidence gathering and information handling. However, these technological advances also bring new types of crime and criminal expertise, and the increased expectations of a more knowledgeable and better informed public.

The goal of improved performance is now the highest priority of all police leaders and this drives the business imperative to look for and implement good practice.

Where is the problem?

In a study of the introduction of best value in the police service, Matt Long's research (2002) uncovered a strong underlying view questioning whether the principles of best value would lead to sharing good practice. His interviews found,

> Good practice was not thought to be easily identifiable or transferable and furthermore several interviewees thought it unlikely that incentives to share good practice would exist in a political climate whereby forces and BCUs were very much in competition with each other.

So there are two possible barriers to good practice being shared. These are:

- recognising it in the first place; and
- the competitive drive for improved performance actually discouraging sharing.

The second point, that the pressure for performance can cause a barrier in itself, is often raised. It would be understandable that a BCU commander who knew that there would be scrutiny and comparison of performance would not easily share successful strategies with the 'competitors' from other BCUs or forces. However, the evidence is to the contrary. In 29 years in the police service, five of which have been spent at Bramshill where he frequently asks people about their ideas and experience, the author of this essay has not found that people are resistant to talking about their initiatives, successes *and failures*. Getting people to write the ideas down for publication or to feed a database is much more difficult but a different matter. The method of communication is significant but the key point is that if you get people together who are interested in a particular issue, they will naturally share ideas.

While pressures for performance may not inhibit people talking about their experiences, they can impede knowledge sharing in a more subtle way. Organizations will often respond to the demands of targets by building stronger control systems. These work against the freedom to experiment and learn.

The first issue highlighted by Long, the problem of recognising good practice, is not easily dismissed. If something is difficult to identify, efforts to share it will start at a disadvantage. Identification of good practice is difficult in this context because of:

- the complexity of decision-making in policing; and
- the type of the information and knowledge which leads to success.

Complexity

Police knowledge is complex rather than complicated. This is an important distinction. Information about how best to paper a wall or make a car more cheaply will usually be quite straightforward. If the information involves a large number of actions it can be complicated, but however complicated it becomes it is always possible to understand the implications and impact of changes. The link between cause and effect becomes clear if you study it sufficiently.

Decisions about police operations are not like this. Responses of people can vary from day to day, or minute to minute. The multitude of potential influences over policing outcomes can make it impossible to be clear about cause and effect. Earl and Hopwood (1980) suggested that this complexity arises from two different uncertainties. These were:

- uncertainty about what success looks like (uncertainty over objectives); and
- uncertainty about the impact of any particular change chosen (uncertainty over outcomes).

Examples of the first can be seen in comparing a supermarket (where success ultimately must be based in profit) to education (where there is constant debate about the benefits of training pupils to gain qualifications versus the development of more rounded young people).

The second type of Earl and Hopwood uncertainty is patent in the police service. What would be the impact on crime of investing 100 hours of overtime in patrolling? The chance that the deterrent effect would cause a reduction has to be tempered with the possibility that other sociological or even meteorological effects would cause crime to rise.

		Uncertainty over objectives	
		Low	**High**
Uncertainty over outcomes	**Low**	Computation *Mathematical Problems?*	Negotiation *Pay Bargaining?*
	High	Judgement *Medical Treatment?*	Inspiration *Policing?*

Figure 5.1: **Earl and Hopwood decision-making matrix**

Both these uncertainties are shown on the matrix (*Figure 5.1*). This illustrates four different types of decision-making: computation, judgement, negotiation and inspiration.

Where the measure of success is clear and the link between different options and the results they bring is clearly understood, the type of decision-making can be called computation. Options can be compared and evaluated and a decision agreed which is obviously the best.

If, however, the link is less clear, deciding between the different options calls for judgement because different participants in the decision-making process may have different views about the best course of action to achieve the agreed outcome.

Where the links are clear but the final objective is uncertain, decision-making will involve negotiation as the different possible objectives are compared and discussed.

If both objectives and outcomes are unclear, then you are in the complex world where inspiration is often needed.

The uncertainty that police leaders have in linking outcomes to inputs has been set out above. It is also quite easy to see that despite significant efforts, objectives surrounding police work are still very uncertain. Take the example of the implementation of a Problem Oriented Policing strategy. How would success be measured? Fewer problems? Fewer crimes? Increased reassurance? Community satisfaction with police? Short term or long term results? Policing is very much in the bottom right hand corner of the matrix.

So how do you share the inspiration that leads to success in the complex world of policing today?

What is the knowledge that leads to success?

Many writers have described the development of society from feudal times where land was the source of success, through the industrial age where capital prevailed, to the information age where what is inside people's minds is the most important resource. The police service has been slow to accept the move into the knowledge environment but the signs of this are now all around us. The focus on control of officers, police stations, extent of powers, and numbers of cars in the 1960s has moved to intelligence, analysis, expertise and leadership today. Successful policing in the twenty-first century is dependent on the use of information and the way in which an organization can build up and make use of its knowledge. Innovation is replacing caution, specialization taking over from walking the beat. Sharing success is no longer sharing tactics; it is about leveraging knowledge—making use of knowledge gained in one part of an organization to improve the performance of another part.

Leveraging knowledge in the police service is complicated by the fact that success often comes from tacit knowledge which can be difficult to describe or even identify. Everyone will have experienced a colleague dealing with a difficult customer, or chairing a meeting, or undertaking a stop and search in the street and thinking, 'I wish I could do it like that'. But the sad fact is that there are some things that cannot be bottled. A book entitled *How to be a Good BCU Commander* would be as limited in its value as one called *How to Ride a Bike* or *How to Plaster a Wall.* All these tasks require some element of natural talent. More significantly, they all contain significant degrees of tacit knowledge that are largely acquired by experience.

The important thing about this tacit knowledge is that it usually cannot be written down. Indeed it is possible that someone will not even realise that they are using it. Michael Polyani (1983) explains this as, 'We know more than we can tell'. It is possible to add to this, 'and we can tell more than we can write'. The principle is well known in the police service. An example would be the importance placed on the period of hand-over for posts.

The success of a strategy or initiative from one force cannot be totally expressed in writing. It cannot be transferred through guidelines and policies. The extent to which the success is dependent on the tacit knowledge of those involved is impossible to measure but it will always be of key importance.

Nancy Dixon recognised four important stages in successful transfer of knowledge learned by one group to another (2000, p. 21). These are:

- using a transfer system that suits the intended receiver and *fits the type of knowledge* [my emphasis];
- translating that knowledge into a form usable by the receiver;
- adaptating the knowledge for the receiver's own use; and
- making use of the knowledge in action.

The key is that the system of transfer needs to fit the type of information. Considerations about the complexity of the task, whether the knowledge is tacit or explicit and how many areas of the organization might be affected, need to be taken into account. Many organizations have experienced the frustration of creating sophisticated technological databases, intranets, message boards etc. to store and share information only to find that they do not get used. In these circumstances the reaction of the leader is often to try inducements to encourage staff to use the system (e.g. you are not allowed to take information off until you have put information on). Usually any improvement generated in this way is short-lived and eventually the organization has to accept that the sort of information it was hoping to share cannot be passed in this way.

Dixon explores how sharing tacit knowledge requires the bringing together of people. She describes organizations which have understood the limitations of the written word or electronic databases (Dixon, 2000 p. 77 *et seq.*) and who have created systems where people are encouraged to get together to talk.

Davenport and Prusak also recognised the importance of people coming together in their study of Dai-Ichi Pharmaceuticals (1998 p.92) where researchers were required to spend 20 minutes every day in talk rooms discussing their work with whoever came in. They describe this as, 'a kind of Brownian motion theory of knowledge exchange, its very randomness encouraging the discovery of new ideas that a more specifically directed discussion would miss.'

Possibly the best lesson comes from the actions of birds. There are those that flock and there are those which have a more isolationist and territorial approach. Arie de Geus (1997 p. 161) explains how in the early part of the last century two types of songbird, blue-tits and robins, each enjoyed drinking the cream out of the tops of milk bottles until the milk companies used aluminium foil caps. Following this setback, robins as a species never learned to gain access to the cream but, within 20 years, the entire blue-tit population of the UK had perfected the art of how to pierce the new bottle tops. This was organizational learning on a massive scale.

Blue tits flock together—robins do not. It is not that blue tits are more clever, bolder or more innovative than robins. The tits learn from each other rather than expend their energy protecting their territory. The flocking behaviour allows knowledge to spread from the few individuals who are inspired, through the rest of the flock.

The songbird analogy can be applied to the police service. There are more than a few innovative individuals, but energy is spent being territorial rather than flocking. If the service is to be effective in sharing the tacit knowledge that is the key to success, leaders need to be able to encourage mobility in their followers. The 'control' approach that senior managers so easily adopt at times of perceived crisis (like when there is a risk of failing to hit government targets) usually only leads to people 'bunkering down' and trying to do the same things a little bit better.

If the service is properly to share good practice and learn from each other and succeed, people need the psychological and organizational space and encouragement to flock.

REFERENCES for *Chapter Five*

De Geus, A (1997), *The Living Company*, London: Nicholas Brealey.

Dixon, N M (2000), *Common Knowledge*, Harvard: Harvard Business School Press.

Earl, M and Hopwood, A (1980), 'Management Information to Information Management' in Lucas H, Land L, Lincoln T and Supper K (eds), *The Information Systems Environment*, Amsterdam: North-Holland.

Her Majesty's Inspectorate of Constabulary (1995), *Obtaining Value for Money in the Police Service: A Good Practice Guide*, London: HMSO.

Home Office (2001), *Policing a New Century: A Blueprint for Reform*, London: Home Office Publications.

Long, M (2002), 'Naming, shaming and the politics of blaming', paper to the British Criminological Conference at Keele University.

Polyani, M (1983), *The Tacit Dimension*, London: Peter Smith.

CHAPTER 6

Values, Self-knowledge and Police Leadership

Robert Adlam, James McKinney and Peter Villiers

In this chapter we shall suggest that a certain type of groundwork needs to be undertaken if the practices of leadership originating from an individual leader are to be consistently effective. Our argument derives from a number of research and theoretical traditions including organizational development, applied behavioural science, humanistic and transpersonal psychology, as well as psychoanalysis. However, we shall refrain from using the type of esoteric and specialised discourse that exists within these disciplines. Instead, we shall attempt to address practical men and women who face pressing problems in police organizations.

We acknowledge that, in principle, anyone is capable of showing leadership—in the sense that every individual has at least some room for manoeuvre in which to drive innovation and change forward within their part of the organization (see Egan, 1988). However, our discussion is nuanced towards the situation facing people who occupy some senior position in an organizational hierarchy. We should also note that we understand leadership in relational terms: leadership necessarily entails followership. Thus we recognise that the leader engages in some sort of communicative and social process with other people. It is also important to underline the fact that effective leadership practice finds ways of meeting the needs of individual persons and groups whilst ensuring successful achievement of tasks.

A first responsibility for the leader

Harold Leavitt (1973) reduced the key activities of senior management to the three processes of 'visioning', 'decision-taking' and 'implementation'. Leadership can be appreciated in essentially similar terms. Leaders want to bring about a better state of affairs than they currently find. They identify goals and work out how they are going to be achieved. They also manage the way in which their designs (or plans) are made to 'happen'. Leadership is a dynamic social enterprise. No longer, in the modern world, is it possible for the leadership of an organization to be seen as merely the occupancy of a role, office or post, the reward for past service, the maintenance of the status quo, or the 'natural' position for a person with political adroitness. Following Hodgkinson (1983) leadership is about making decisions that fit into an over-arching and consistent framework—*which is readily perceived, understood and approved by the workforce.*

That framework must convey purpose and provide motivation. It should excite and inspire. It should 'connect' with untapped or underused potential. Not only should the motivating vision win the enthusiasm of the police service but it must also win the approval of its stakeholders—the public.

The personality of the leader

The framework for leadership that is outlined above places great demands upon the inner resources of the personality at the heart of the extended decision-making process. A fully articulated motivating vision cannot be generated overnight. Nor can it be conjured up from outside the position of leadership: for the leader must be aware of, but not subservient to, the realities of the situation in which the vision needs to be generated.

Leaders' appreciation of their effect on others and the rationale underlying their decision-making thus become crucial resources to the whole organization. Indeed, the personality of the leader is perceived by colleagues and subordinates alike, prior to any articulation of a coherently elucidated vision, and inferences are drawn. Thus, we arrive at an irreducible factor in leadership: personality.

Values and the leader's value system: the need for self-knowledge

It would be very strange if the value system expressed in the vision were to be disconnected from the leader's own system of values. If it were, it would be both hollow and alienated. Thus, if the vision is to be genuine and capable of motivating others it ought, at the very least, to be capable of motivating its originator, who must be aware both of his or her own values and how they influence one's actions. This sounds relatively straightforward—values are what we value, and it should be simple enough to find those out—but in fact it can be surprisingly difficult.

Problems of moral elucidation

Why do we act as we do—and what are the moral values that motivate or influence our actions? Philosophers, economists and psychologists—to say nothing of poets, novelists and historians—would agree that these are some of the most difficult questions we must face: and they have found very different ways of addressing them. Let us confine our speculations to the experienced police officer, and assume that we have gathered that status for ourselves.

We belong to a culture that is not inclined towards introspection and may dispute its validity. Our disinclination towards introspection may have been reinforced by our professional experience so far, in which we have devoted the bulk of our attention to understanding others rather than ourselves—which is often a simpler task, and more likely to lead to career-enhancing rewards. We have a penchant for action and a need to solve problems as they arise. Moreover, we very often believe that the right solution is not in question, and any difficulties of achievement will arise over means and not over ends.

We may have joined the police service itself, at least in part, because of its apparent moral certainty: only to find that things are not as they appeared. Right and wrong may not be so easily separated as we had thought. Our colleagues, being human, may not be so virtuous as we had hoped. And the work itself, which we had expected to be a relatively straightforward affair of upholding the law, may be proving infinitely variable in the combinations and permutations that it thrusts before us, and the demands on our decision-making powers that we had not anticipated.

We may have identified an incongruity between the official values of the organization and profession to which we belong, and the factors that appear to motivate at least some of those who work for it—and here we do not refer to those police officers who are widely perceived to be corrupt, brutal or vicious. The police service, for example, may laud the values of selflessness, justice, impartiality and truth, whilst its officers are in reality motivated by a quite different, if much more understandable set of values. These may be taken to include the avoidance of stress and the pursuit of a reasonably comfortable and not too demanding way of life—and one in which loyalty to colleagues features rather more prominently than an obligation to serve the community without concern for personal or organizational gain.

As experienced police officers, we may be a little uncomfortable with the wider notion of examining values, since our acquaintance with the criminal justice system in operation has encouraged us to believe that the good are not always rewarded and the wicked punished: and we may not hold the profession and administration of the law in the utmost respect. We may fear, consciously or subconsciously, the possibility that other assumptions that have so far comforted us by their apparent certainty are of similar untruth: and restrict our pursuit of ethics to situations in which the inculcation of a simple moral code is more a matter of repetition than analysis. (Stop kicking your brother!)

We may further believe that we have a contract with society, all the more powerful in that it is no longer openly declared. Just as in Victorian times, although today with less candour, it is the police task to protect the respectable and law-abiding sections of society against what used to be called 'the dangerous classes': which means not just habitual criminals, but the deviant, the marginal and the dispossessed. Despite the current emphasis on diversity and multi-culturalism, the astute police officer soon realises that there are limits to tolerance, and that the more successful members of society, whatever their own origins, do not actually want gypsies living in their backyard.

These reservations must be explored and overcome if as practical people we are to make practical progress. We have noted in the course of our all-too-lengthy contact with working police officers that they may be somewhat hesitant to embark upon the path of moral evaluation, but do not necessarily lack the ability to do so. The best way forward is to reduce and simplify the problem. How to do so? The first step is to gain some sort of purchase on the origin of values. Where do they come from?

The derivation of values

Initially personal values derive from the child's interaction with its family or significant others who induct the child into a culture. Fundamental dispositions, codes of conduct, notions of right and wrong are forged in the early definition of personhood. These initial values are so basic to our personality that they could be defined as the foundations of our very self-hood. Developments in the fields of psychoanalysis and humanistic psychology provide remarkably illuminating analyses illustrating how values can be traced to distinct patterns of parent-child interaction.[1]

---

1 Readers will already have found a spontaneous discussion of the personal development of values in the interview with the former Director of Public Prosecutions, Sir David Calvert-Smith (*Chapter 2*) who volunteered the information that he first formed his idea of justice from the family trial for misconduct within the home, which gave him his first notions of fairness, impartiality and retribution.

The next crucial adoption of our values occurs through interaction with our peers—usually within the environment of the educational process. Our peers communicate values such as loyalty, recognition, competition and achievement. The educational process mediates the values of order, coherence and enquiry amongst many others.

Values acquired in adult life will also be partially drawn from the organization for which one works. Usually adults become socialised or inducted into the occupational values unique to each profession.[2]

All the values mentioned so far derive from personal interaction. In addition, we acquire values through the traditions and procedures that are embedded in our wider culture. The mass media also functions as an extremely powerful generator of values.

Thus, there are various sources for our values, which are absorbed and internalised by us in different ways and with different degrees of impact. The acquisition of values is largely an unconscious process based on behaviour drilled into the individual as a child, deliberately 'taken on board' in imitation of an adolescent role model, accepted as if by osmosis through the lyrics of a song, or intellectually accepted through argument and debate with colleagues at work. Some of these processes are rational whilst others are not. It is worth underlining the fact that depth psychologists encourage individuals to search for the unconscious 'drivers' that underlie aspects of their values—whilst semioticians sensitise us to the subtle ways in which a culture constructs the values of its people.

Values and leadership

In any event the value system of an individual is more like a haphazard accumulation of personal experiences, many of which are highly idiosyncratic, than a rationally ordered hierarchy arrived at through personal choice. Thus, it can be seen that a person's value system is a problematic area. Values cannot simply be 'read-off' as details from someone's *curriculum vitae*. The individual concerned has to undergo a process of self-questioning of a particularly demanding nature in order to bring to the surface the complex of interacting and conflicting values that constitutes a major aspect of their activity and motivation. We should underline the fact that ego-defence mechanisms are likely to intervene in the process of value clarification. Freud advised us to pay close attention to what people do, rather than what they say motivates them, since the former may be a better guide to their values. However, self-awareness and knowledge can be both fostered and developed by the appropriate means, of which we shall say more later. At this point we must stress that since the personality and manner of decision-making of its leaders are such an important factor in the functioning of any organization it is crucial that they be able to take their value systems into account.

---

[2] In *Chapter 4*, Professor MacIntyre discusses the development of values in such a setting as the Third Reich, wherein those of conformity, obedience and industriousness in one's delineated sphere encouraged officials to disregard examples of immoral behaviour by the state which fell outside their official concern. The inculcation of values in the Third Reich was at least partly the 'natural' result of the authoritarian nature of German society up to that point, and partly the result of the deliberate policies of the Minister of 'Enlightenment', Joseph Goebbels. In such circumstances, upbringing, education, work and social propaganda reinforced each other to produce a rigid and unquestioning conformity to the will of the Leader as the embodiment of Germany.

Clearly, a major aspect of any value system concerns those values that are 'moral values'. Moral values, such as benevolence and justice, constitute, in part, the conscience and ego ideal of the person. A person's value system can be described as a complex compound of moral and non-moral values. To the extent that values-clarification will seek to make explicit this compound it will, necessarily, entail ethical reflection.

A note on ethical reflection

Ethical reflection in today's society is a more complicated process than it has been in previous times (see MacIntyre, 1982). Durkheim (1897) characterises society since the industrial revolution as one dominated by 'anomie' or normlessness. We live, he suggests, in a society where integrating norms are open to question, fluctuation and revision. The frameworks of shared outlook and values are now part of the rapid 'mutation' that characterises modern society. So, for example, norms generated by the traditions of locality, community and interest have been eroded through the process of economic development, with its requirement for the physical mobility of labour. The norms established through the interactions and relationships of the extended family have 'suffered' in a similar fashion. The increasing individualisation of society has further accentuated the demise of shared norms. The psychological and intellectual integration offered by religious belief and doctrine has been attenuated and no commonly accepted philosophical system has filled the gap. A philosophical and intellectual relativism obtains, which allows each individual to 'take on board' whatever ideas appeal and to craft their own code of conduct and moral outlook.[3]

We should note that the mood associated with this relativism is inherently suspicious of the systematic investigation of beliefs and values; in consequence, there has been little sustained practice of rigorous value analysis to aid us in the process of ethical reflection. Nonetheless, over the last decade and a half, the authors of this text have developed structures to aid police leaders and managers to undertake the process of ethical reflection. We should add that there are plenty of other resources developed for this kind of 'personal work' (see Pfeiffer 1972–2003).

Values and the organization

Ethical reflection and value clarification cannot stop at the individual. Organizations have purposes and thus have value systems, of which the leader must be aware. Through this process can be highlighted the actual priorities (declared or tacit) which motivate or constrain the organization's members. Structural value conflicts and value omissions can be identified. Diagnoses of fundamental procedural malfunctions can be brought to the surface.

We think that the organization's value audit is the 'raw material' upon which leaders need to work, in their principal task of developing their organization in line with their vision. We accept that this might appear to place an unrealistic onus upon the individual leader and that it might be more realistic if the process were to be reversed i.e. the leader should develop his or her value system in line with the

---

[3] The philosopher Richard Rorty has in our view been over-accused of a tendency to moral relativism, as we discussed in our previous volume (Adlam and Villiers, 2003). Rorty has argued consistently that any moral system should aim to reduce cruelty—hardly a relativist position, and in fact a good basis for a police 'mission statement'.

organization. The police service has, for example, developed a statement of common purpose and values, and there is now a European Code of Police Ethics that outlines a framework designed to establish a moral basis for pan-European policing. However, since it is the individual leader who breathes life into the words and concepts of official stipulations, then it makes more practical sense to focus upon the leader as a shaper and creator of organizational values (see Schein, 1985). We are currently developing a number of instruments designed to help begin the process of taking an initial value audit of the police organization, and we suggest that interested readers contact us for further information and guidance if they so wish. We should emphasise that many such structures are available and we recommend that police leaders explore the literature on organizational development and transformation for examples.

Vision and values

The leader's value system underpins his or her visioning and decision taking. It also shapes and orders the way decisions come to be implemented. In practice, of course, leaders also need to take stock of the raw material upon which they have to work, i.e. the organization's values. But these are static analyses. They are snapshots of the present. They can be of no use to the process of leadership unless they can be related to a vision of the future. Or, to put it another way, a vision of the future can be of no value unless it is in constant interaction with the present values of the organization and its leaders.

How might leaders go about the task of elaborating this vision? We have remained uncertain as to how police leaders and managers actually construct their image and designs for the future, since so much of police leadership seems to be either reactive or defensive—a means of absorbing latest governmental initiative, rather than a 'home-grown' and authentic creation (see Elliott, 2003). Notwithstanding, it is clear that there are a number of sources from which to draw in order to arrive at a genuine vision. Police leaders can trawl their experience and decide to model themselves on some exemplary practitioner. They can attempt to elucidate the 'formula for success' that they perceived to characterise the police leader whom they most admire. Or they can use other resources, drawing upon the identification of deeper personal 'drivers' on which we have already touched.

Implementation and values: a link with transformational leadership

It seems that the current police organization is experiencing at least two sorts of value clash. On the one hand the demands of 'managerialism' can conflict with the ethos of police-as-a-profession. On the other hand the requirements of 'partnership' can come up against the cherished sense of independence that characterises the police.

There is no point in inspecting organizational values if one cannot change them. The values of the existing organization must be capable of alteration into those of the envisioned organization if the leader's vision is to be realised. The values inherent in the vision must become the shared values amongst the organization's three fundamental constituencies: its members, its sponsors and its 'customers'. The leader's task is to transform the present organizational values into the envisioned values through his or her skills as negotiator and communicator. The task is to promote co-operation with and commitment to the vision.

In dealing with co-operation and commitment, however, whole 'new' sets of values are brought to the fore. These are the transcendent or overarching values that maximise co-operation and the flourishing of individuals. They are the moral values. Moral values function, in part, to provide the frameworks whereby personal values are allowed to become actualised and shared (see Warnock 1971). The most widely held moral values include the following: benevolence, justice, freedom, courage, equality, loyalty, truth, tolerance, wisdom, prudence, integrity, and industriousness.

These transcendent or co-operative values are those by which the co-operation and communal interchange that marks our lives are carried on. There exist (now) minimal standards of justice, tolerance, integrity and truthfulness without which human beings refuse to take part in any corporate endeavour. They will either withdraw explicitly by means of a walk-out (or some other form of 'exit') or they will simply 'go through the motions' with no sense of obligation or commitment to any worthwhile purpose for which the organization was established.

Conclusion

In this chapter we have outlined a framework for organizational and leadership development. We suggest that leaders need to build a comprehensive understanding of their own value system in order to appreciate the vectors that will influence their vision and decision taking. We suggest that they conduct an organizational value audit in order to establish the 'raw material' which they have to transmute. We recommend that the vision that they build for the organization includes explicit reference to moral values. We note the significance of moral values in the struggle to implement the organizational vision. Finally, we draw a positive relationship between moral values and fundamental human rights and freedoms.

REFERENCES for *Chapter 6*

Durkheim (1893), *The Division of Labour in Society*.

Egan, G. (1988a), *Change Agent Skills A: Assessing and Designing Excellence*, San Diego: California: University Associates Inc.

Egan, G. (1988b), *Change Agent Skills B: Managing Innovation and Change*, San Diego: California: University Associates Inc.

Elliott, G (2003), 'Mission Statements and Other Fairy Tales', *Policing Futures*, Vol. 1, No. 3, National Police Leadership Centre, Bramshill: The New Police Bookshop.

Hodgkinson C. (1983), *'The Philosophy of Leadership'*, Oxford: Basil Blackwell .

Leavitt, H. J. (1973), *The Organizational World*, Harcourt Brace College Publishers

MacIntyre, A. (1982), *After Virtue'*, London: Duckworth.

Pfeiffer, J. (1972– 2003), *Annual Handbooks for Group Facilitators and Consultants*, San Diego, California: Pfeiffer and Company.

Schein, E. (1985), *Organisational Culture and Leadership*, Oxford: Jossey-Bass Publishers.

Warnock, G. (1971), *The Object of Morality*, London: Methuen and Company.

CHAPTER 7

Virtue, Shame and Privacy

William C Heffernan

'O shame, where is thy blush?' Hamlet asks despairingly as he considers his mother's manifest pleasure in her new marriage to his step-father. Hamlet's question has more general implications. In western civilization, and perhaps in all human societies, shame can produce physical symptoms—blushing, in particular—that deter wrongful behaviour. Because of this, shame links individuals and social norms in a way that is both emotional and physiological. Anticipation of it inhibits people from violating those norms. Anticipation of shame also has the effect of shaping people's character, for to the extent that shame is a public experience—to the extent it depends on anticipation of humiliation in the presence of others—then shame can stimulate people to reflect on what they want to be, in particular on what specific traits they wish to possess. To speak of character traits is, of course, to speak of virtues (and vices). Shame, one can say, enforces virtue; it makes vicious character traits less likely and virtuous ones more so given each person's anticipation of public scrutiny. Burke captured the shame/virtue connection well when he remarked, 'Whilst Shame keeps its watch, Virtue is not wholly extinguished in the heart' ([1790] 1968 p. 218).

Although shame may well be a universal phenomenon, its sources have varied over time, as has its threshold. As many observers have noted, contemporary western history has been marked by a dramatic elevation in the threshold of shame. What observers have less frequently pointed out is that privacy is the device that has facilitated this increase in the shame threshold. Respect for privacy is also a social norm, but respect for privacy has unusual consequences in that privacy makes it easier for people to escape the public scrutiny that leads to shame. Burke, it will be noted, speaks of 'shame keep[ing] its *watch.*' To the extent that privacy norms are honoured, that watch—the system of social surveillance so necessary for the enforcement of individual virtue—is compromised. Whether observation of privacy norms generates a net social value is something that need not concern us here. My opinion, which is not critical to the points advanced in the remainder of this chapter, is that privacy is *on balance* socially valuable in modern life. All that should be considered now, however, is the straightforward point that privacy norms undermine the shame/virtue connection.

My aim in this brief (and so highly schematised) chapter is to examine the shame/virtue connection that Burke posits in his provocative remark. In particular, I advance four arguments as follows.

First, the connection that Burke asserts is direct for what I shall call 'Aristotelian virtues.' Whether any connection can be established for Christian virtues is a more difficult issue. Burke's dictum is most plausible for the virtues esteemed in the classical Aristotelian *polis* or city state; it is less persuasive for the inward-looking virtues esteemed in the New Testament.

Second, privacy is indeed a subversive force for Aristotelian virtues. Not only is privacy a paradigmatically modern value—one that can be applied only awkwardly to the classical *polis*—it also directly undermines the virtues Aristotle and other ancients held dear. For those virtues, at least, privacy is an unmitigated threat to the possibility of the good life.

Third, however, I contend that despite the force of this point, privacy can be classified as a positive ethical value when considered in either one of two different moral frameworks. Whether morality is defined either deontologically or consequentially—the two frameworks most commonly used in modern thinking about morals—privacy can be treated as one of the many values that should be considered in the general menu of what is worthwhile. Its inclusion, though, comes with an important caveat: for whereas Aristotle reasoned in terms of an integrated, coherent version of the good life, modern ethical frameworks, particularly when they include privacy as a positive value, make no such attempt. They focus on specifically targeted acts—rights and duties, for example, or costs and benefits—and make no attempt to establish the general ethical coherence of life that is a particularly attractive feature of Aristotle's thought.

In the final section, I apply these points to issues in modern policing. In doing so, I consider an intriguing argument for the enduring relevance of the Aristotelian virtues for individuals who serve in paramilitary organizations. In some respects policing continues to emphasise not only the specific character traits prized in pre-modern societies but also the very notion of character-development itself as the primary focus of ethics. However, the Aristotelian framework is insufficient by itself to provide a foundation for police ethics. Police work in the twenty-first century is sufficiently bound up in the dilemmas of modern life that one cannot dispense with the insights of targeted ethical systems when reflecting on the choices officers must make. Moreover, the police, like other individuals in modern society, enjoy a substantial degree of privacy insulation from others, thus weakening their incentive to take seriously the notion of character as the critical feature of the moral life. Policing, I thus suggest, stands at an interesting mid-point on the continuum between pre-modern and modern ethical systems. One can come to terms with its complexities only by thinking about the interplay between frameworks that emphasise the development of character and those that are targeted on specific acts.

1. THE SHAME/VIRTUE CONNECTION: ARISTOTELIAN AND OTHER VIRTUE-BASED ETHICAL SYSTEMS

'Virtue,' Aristotle asserts, 'is concerned with passions and actions in which excess is a form of failure and so is a defect, while the intermediate is praised and is a form of success; and being praised and being successful are both characteristics of virtue.' (1941, 1006b, pp. 24-8). This oft-cited definition of virtue helps introduce us to the Aristotelian approach to ethics, in particular to its emphasis on the ethical mean. It is not, however, sufficient to provide a general introduction to the notion of virtue. A virtue, Timmons (2002, p. 212) has helpfully suggested, can be defined as '(1) a relatively fixed trait of character or mind, (2) typically involving dispositions to thought, feeling, and action in certain circumstances, and which furthermore (3) is the primary basis for judging the overall goodness or worth of persons.'

What, in particular, are the central virtues? Aristotle lists more than ten in the *Nicomachean Ethics,* but there are four he considers central: justice, courage, prudence, and temperance. Each of these he deems an ethical mean (as he does all other virtues). Courage, for example, stands on a continuum of character traits, with the defect (a vice) of cowardliness at one end and the excess (also a vice) of rashness at the other. More important for our purposes is Aristotle's claim that the virtues are objects of praise. Indeed, Aristotle speaks not only of praise but also of success: the definition quoted at the outset presupposes an audience that passes judgment on an individual because of the traits that person displays. For Aristotle, individual character is an object of evaluation; arguably, he views it as the most important of all matters for evaluation. The criteria for evaluation are the virtues; the judges are a person's contemporaries; if someone achieves renown, then history itself adds a further judgment.

Lest there be any doubt about the importance of public scrutiny in Aristotle's ethics, we should consider his remarks about shame's role in enforcing virtue. Shame, he says, is 'a kind of dishonour and produces an effect similar to that of fear of danger, for people who feel disgraced blush and those who fear death turn pale' (Aristotle, 1128b, pp. 10-13). For Aristotle, the contrast is clear. Although he does not deny the possibility of private virtue and private shame, his own remarks treat each as social in nature. Virtue is *praised;* shame is a form of *dishonour*. Thus for him, shame functions as a spur to virtue. While otherwise undesirable, shame is useful because it is a deterrent to vice. 'Shame,' Aristotle states, 'may be said to be conditionally a good thing [for] if a good man does such actions, he will feel disgraced' (*idem,* 1128b p. 33).

Here, then, is a quite plausible account of the shame/virtue connection. On Aristotle's account, the link between the two is not coincidental but necessary. As long as virtue is conceived in terms of traits that are publicly honoured, shame provides an indispensable incentive to act virtuously. Needless to say, this is not a logical point but rather a sociological one. There are occasions when people want their courage not to be an object of attention, when they want their fairness to others to be kept secret, and so on. There are also occasions when shame is felt apart from others—when it is a source of purely personal torment. But Aristotelian ethics is not built on these possibilities. Indeed, as long as attention is focused on virtues (such as courage and justice) that are fundamentally social in nature, Aristotle's indifference to the possibility of undisplayed virtue seems sound. For if our attention is limited to traits such as courage and justice, then the prospect of public scrutiny does in fact seem to be an essential spur to their acquisition. Courage without the expectation of subsequent notice is only a remote possibility. By contrast, courage undertaken in anticipation of an audience's favourable response is a routine feature of life.

Christian virtues

Is a different approach to virtue ethics possible? Of course. In fact, many different catalogues of virtues can be imagined, and only some of these virtues hinge on public scrutiny. Rather than canvass the many alternatives, let us focus on the most important one: the Christian list of virtues. To the standard Aristotelian catalogue of justice, courage, prudence, and temperance, medieval thinkers added at least three more: faith, hope, and charity. Many added another as well: humility. [For a sustained discussion in this area, see MacIntyre (1982, pp. 156 and 170).]

Scholastic philosophers tended to treat these New Testament virtues as compatible with the ones Aristotle identifies, but it is easy to see why they are not. Humility—a virtue central to New Testament ethics—poses the most obvious problem. In the *Nicomachean Ethics*, Aristotle singles out humility as a defect/vice; vanity is its excess/vice; and proper pride is the ethical mean (1125a, pp. 18-20). But even if we set aside humility, the other Christian virtues can also be said to fit uncomfortably with Aristotle's original four. The spur to faith, hope, and charity is to be found primarily in a person's relationship with God, not in that person's hope for the esteem of others. Indeed, if one were to try to identify the fear that induces these Christian virtues, fear would have to be said to centre on guilt rather than shame. For most people, shame hinges on the prospect of losing face—thus the significance of Hamlet's question about his mother. Though secret shame may be logically possible, the wellsprings of shame are far more commonly found in the dishonour (Aristotle's term) associated with public exposure.

The sense of guilt can be exacerbated by public exposure, but guilt's centre of gravity lies in individual conscience, in an inward reckoning with one's own standards of conduct. The Christian virtues of faith, hope, charity, and (above all) humility all centre on this inwardness; in turn their spur is guilt rather than shame. One might argue, of course, that the inwardness of Christian virtues presupposes a highly developed social sense—that these virtues play out an *internalised* drama of honour and dishonour in which someone attributes to his or her conscience impulses originally developed in social interactions. But even if this notion of conscience, whose origins are to be found in the thought of George Herbert Mead (Strauss, 1964), is granted for purposes of argument, it surely differs in important respects from the genuinely public spectacle that Aristotle anticipates for the exercise of virtue. Actual public honour matters in the Aristotelian account. In employing Mead's interpretation of Christian ethics, the most one can say is that public honour is transmuted into private conscience.

It is certainly possible, then, to analyse virtues without regard to either publicity or shame. But while this is possible, Aristotle's account provides a compelling reason for treating public scrutiny as central to an understanding of socially valued, secular character traits such as courage and justice. When traits such as these are the focus of attention, then surely the key incentive for their acquisition is the expectation that they will be appreciated by others. Correspondingly, the factor most likely to be feared in the event that they are not acquired is shame. For the Aristotelian virtues, at least, Burke's shame/virtue connection holds true.

2. THE ADVENT OF PRIVACY

Privacy is a modern value. As Arendt (1959, p. 35) has noted, for the ancient Greeks 'the trait of privacy ... meant literally a state of being deprived of something'. Although some ancient societies (Rome in particular) showed marked respect for private life, the notion of *private liberty*—of an individual's right to cultivate a unique way of life—did not emerge as a central value in western thought until the mid-to-late-nineteenth century. Even the American Constitution, one of the key political documents of the late-eighteenth century, contains no reference to privacy.

The Fifth Amendment states that private property 'shall not be taken without just compensation,' thus anticipating that there will be a realm of private activity free of state control. But unlike twentieth-century constitutions (think, for example, about the German Constitution of 1949 or the European Convention On Human Rights of 1951), the American one makes no reference to the non-economic liberties associated with private life, nor does it explicitly command that privacy rights must be respected independently of property rights.

In modern parlance, the word 'privacy' is used in both broad and narrow senses. In its broad sense, 'privacy' refers to the cluster of rights associated with personal autonomy: to rights that protect each individual's interest in cultivating a unique way of life regardless of pressures imposed by others. More narrowly, 'privacy' refers to two different devices: the methods individuals use to avoid disclosure of information about themselves (informational privacy) and also those used to avoid disclosing parts of their bodies (privacy of the person). These more limited types of privacy sustain the broader one, for there are many occasions (Heffernan, 1995) in which people want to cultivate a special identity but are reluctant to present this to the public-at-large. But the narrower types of privacy do not have to be viewed simply as handmaiden for the broader type. Informational privacy and privacy of the person not only shield people in the construction of their unique identities, they also provide shields for activities that have nothing to do with identity-creation—indeed, they routinely shield people (Heffernan, 2001) who are engaged in *illegal* activities. Privacy is so central a value of modern life that one of the key questions that courts of all advanced industrial societies must confront—one that simply was not of judicial concern prior to the twentieth century but that has become particularly urgent in an age of terrorism—is when to permit the government to pierce the shields of informational privacy to apprehend those engaged in criminal activity.

If we concentrate on the narrower types of privacy, we can readily discern their effect on the shame/virtue connection. Informational privacy and privacy of the person shield individuals from public scrutiny, and public scrutiny—sustained, intense, probing examination of individuals' lives—is essential to shame and so to the exercise of the Aristotelian virtues. Privacy's subversive effect is not a matter of coincidence. Each of the narrower types of privacy facilitates the transgression of social norms. When Virginia Woolf wrote of the importance of 'a room of one's own,' she was suggesting that the physical and psychological distance secured by means of privacy of the person makes possible the flourishing of unique ways of life that diverge from what is publicly honoured and respected. Indeed, as already noted, informational privacy and privacy of the person can facilitate criminal activity.

But even if we set this point to one side, we can see that privacy has a more moderately subversive effect on all activity that engenders public honour. In placing a barrier between the individual and the larger society, the narrower types of privacy provide each person with an opportunity to transgress quietly the social norms essential to public honour—to avoid unobtrusively opportunities for courage, to be less than just in dealings with others, to be intemperate and imprudent (at least on some occasions) without having to risk public censure. Virginia Woolf's Bloomsbury circle provides a fitting symbol of all this. In practising 'the higher sodomy,' in openly advocating the priority of friendship over patriotism, they mocked their era's public system of honour in favour of an ethic of privatised, personal affection. That the Bloomsbury Set continues to fascinate later generations underscores its importance as a symbol of the move away from Aristotelian virtues.

Needless to say, informational privacy and privacy of the person have not been sufficient by themselves to reduce the importance of a public system of shame. The narrower types of privacy only indirectly challenge public shaming. Direct assaults on public shaming have complemented the growing emphasis on privacy. Perhaps the most significant of these efforts was the one undertaken by nineteenth-century penal reformers to eliminate punishment as a public spectacle: think, for example, about the abolition of stockades, the elimination of public executions, the rise of prisons (which are usually enclosed, although 'open prisons' now exist), and the development of juvenile courts (with the concomitant sealing of adolescents' criminal records).

In the twentieth century, efforts to avoid public shame focused on different matters. The progressive education movement sought positive motivators rather than public humiliation as a spur to academic achievement. Psychotherapists treated shame as a disorder that required professional treatment. And advocacy groups argued that previously scorned ways of life—homosexuality is the best-known instance of this—should not be treated as an object of public scorn. Reform movements of the last two centuries have thus raised the threshold of shame. Compared with the past, we live in what can now be called (Twitchell, 1997) a low-shame society. The prospect of public shame has not been eliminated. It has been reduced, though, in part because of direct efforts to control its sources, in part through the indirect effect of informational privacy and privacy of the person.

3. ALTERNATIVE FRAMEWORKS FOR ETHICS: TARGETED ETHICAL SYSTEMS VERSUS COMPREHENSIVE ONES

Conservatives often wax nostalgic for the sturdy days of yore in which virtue ethics was the dominant framework for thinking about morality. The conservative complaint is at least factually correct: virtue ethics once was, but is not today, the dominant framework of moral reasoning. To paraphrase Burke ([1790] 1968), we can say that shame no longer keeps its vigilant watch on social life—with the result that the Aristotelian virtues no longer play the dominant role in public consciousness they once did. As an aside, it should be noted that belief in an omniscient, intervening God does not dominate popular thought as it once did, thus draining Christian ethics of their vitality as well. If our focus is limited to virtue ethics, these developments may seem to herald a momentous moral decline. An expansion of our range of attention should be sufficient, however, to establish that alternative ethical systems have been developed in the modern world, systems that emphasise not the overall evaluation of individual character (this is the perspective of virtue ethics) but rather the moral questions that surround individual acts. The most important of these systems are either deontological (that is, they treat right and wrong as the fulcrum of moral inquiry) or consequentialist (maximization of good states of being as the fulcrum of inquiry) in nature. These systems are *targeted* in that they focus attention on the merits and demerits of specific acts. Given their different starting points for inquiry, they can take privacy into account as a positive moral value, a point that distinguishes them from Aristotelian virtue ethics.

The Aristotelian framework can work effectively only if it appears reasonably likely that an outsider observer will be able to render a well-informed judgment of the overall character traits of a given individual. It is never enough, given Aristotle's approach, to say that an individual has manifested courage or has acted justly, for one must ask whether these virtues are outweighed—or even merely substantially weighed down—by personal vices. A comprehensive judgment is possible in societies where sustained scrutiny of the contours of an individual's life seems likely. As we have seen, though, with the advent of privacy, such comprehensive judgments have become increasingly untenable. Virtue ethics, however, remains a plausible moral framework in settings where substantial amounts of information about an individual are available. It is not uncommon, for example, to hear family members render character judgments about others within their family circle. Similarly, character—rather than, say, duty—is often the organizing concept for judgments within circles of close friends.

When, however, we turn to the impersonal relations that characterise life within the public sphere of modern societies, targeted ethical systems provide the measure for moral evaluation. In focusing on particular acts, targeted frameworks make it possible to sidestep the overall assessments essential to virtue ethics and instead to concentrate on the merits and demerits of a unique intervention or omission. As I use the term, 'a targeted system' can cover a wide variety of ethical theories. Although there is much on which partisans of these theories disagree, targeted systems have the following in common besides their commitment to the assessment of individual acts. First, they allow for the possibility of morally conflicting judgments concerning an act. Deontological theories, for example, make allowance for a conflict between rights; consequentialist approaches have been known to treat an action as cost-incurring in one context and benefit-producing in another. Second, targeted systems presuppose the possibility of morally neutral acts: that cannot be placed on the 'plus' or 'minus' side of the moral ledger but that have no positive or negative value. And third, they also make it possible to treat privacy as a worthwhile moral variable. On a deontological account, privacy rights are justifiable as important props to personhood; they can be overridden only on a showing of an even weightier right. On a consequentialist account, privacy rights can be defended as devices essential to individual happiness. In accommodating the peculiar, often disquieting value of privacy, each type of system also demonstrates its compatibility with the strongly individualist character of modern life.

Clearly, there is an incommensurability between targeted ethical systems and comprehensive ones. Even more important, though, is the gradual obsolescence to which comprehensive systems have fallen prey in modern societies. One cannot say that virtue ethics is 'mistaken.' This adjective can readily be applied to Aristotle's theories about, say, biology or physics. In these areas, Aristotle has to be deemed flat-out wrong given the presuppositions of modern science. The more qualified word 'obsolete' is needed when dealing with his moral framework. His framework is appropriate for premodern societies—that is, for societies in which an individual can expect to be appraised for his overall character by a large segment of his peers. Moreover, virtue ethics provides a viable framework for character assessments in familiar, long-term relationships in modern societies—for assessing family members and friends, for example. Virtue ethics is not, however, appropriate for the socially fragmented way of life characteristic of the modern era. Not only is comprehensive judgment of character more difficult now, the very focus on character is less socially useful given the importance of resolving thorny moral dilemmas. An abortionist can have a good character, as can a pro-life advocate. A libertarian may be suffused with virtue (including even liberality), as can a socialist. To the extent that disagreements about, say, abortion or wealth-distribution are resolvable at all, they will come about through debates over the merits of specific acts and policies—targeted debates, in other words, that try to unravel the knotty disagreements characteristic of modern life and that treat character as a side issue.

4. POLICE ETHICS: TARGETED ETHICAL SYSTEMS VERSUS COMPREHENSIVE ONES

Most ethical reflection on the police (Heffernan and Stroup, 1985; Kleinig, 1996) has been grounded in targeted ethical systems. Some efforts have been made, however, to revive the Aristotelian framework and to examine police conduct in terms of virtues that bear a rough resemblance to the ones prized by Aristotle himself—and here we consider particularly the work of DeLattre (1994), to which he has returned in this volume. In this section, I consider an argument which maintains that Aristotelian virtue ethics, while not perhaps sustainable in modern societies at large, continue to be relevant to paramilitary organizations such as the police. I conclude that the argument has some merit, but that even for an occupation such as policing targeted ethical systems are of critical importance as well.

In responding to the points made so far, an advocate of virtue ethics for the police could concede the merits of the central argument I have advanced but maintain that it is nonetheless not applicable to policing and other paramilitary organizations. Modern social life is indeed fragmented by comparison with life in premodern societies. Privacy is an immensely important shield against shame. The result, an advocate of virtue ethics could contend, is that the Aristotelian system has been drained of its vitality as it is applied to most aspects of modern public life. But Aristotelian virtues remain pertinent, the critic could continue, when applied to service occupations that call for courage and a sense of justice. The most obvious of such occupations is policing. Police officers are routinely called upon to act courageously in their lives. The events of 11 September 2001 provide an obvious example of this, but acts of courage are required on an everyday basis in settings far more obscure than the World Trade Center attack. Also, police officers are called upon to act justly in all their work—such as when exercising discretion as to when to arrest, when intervening in family disputes, or when seeking to conciliate hostile neighbours.

A critic could note one other point as well. Personal life in modern society may be sufficiently fragmented as to make it reasonable for an individual to expect to be free of sustained scrutiny in his everyday dealings with others. The same expectation is not as reasonable, however, (the critic could maintain) for police officers in their professional lives. The public scrutinises policing as it does few other occupations. Line officers are subject to careful review by their superiors.

Police executives are routinely questioned by legislative bodies and, in most jurisdictions, subject to at-will dismissal by the government executives to whom they report. The conditions for the exercise of virtue are present within the policing occupation, it could be argued. Following Burke, one could maintain that *because* shame keeps its watch on the contemporary police, the incentive exists for police to practise the Aristotelian virtues in the course of their work. This argument, it should be clear, concedes the merit of the larger claims advanced in the earlier sections of this chapter while suggesting that police work—as well as that of other paramilitary and even military organizations—stands as an exception to those claims.

Intriguing as this argument is, it proves on inspection to be only partially satisfactory. There are indeed occasions—September 11 is the most prominent recent one—when the police are called upon to act heroically, but one fails to come to terms with the humdrum nature of most policing if one gives pride of place to heroism. There are also occasions in which officers must exercise discretion according to their own sense of justice, but, again, one would distort the nature of contemporary policing if one were to ignore the converse: the far more frequent occurrences in which officers are called upon to implement detailed rules promulgated by their superiors. The claims advanced concerning scrutiny of the police are also one-sided. True, the police are subject to careful oversight. However, it is also true that the very nature of patrol and detective work has made it possible for many dishonest officers to evade oversight by their superiors as well as members of the executive branch and the judiciary. The argument for a paramilitary exception is thus less than compelling—though still not wholly implausible—on even moderately close inspection.

More difficulties with the argument become apparent once other factors are taken into account. One has to do with the privacy shields built into contemporary policing. Although officers are in principle open to sustained legal scrutiny concerning the performance of their roles, in fact many officers, on being challenged as to the propriety of their conduct (through charges of corruption or brutality, for example) are permitted to retire with no clear finding as to wrongdoing, so that, *inter alia*, their pensions are intact—an outcome on which it would be interesting to read Aristotle's comments. Knowledge of this possibility significantly undercuts the shaming effect of public scrutiny. The officer who is tempted by vice knows that the chance of public condemnation is unlikely, or at least less than certain. In the modern world, shame does not keep a *constant* watch even on members of paramilitary organizations.

Finally, it is essential to bear in mind that the virtue ethics argument for the police is most plausible for the lower, not the higher, ranks of police officers. If we consider the policy questions confronting police executives—how to allocate scarce resources, for example, or whether to implement affirmative-action programmes—it readily becomes apparent that virtue ethics is vacuous rather than helpful in offering solutions to them. By contrast, targeted ethical systems are often quite helpful in this context. Their focus on acts rather than character is appropriate for policy makers. Indeed, consequentialist ethical systems are perhaps most useful in the policy context, given the possibility they hold out of calibrating with precision the costs and benefits associated with a given initiative.

The sceptical points just advanced should not be understood as a full-scale rejection of the argument for applying virtue ethics to police work. Policing is perhaps best conceived as a hybrid field, one in which virtue ethics speaks to the occupational norms of line-officers while targeted ethical systems provide guidance for the problems associated with bureaucratic management. Virtue ethics thus establishes part of the ethos of policing. It is, however, perhaps best classified as an atavism within modern life, one that reminds us of the enduring importance of the classical *polis* even in a world of impersonality and bureaucratic rigour.

REFERENCES for *Chapter 7*

Arendt, H (1959), *The Human Condition*, Chicago: University of Chicago Press.

Aristotle (1941), *Nicomachean Ethics*, W D Ross, trans., in R P McKeon, ed., *The Basic Works of Aristotle*, New York: Random House.

Burke, E [1790](1968), *Reflections on the Revolution in France*, C Cruise O'Brien (ed.), Harmondsworth: Penguin Books.

Delattre, E (1994), *Character and Cops*, Washington DC: AEI Press.

Heffernan, W (1995), 'Privacy Rights', 29 *Suffolk University Law Review*, 737.

Heffernan, W (2001), 'Fourth Amendment Privacy Interests', 92 *Journal of Criminal Law and Criminology* 1.

Heffernan, W, and Stroup T (eds.) (1985), *Police Ethics: Hard Choices in Law Enforcement*, New York: John Jay Press.

Kleinig, J (1996), *The Ethics of Policing*, Cambridge: Cambridge University Press.

MacIntyre, A (1982), *After Virtue: A Study in Moral Theory*, Notre Dame: University of Notre Dame Press.

Strauss, A (ed.) (1964), *George Herbert Mead on Social Psychology*, Chicago: University of Chicago Press.

Timmons, M (2002), *Moral Theory: An Introduction*, Lanham, MD: Rowman and Littlefield.

Twitchell, J (1997), *For Shame*, New York: St. Martin's Press.

CHAPTER 8

The Problematic Virtue of Loyalty

John Kleinig

Professor Kleinig returns to the enduring theme of loyalty in the context of policing. He argues that loyalty is an associational virtue, which is necessary in terms of police bonding but must be reconciled with other necessities. A police service whose officers practise absolute loyalty to each other can neither uphold nor sustain a safe, just and tolerant society, since it will put its own interests above those of all others. The collective value of loyalty must be tempered by the individual virtue of integrity.

INTRODUCTION

Formal ethical constraints on police conduct—often characterised as codes of conduct or statements of values—are sometimes distinguished as 'rule-driven' or 'value-driven.' The 'or' is not exclusive: a well-formed formal document will include reference to both rules and values. Broadly speaking, a code will be rule-driven to the extent that it focuses on prescribed or (more commonly) proscribed behaviour. It will, for example, prohibit the taking of gratuities or smoking in public while on duty. A code will be value-driven to the extent that it focuses on the need for certain dispositions of character that might be expected to figure prominently in occupational decision-making. It will, for example, advocate team work, integrity, or, more generally, professionalism. Such values are often characterisable as virtues—excellencies of character that it is good for a person to have. In the case of professional virtues, they will be excellencies that help to constitute a person a good member of an occupational grouping.

Here we will prescind from questions about whether, for dispositions to be virtues, they have to be morally charged. Even if the so-called intellectual virtues (such as open-mindedness, thoroughness and imaginativeness) are not exclusively moral, the classic moral virtues (such as compassion, justice, and courage) are likely to be impoverished in the absence of the intellectual virtues. We shall also prescind from ongoing debates about the relation of rules to virtues and their relative priority. Again, it is generally accepted that any adequate ethic must give consideration to both: rules without appropriate dispositions will be eviscerated and dispositions without rules will be rudderless.

In the case of police ethics, development of the virtues is of particular importance. Police work involves a great deal of interpersonal interaction, often in ways that bear on sensitive areas of life. Moreover, such work involves discretionary judgment in which complex sets of facts must be accommodated in the process of decision-making. In addition, decisions will often have to be made under conditions that do not allow the luxury of casuistic deliberation, but instead demand that 'rightly trained instincts'—well-modulated virtues—are brought to bear on a complicated situation requiring a rapid response. Even if a course of action is, in some sense, rule-bound, determination that the rule is applicable and how it is to be implemented will require judgment informed by appropriate virtues. There are issues of spirit as well as letter.

Formal statements of virtues that are important to good police work are diverse and to some extent conditioned by local experience and needs. Codes of ethics are covenants between police and the communities they serve and are designed to assure those communities that the powers vested in police will be used in a manner that accords with communally recognised values. If the formal statement pledges compassion, courtesy, integrity, fairness, and respect, it is because these are considered significant as well as sensitive factors in good police–community relations. Good police work will manifest such virtues and is jeopardised if they are absent.

Although loyalty figures prominently in police culture, it is a virtue that has a much more ambiguous place than those already mentioned. Students of police culture will not usually characterise the 'working personality' of police officers in terms of their compassion, courtesy, and so on. They are, however, very likely to draw attention to their loyalty (or, more generally, solidarity). Formal statements of police values tend to be reticent about including loyalty—and the relatively few exceptions often underplay the importance that loyalty actually has in the dispositional life of police officers. One reason for this may be the fact that these formal statements tend to focus on 'sticking-points' in police conduct—dimensions of police behaviour that cause difficulties in police–community relations. If there is no lacking in loyalty as there may be in integrity or courtesy, there is little reason to emphasise it in a code or statement of values.

But the issue is almost certainly more complicated than this. Loyalty as a virtue, and particularly loyalty as a virtue in policing, has proven deeply problematic. In police culture loyalty has often functioned more actively as an underground virtue than as a public one, as a corruption of integrity rather than an expression of it. The community served by police most readily associates police loyalty with the blue wall of silence, a conspiracy to shield officers from public scrutiny and judgment. As one officer—no friend of the blue wall—put it to me: 'If an organization wants you to do right, it asks for your integrity; if it wants you to do wrong, it demands your loyalty.'

But even as a general virtue, loyalty has had its detractors as well as supporters. It is often considered a 'sham virtue', a form of commitment that is invoked to lend a patina of virtue to immoral behaviour—'the last refuge of rogues and scoundrels,' as Dr Johnson said of its political manifestation, patriotism. And even if not viewed as a cloak for immorality, it is interpreted as a flight from responsibility, the surrender of one's own judgment and freedom to that of another.

What, therefore, I propose, is first to focus on the problematic virtue of loyalty, exploring its nature and foundations. I then review its appropriateness to policing contexts, looking particularly at excesses and deficiencies. I conclude with a consideration of ways in which loyalty may be appropriately constrained.

LOYALTY AS A VIRTUE

As noted, not everyone considers loyalty to be a virtue. The cynical quotation above, in which loyalty is contrasted with integrity, captures one strand of the critique to which it has been subjected. Loyalty is construed as an amoral tribal bond that trumps the demands of moral conduct—a commitment to the 'us' that rides roughshod over 'them.' Such tribalism also lies at the heart of Dr Johnson's invective. An alternative critique sees loyalty as blind adherence—a sacrifice of one's independent judgment to the will of another, whether individual or collective. These claims reflect important concerns, and I will return to them later. For the present, though, it is more helpful if we become clearer about the kind of disposition that loyalty is, why it is a virtue, and how it may function as part of an ethical life.

At its most fundamental level, loyalty is an associational virtue. It is a virtue of interpersonal relations. What I mean by that is not simply that it is social in nature—as justice, kindness, or courtesy might be—but that it is a virtue of bonded groupings or associations, and particularly of groupings that have come to be considered intrinsically valuable by those who are members of them. Loyalty cannot exist apart from a sense of identification with those to whom one is loyal. I can be loyal only to my friends, my group, my community, and my country. I cannot be loyal to yours, unless they are also mine. It is in this sense that loyalty can be said to be a tribal virtue, though without the derogatory overtones. More neutrally, it is a particularistic virtue in the same way that gratitude is: one may owe it only to some other with whom one has a special relation.

Within such relations, loyalty is constituted by a disposition to secure the valued association against the ravages of self-interest that might otherwise tempt one to opt out. Those to whom I am loyal can count on my support in hard times, hard times for me as well as for them. Loyalty is no fair weather virtue: my loyalty is called for when someone to whom I regard myself as associationally bound needs my assistance in circumstances that may burden me also. Loyalty is shown when I render such assistance as I am able, despite the burdensomeness of doing so. Disloyalty occurs when I allow the blandishments of self-interest to override the claims of my bond to the other.

Loyalty is essential to some associations. Friendship, or, more narrowly, what is sometimes spoken of as end-friendship[1], is a relation in which the parties to it have each other's interests at heart. A so-called disloyal friend is often said to be no friend at all: disloyalty undermines the friendship. Certain other associations also tend to presume loyalty, though they have an ambiguous character that complicates the connection. Familial relations are frequently suffused with expectations of loyalty, but are more complex because they tend to be constituted by biological as well as social relations. To the extent that one focuses on the nurturing and supportive aspect of family relations one will expect loyalty to develop among family members. If that social dimension has been badly corrupted, and not much more exists than the biological connection, then loyalty will not seem so important.

---

1 To be distinguished from means-friendship, an association forged only with the purpose of securing certain ends.

There are other associations, however, for which, even if loyalty is nonessential, it is often considered desirable. Teams, occupational societies, and employing organizations are primarily instrumental associations, but frequently operate more effectively if their members possess some loyalty to them. Indeed, if we assume that they have an endemic tendency to decline, then loyalty may be important for their long-term health. When members of such associations are committed to them to the extent that they are willing to make sacrifices to further the interests of such associations, the association will be more resistant to competition and more likely to achieve its goals.

It can be seen, then, that the virtue of loyalty possesses the important moral and social function of countering the corrosive effects of self-interest. The underlying presumption, of course, is that the associations to which loyalty is given are not merely *valued* by those who are party to them but also *valuable* in some more general sense. But that presumption cannot always be sustained. Even if friendship is a good to be realised, a valuable natural association, it is not the case that every friendship is a worthy one and that the loyalty of those who are participants is therefore justified. In the case of friendship, the point is not sometimes that the friends should be disloyal but that the friendship should not, or no longer, exist. In the case of other associations to which loyalty is not integral, it might be said that, when corrupted, the associational other cannot legitimately demand loyalty or has forfeited any claim to it.

This capacity for the objects of associational loyalties to fall short of or lose claim to the allegiance of others has led to the dissociation of loyalty from personal objects and its consignment to impersonal objects or the abstractions that might otherwise have been presumed to be exemplified in the primary associations. When mediaeval writers began to make a distinction between loyalty to the king and loyalty to kingship, their distinction reflected the painful reality that those vested with regal powers did not always possess the personal qualities that one might assume to be integral to the particular association. The distinction in such cases was intended to show that acts of disobedience—no doubt seen as acts of disloyalty—meant no disrespect for the office. They were therefore not to be seen as anarchistic or revolutionary, but were simply expressions of the fact that a particular officeholder had failed to live up to the demands of the office. If anything, they represented an effort to recall the officeholder to the high terms of his office. This dissociation has led to ideals and principles becoming secondary objects of loyalty.[2] It is reflected in Donald Schultz's dedication of his book on law enforcement 'to those police officers whose first loyalties are to principles, not men,' an interesting inversion of the original object.[3]

The vulnerability of loyalty to unworthy associations—and therefore the need to form associations worthy of loyalty—points to a further distinction between it and a number of other virtues, such as kindness and courage, in which there exists a greater presumption of appropriateness. Like sincerity, conscientiousness, and industriousness, loyalty is an executive virtue. It does not constitute a virtue of

---

[2] Sometimes this is taken even further. A person is said to be loyal to his or her own principles. But being true to oneself in this way is probably better characterised as a form of integrity.

[3] Schultz, D O (ed.) (1975), *Critical Issues in Criminal Justice*, Springfield, IL: Charles C Thomas, epigraph. A similar reversal is argued for in Souryal S S and McKay B W (1996), 'Personal Loyalty to Superiors', *Criminal Justice Ethics*, 15(2) , Summer/Fall, pp. 44-62.

relations in general, but only of particular relations, and then only if those relations possess other features that constitute them as worthwhile. This is why the classic contexts for loyalty encompass relations such as friendship, family, tribe, or nation—generally considered to be valuable in structuring and supporting human experience. But they can go wrong, as we well know, and so too can other associations that we enter into—teams and organizations that we join.

LOYALTY AS A POLICE VIRTUE

As noted earlier, police generally view loyalty as an important virtue within their own organizational culture. Indeed, I am tempted to say that it is informally viewed as the most important virtue. A considerable portion of police socialisation is devoted to the forging of loyal bonds among officers. At a certain level, that is both understandable and desirable. By its very nature, police work is hazardous. As a society we ask of police that they secure us against the encroachments of disorder and threat. As police often put it of themselves, they represent the thin blue line between civilisation and the jungle. To a degree, they occupy a social space in which they have only their fellow officers to rely on, and so, to cope with the emotional and physical demands individually placed on them they develop deep associational bonds through which they are assured that, should their well-being be jeopardised, they can rely implicitly on their fellows. Policing is an associational enterprise that unlikely to succeed in the absence of loyal bonding among its members.

Loyalty and fidelity

Police officers are called to be loyal to their communities, local or national, their departments and occasionally to their families. More often—no doubt in recognition of the ways in which personalised objects can fall short of the values that are supposedly implicit in them—they are called to be loyal to the Constitution, the law, their oath of office, their profession, their goals or mission, and sometimes to their own beliefs and ideals.[4]

---

[4] For statements in which loyalty is advanced as a professional value, see Singapore Police Force, Core Values (http://www.spinet.gov.sg/aboutus/mis/01mission.htm) (4/29/03); Pennsylvania State University Police Department, Organizational Values (http://www.psu.edu/dept/police/values.htm), (5/25/03); Garland (TX) Police Department, Conduct and Performance Values (http://www.ci.garland.tx.us/police/gpd1000.htm); Norton Police Department, Our Values (http://www.cityofnorton.org.Police/Values.htm) (5/25/03); Monroe (NY) Police Department, Our Mission (http://www.monroepd.org/ourmission.htm) (5/22/03); Punta Gorda (L) Police Department, Values (http://www.ci.punta-gorda.fl.us/police/police_about.htm) (3/14/03); Lake Havasu City (AZ) Police Department, Values (http://www.ci.lake-havasu-city.az.us/PD/Police.htm) (3/14/03); Pocatello (ID) Police Department, Department Values (http://www.ci.pocatelloid.us/departments/policedept/) (3/14/03); Ewing Township (NJ) Police Department, Organizational Values Statement (http://www.taylorapp.com/ewingpolice/mission.html) (3/14/03); Santa Monica (CA) Police Department, Values (http://santamonicapd.org/information/mission.htm) (3/14/03); Mountain Brook (AL) Police Department, Values (http://www.mtbrook.org/Pd/mission.htm) (3/14/03); Fremont (CA) Police Department, Our Values (http://www.fremontpolice.org/M_V_V/M_V_V.htm) (5/1/03); Calexico (CA) Police Department (http://www.calexicopd.org/mission/mission.htm) (5/1/03); and Fairfield (ME) Police Department, Values (http://www.fairfieldme.com/users/pd) (4/8/03) (almost identical to the Santa Monica PD statement).

These are all eminently understandable objects. We can easily accept that officers ought to be loyal to their communities, departments and families. Their role is to serve their communities, and to risk themselves in securing the members of those communities against the forces of disorder. Their departments will flourish only if their members can work together as a supportive team, subordinating personal ambitions to the larger structure. Their families promise an important source of personal stability, an intimate social centre that helps to steady them for the daily demands that are placed on them.

For the most part, our loyalties cohere with each other and also with other virtues and values that we possess. That is to be expected and desired: the choices we make—of friends, of occupation, of the community in which we reside—will be made against the background of values that we hold, leading to a relatively cohesive set of relations. And in the broader sphere, it is likely that the values that inform these choices will themselves reflect the associations that have nurtured us. Were this not the case, our lives would be characterised by anguished choices as one part of our identity was played off against another. Even so, there will almost certainly be occasions on which our loyalties will come into conflict with each other and also, perhaps, with other values that we hold, and we will confront a hard decision about the kind of person we will be.

Leaving aside for the moment how such decisions should be made, are there any generalities to which we might appeal—any ordering of loyalties that might assist in our decision making? Formal codes of ethics are often poorly crafted for such eventualities. They enunciate values to be observed without indicating how conflicts among them should be resolved. That is almost always true of conflicts between the general values they espouse, but it is also true of conflicts of loyalty that might arise.

However, not every code is deficient in this regard. In the *Conduct and Performance Values* promulgated by the Garland, Texas, Police Department, it is stated:

> Loyalty. Members shall recognise that their allegiance is first to the community, then to the department's mission and the government agency that employs them. Commitment to the department must be over and above that of any individual member of the department.

This is a worthy attempt to accommodate the potential for conflicting loyalties. In giving first place to the community, the statement acknowledges the source and purpose of police authority. Policing does not exist as a natural association, as friendship or even familial relations might be construed. It is a purpose-oriented institution, formed to serve specific even if broadly defined communal needs. Without that justification, policing lacks a *raison d'être,* and should it lose sight of its *raison d'être,* it loses its legitimacy. Wisely, it does not identify the department's mission with service to the community or the organization with the mission. Community needs may change; the mission may need to be rethought; and the agency may lose sight of its mission. What then follows addresses the most likely conflict of loyalties: that between the department as it seeks to fulfil its mission and the individual loyalty that members will come to have to each other. That loyalty is taken for granted: what cannot be taken for granted is the priority of other loyalties.

We might of course take issue with the statement if interpreted strictly. Communities may lose their legitimate claim on the loyalty of those who serve them. Thankfully, this will be rare, though statements that focus on loyalty to the Constitution or law might be said to grasp such possibilities. As is almost always the case with codifications of values and their prioritisation, any rankings will be presumptive or defeasible. Although we may generally wish to give departmental loyalty priority over loyalty to a fellow officer, it is surely possible to envisage cases in which corrupt departmental politics or the vindictiveness of superiors makes it reasonable to back up a fellow officer. For all its perversity, the blue wall of silence is often reinforced by the sense that departments operate in unfair and self-serving ways.

Nevertheless, by addressing the issue of loyalty and seeking to offer some prioritisation of the multiple loyalties that officers might be presumed to have, the Garland statement confronts what many other codes avoid, and does so about as well as one might expect from a formal statement. Codes of ethics are never complete manuals of decision making. They set parameters, at best, and if they try to do too much they may come to be treated as substitutes for judgment. Ethics will collapse into law.

EXCESSES AND DEFICIENCIES OF LOYALTY

Critics of loyalty tend to view it as blind adherence. Not only blind, but also absolute. There is some social basis for this criticism, particularly if one's focus is the blue wall of silence. Although the blue wall is buttressed by a variety of considerations, among them is the loyalist notion that one ought *never* to hurt another officer. Loyalty to fellow officers is deemed to override all other claims. It is the seeming detachment of such loyalty from moral boundaries that contributes significantly to the ambivalence, if not disdain, that loyalty attracts. It is not helped by the fact that loyalty has often been associated with what are seen as intrinsically distasteful objects—the loyalty of the Nazi, Mafioso or gang member is likely to exacerbate the evil they do. Loyalty appears to be particularly susceptible to excess.

Understandable though such reactions may be, they fail to show that there is something inherently problematic with loyalty. The fact that one may be sincere in one's devotion to Nazism or industrious as a gang member is not sufficient to exclude sincerity and industriousness from the pantheon of virtues. Sincerity may not be enough. That is true of the executive virtues in general: their limited or focused role cannot be used to criticise them for failing to be what they do not profess to be. Moreover, blind loyalty is just that: blind. But loyalty need not be blind, and a person in whom other virtues are strong will have reason to ensure that loyalties are well placed. There is nothing to prevent us from subjecting the objects of our loyalty to the kind of scrutiny that will determine whether they are worthy of it, or of our loyally seeking to make such objects more worthy in the event of their falling short.

For the most part, the process of developing a particular association will provide ample opportunities for assessing the worthiness of the object of our association. Friendships, though they may develop slowly and almost imperceptibly are not entered into in an ethical vacuum. To the extent that we become aware of deficiencies in the person with whom the association is developing we have opportunities to pause and reconsider or withdraw. Even if we have formed an association with others that has given rise to a loyal commitment, there is no reason to disengage our moral antennae. Although the loyalist will be inclined to support the object of loyalty, and might therefore not ask some of the questions that could be expected of a stranger, becoming aware of some problematic features in the situation might reasonably prompt questions that affect the response. In some cases, the loyal response might be to question what is being asked for; in other cases, continued loyalty may be inappropriate—what has been done or what is asked for may undermine the loyalty.

It is true that certain associational bonds—those to family and community—tend to be fostered before our abilities to assess them are fully mature. This can cause difficulties down the line. And some associational bonds may be demanded as a condition of membership. One suspects that those who enter police work will not always be aware of the associational demands that are going to be placed on them. Still these are practical challenges rather than deficiencies in loyalty as such. In his memoir, Bill McCarthy indicates how he avoided the awkward kinds of situations in which officers sometimes find themselves, such as when unexpectedly faced with the burden of protecting an errant officer:

> *Loyalty* in the police department means you're willing to lie for someone else. Loyalty to me meant that I would always be the way I promised to be for another person. I would never be an ambush. Any person I worked with, I had to tell them right away that I wasn't on any pad. They had to know from me that if I caught them stealing, *I* would be the one to lock up their ass.[5]

Although the executive virtues are particularly vulnerable to excess or misplacement, even the substantive virtues are not immune to subversion. One may be generous to a fault, or exact justice untempered by mercy. Any virtue, if not moderated by others, will result in excess. The implicit lesson of police codes, to the extent that they are value driven, is that the values they uphold are not to be viewed in isolation but as practical dispositions to be kept in some kind of balance. When the Garland Police Department advertises its commitment to: 'integrity, professionalism, loyalty, courage, compassion, fairness/equality, leadership, and teamwork,' it does not treat these as unbounded obligations, but as integrated pledges, in which loyalty will not undermine integrity, compassion will not subvert professionalism, courage will not undermine teamwork, and so on. The problem of course is to determine what that appropriate balance is, a determination that will depend on the particulars of situations and require judgment rather than the mechanical application of some formula.

If virtuous excess is a permanent danger, so too is virtuous deficiency. In some respects they are two sides of the same coin. Excessive loyalty is likely to involve a deficiency in integrity. But an excessive concern for integrity may also be associated with a deficiency in loyalty. Early in life we are taught the distastefulness of tattle telling. Although the tattle tale may be morally deficient in a number of respects, a key deficiency is his or her failure to stand on their own moral feet—a failure to

5 McCarthy B and Mallowe M (1991), *Vice Cop: My Twenty-year Battle with New York's Dark Side*, New York: William Morrow, p. 42.

confront violations as breach of relationships calling for restoration rather than as infractions requiring outside intervention.

If the blue wall of silence represents an excess of loyalty, the reporting of every infraction—as departmental regulations often demand—can express a deficiency. Where loyal bonds exist, there is at least a *prima facie* reason to address infractions in a way that is compatible with a continuation or rejuvenation of the association. If I catch my daughter shoplifting, it is unlikely that I will respond by delivering her to the store security for arrest and charging. It is more likely that I will deal with the situation privately—no less seriously perhaps, but in a way that reflects and does not jeopardise the associational bond of father and daughter. So, too, one might expect police who become aware of relatively minor fraternal failures to deal with them 'horizontally' rather than 'vertically.' Obviously, as will be the case even between parent and child, there will be limits to the private handling of breaches.

The problem of course is that police culture is frequently hostile to any kind of vertical or even horizontal criticism, let alone criticism of a public nature. There is no room for a loyal opposition or 'second guessing.' As is it is understood in certain organizational contexts, loyalty is taken to demand unquestioning support, a 'yes-man' response to those to whom one is expected to be loyal. But this involves a corruption of loyalty.

CONSTRAINING LOYALTY

Even though loyalty is the source of many ethical problems in policing, it is not a dispensable virtue. The work to which police are called is often onerous and sometimes dangerous. We expect of them devotion to the community somewhat analogous to the devotion to country we expect of the military. But it is not only the community that lays claims on police loyalty; it is also expected by their departments and their fellow officers.

How are we to resolve such conflicts, and others that might arise between loyalty and other virtues? One partial solution is provided by the kind of prioritisation we observed in the Garland Police Department's statement of values. We can look at an occupation, determine its fundamental purposes, and then see how those purposes are best served by various personal characteristics possessed by those who enter it. If we see police fundamentally as social peacekeepers, we will give priority to certain communal commitments, recognising that they might be most effectively advanced by certain other commitments, but acknowledge the subordination of the latter to the former. That is the Garland strategy and it goes someway to providing a check on the development of loyalties.

Another way is to recognise that loyalty as a virtue does not exist in isolation from other virtues but must be expressed in ways that take account of those other virtues. And so, should loyalty and integrity conflict, the moral costs of compromising integrity should be given serious consideration. Even though loyalty to others may be a constituent of a person's integrity, it is unlikely that unfettered loyalty will be.[6] Or, to take a more generalised virtue, that of professionalism, we

[6] For an interesting discussion of this, with which I am in only partial agreement, see Thomas Wren, 'Whistleblowing and Loyalty to One's Friends,' in William C. Heffernan and Timothy Stroup (eds.), *Police Ethics: Hard Choices in Law Enforcement*, New York: John Jay Press, 1985.

will see that the public service ends of professionalism, the evolving commitment to providing the best service one can, will be compromised if certain loyalties are permitted too much influence. The blue wall of silence generally has a corrosive effect on police professionalism.

Whatever strategy we adopt, judgment will be involved. Officers will have to judge how their loyalties relate to each other and how those loyalties are to be balanced with other virtues they might, as officers, be expected to have. Occasionally those decisions will be very difficult. The case of an officer who sought release during a flash flood so that he could attend to the needs of his family—residing in the flood area—provides a poignant example. After having permission to leave his post twice denied, the officer decided that his family took priority and went to provide assistance to them. He was suspended and charged with insubordination, an offence justifying dismissal. Did he act improperly? One might argue that his professional responsibility (especially in an emergency situation) was to follow orders. On the other hand, had he been a member of the Queensland Police Service, he would have been able to take account of a provision allowing that 'while an officer will put his family responsibilities first, duty to the community of Queensland will always be given priority over the other private interests of officers.'[7] Judgment is required: not every family responsibility will take precedence over professional responsibilities any more than every professional responsibility will take precedence over family responsibilities.

Cultivation of the virtues does not relieve police officers of the need to make ethical judgments. What it does is to identify those virtues of which police ought to be particularly mindful, demanding that they be exercised in ways that give due weight to the purposes of policing and the particulars of a presenting situation.

[7] Queensland Police Service, *Code of Conduct*, issued by the Commissioner of Police, 1990, Sect. I.

CHAPTER 9

Ethics, Education and Integrity[1]

Milan Pagon

This chapter deals with the importance of police ethics and integrity in contemporary policing. It first describes the field of applied ethics in general. It explains the basis for the structure of professional moral obligations, briefly depicts the core imperatives of applied ethics and describes the process of moral reasoning. It then defines police ethics, discusses the reasons for its relative underdevelopment, and delineates its future development in three interrelated directions: (a) applying the principles of applied ethics to the police profession; (b) establishing standards of ethical conduct in policing; and (c) defining the means and content of education and training in police ethics. Next, it discusses the organizational environment that is conducive to police ethics and elaborates on the concept of integrity. The chapter concludes that police ethics and integrity are of critical importance in the professionalisation of policing and the best antidotes to police corruption, brutality, neglect of human rights, and other forms of police deviance.

INTRODUCTION

In the field of police and security studies, it has become clear that we are witnessing a paradigm shift. While we cannot expect this shift to result in a uniform approach to policing everywhere in the world, we can assume that all the various approaches will be based on the same set of assumptions of modern policing, namely community involvement—a proactive approach that emphasises a problem-solving approach and an integrated view of criminal justice (Pagon, 1998). As various authors (e.g. Hahn, 1998; Vicchio, 1997; Murphy, 1996; Delattre, 1996; Fry and Berkes, 1983) point out, aspirations by the police to become professionalised either create or at least re-emphasise several requirements, such as a wide latitude for discretion, higher educational requirements, higher standards of professional conduct and self-regulation.

At the same time, however, there have been countless accounts of police brutality and abuse of authority, some of them making the headlines, and others taking place outside the public eye. In some countries, police corruption has already reached epidemic proportions. It is obvious that corruption, brutality, and other forms of police deviance go against the above-mentioned efforts to achieve police professionalisation and community involvement. The community cannot trust nor attribute a professional status to deviant police officers. No wonder then, that modern police organizations all over the world are fighting police deviance and trying to achieve the proper conduct of their members. However, according to

---

[1] This chapter is a revision of the author's keynote presentation at the third biennial international conference *Policing in Central and Eastern Europe: Ethics, Integrity, and Human Rights*, organized by the College of Police and Security Studies in Ljubljana, Slovenia, September 2000.

Sykes, a brief history of these efforts to enhance police accountability reveals that they relied on rules and punishment:

> Although each of these reform efforts had an impact, the sum total fell short of providing assurances that they were adequate and serious incidents continued ... In short, the various rule-based systems of accountability seem insufficient if officers hold different values or there is a sub-culture which nurtures values different from the ideals of democratic policing. (Sykes, 1993, p. 2)

This author believes the answer lies in approaches based on ethics, where accountability rests more on individual responsibility than it does on external controls and the threat of punishment. It has become clear that only properly educated and trained police officers are able to respond adequately to the ethical dilemmas of their profession. Only police officers who are able to solve these dilemmas appropriately can perform their duties professionally and to the benefit of the community. In doing so, they cannot rely solely on their intuition and experience. Not only have they to be well acquainted with the principles of police ethics and trained in moral reasoning and ethical decision-making: they also need clear standards of ethical conduct in their profession.

In this chapter, I will try to show that a proper development of police ethics and integrity is one of the most important steps toward the professionalisation of policing, and one of the most powerful antidotes to deviance and neglect of human rights by the police. To introduce the field of police ethics, however, I first have to describe the field of applied ethics in general.

APPLIED ETHICS

Police ethics is a branch of applied, normative ethics. The best known branches of applied ethics are medical and business ethics. The link between 'theory' and 'practice' is what makes applied ethics different from philosophical ethics. Applied ethics is the field that holds ethical theory accountable to practice and professional practice accountable to theory. Therefore, the philosophers should not dictate to professionals the norms that are supposed to govern their professional practice, without a very thorough knowledge of that practice. On the other hand, the professionals have to understand that their experience and intuition are insufficient for defensible judgment, and that the constraints under which they work do not exempt their decisions from ethical scrutiny (Newton, 1998).

According to Newton, there are three fundamental imperatives of applied ethics—to which we might add that they are also the foundations of a safe, just and tolerant society. Those imperatives are beneficence, respect for persons and justice.

Beneficence

Professionals must take care of, or look out for the interests of, the client. Beneficence has several sub-imperatives conjoined in it: first, to do no harm, second, to prevent harm or protect from harm, and third, to serve the interests or happiness of the client.

Respect for persons

The command to respect the autonomy and dignity of the individuals with whom we deal, to attend to their reasons and honour their self-regarding choices, is the command underlying all of our interpersonal dealings. In professional relationships, however, it also limits the boundaries of professional beneficence. Professional expertise may tell us that the client's best interests will be served by certain services that we are able to provide; it may even tell us that the client needs, on pain of loss of life or liberty, certain of our services. But if the client chooses not to avail himself or herself of them, and only his or her own interests are concerned, the professional may not impose those services on the client. This implies a combination of justice and tolerance for the wishes of the client, even if the judgement of the professional indicates that those wishes may be wrong. In the case of medicine, the patient may choose a course of action or inaction which leads to harm or death. This could also apply to the citizen who ignores, flouts or simply chooses not to follow the advice of a police officer. Consider, for example, the police officer who is attempting to protect members of the public against a possible threat to their safety…

> I wouldn't go up that lane at the moment, Sir.
> —Why not?
> We have a suspect package.
> —But I have to get home!
> Not that way, Sir.
> —Are you ordering me not to use this street?
> No, Sir. I'm advising you.

Justice

This imperative demands that the professional looks past both art and client, and takes responsibility for the effect of professional practice in society as a whole. In every profession or practice, we can find examples of injustice. For example, in medicine in some societies, the rich get immediate and adequate care while the poor get late and inadequate care. The demand of justice upon professionals is that they work within their professional associations, and in their individual practices, to blunt the effects of injustice in their fields. The professional who ignores this demand fails to fulfill all the duties of professional status.

Because these imperatives are logically independent, they can be (and often are) in conflict. Yet, as Newton (1998) says, we may not abolish one or another; we cannot even prioritise them, which leads her to conclude that applied ethics is not the science of easy answers. As professionals are struggling to solve moral and ethical dilemmas, they engage in the process of moral reasoning.

Applied ethics does not specify for each profession how its imperatives should be reflected in professional practice—nor what are the values and virtues of that particular profession. These will (and should) differ depending on the function of the profession in the community. That is why we need branches of applied ethics, tailored to individual professions. Let us take a look at police ethics.

POLICE ETHICS

Police ethics applies the principles described above to the field of policing. Compared to medical or business ethics, police ethics is relatively underdeveloped. There are several reasons for this, the major ones being the paramilitary philosophy of policing which has been prevalent until now[2], and a misunderstanding of the need for police ethics (Pagon, 2000).

First, within the paramilitary philosophy of policing, officers are assigned the role of executors of orders from their supervisors. They are not supposed to question those orders, so there is not much need for moral deliberations. The basic virtue of police officers within this framework is obedience. Police leaders, on the other hand, are either not accountable to anybody (since they are setting their own goals and can always tailor the statistics to fit their needs[3]) or they are accountable only to the party in power, with which they are in a symbiotic relationship. It is not surprising that police ethics does not thrive in such a context.

Second, some practitioners are misled by a belief that as far as police officers perform their work strictly by the law, they need no police ethics. Proponents of this view also deny police officers the right of discretion. Unfortunately, when one is faced with an ethical dilemma, the laws prove themselves to be of little use. As Newton (*idem*) puts it,

> our first job... in all fields of practice, is to distinguish, in every context, between the demands of law and the demands of ethics—between the danger of being sued, prosecuted, jailed or defrocked, and the much subtler, but more pervasive danger of being systematically and cruelly wrong. One of our first lessons was that we must think beyond the law and teach nervous professionals to do the same.

With the rise of the new philosophy of policing (i.e., community policing and problem-oriented policing) and with the acceptance of police discretion as a necessary part of police work, the importance of police ethics is gaining acceptance. Nowadays it is hard to find a curriculum at a police academy or a programme in police studies at a university that does not include the subject of police ethics. At the same time, the number of police agencies with a department, task force or a committee on police ethics is rapidly increasing. The majority of these agencies have also adopted a code of police ethics, in a more or less articulated form.[4]

---

2 The reader might assume at this point that the author has been influenced in his description of the 'prevailing' paramilitary philosopy of policing by his experience as a police reformer in Central and Eastern Europe, so recently released from the oppression of authoritarian communism. However, as is explored in Adlam and Villiers (2003) by Pagon and others, paramilitary policing may also be the norm in non-communist societies such as France and the USA.

3 A phenomenon not unknown under the contemporary 'reforming' performance management culture: see Adlam and Villiers (2003, *passim*).

4 There are, of course, a number of internationally based codes of police ethics, produced by such organizations as the United Nations, and which have been explored in depth by Kleinig (see *Chapter 8*). The European Police Code of Ethics produced by the Council of Europe was endorsed by the Committee of Ministers of that council in September 2001. However, it should be noted that some member-states of the Council of Europe, of which the UK is a notable example, have failed to take this code any further on the domestic front. This is not to imply that British policing is an ethics-free area—quite the reverse, in fact—but that the UK is failing to take full advantage of the possibilities offered by a European code.

But, as I have already mentioned, police ethics is still at the beginning of its development. A lot of courses on 'police ethics' are mainly dealing with philosophical ethics, while the word 'police' in the name simply means that police officers or students of police studies are the target group of the course.

(a) The core virtues of policing

What are the core virtues of policing? No educational or training programme in applied ethics for police professionals can be successful before this question is both addressed and resolved. Vicchio (1997) believes that if the goals of police organization are to be met, the following virtues must be required of officers: prudence, trust, effacement of self-interest, courage, intellectual honesty, justice and being open to choice. Delattre (1996) describes the importance of the following virtues for police officers: honesty, trustworthiness, justice, fairness, compassion, temperance, courage, wisdom and integrity. Whichever virtues are finally chosen must rest upon the identification of what is most needed for the proper functioning of the police in society.

(b) Establishing standards of ethical conduct in policing

Expectations regarding ethical conduct have the greatest impact upon actual behaviour if they are not simply assumed, but are clearly and unambiguously communicated. Based on the imperatives, values and virtues of the profession, police ethics has to establish clear and unambiguous standards of ethical conduct. A code of police ethics can be very important within this context. For example, research shows that the mere existence of a code of ethics positively influences employees' ethical behaviour (Ruch and Crawford, 1991). The simple declaration of a code is, however, not enough. Police management and leadership must embody, and demonstrate in action, the principles of that code.

(c) Defining the means and content of education and training in police ethics

This has to be accomplished by a joint and sustained effort of police ethicists and practitioners. We have to keep in mind that listening to a single lecture on police ethics or skimming through some literature on the topic will not make police officers moral or their behaviour ethical. A lot of time and effort need to be put into education and training in this field, before police officers—when faced with a moral problem or dilemma—will automatically consider all the alternatives available to them; will not make decisions based on prejudice or impulse; will submit their decisions to reason and change them, if such a change seems reasonable; and will give equal consideration to the rights, interests and choices of all parties to the situation in question.

Furthermore, as Delattre (1996) points out, even the mastery of the process of moral reasoning and decision-making does not, by itself, guarantee ethical conduct, nor do all of the situations require moral reasoning and deliberation. An individual has to have good character (i.e. appropriate virtues) to be motivated towards ethical behaviour. This realisation imposes two additional requirements for police ethics training. Firstly, in addition to teaching moral reasoning and decision-making, training has to emphasise and develop virtues characteristic of the profession of policing. Secondly, the task of ethical training should also be the development of moral habits.

So, the task of *police ethics education* is to teach the principles of applied ethics in general and police ethics in particular. It has to cover the imperatives, values and virtues of policing; the process of moral reasoning and decision-making; and the difference between moral problems and moral dilemmas.[5] It has to explain and justify the standards of ethical conduct in policing, the code of police ethics and the process of code implementation. Other vital topics are strategies for managing ethical behaviour in police organizations, and ethics training and education.

The tasks of *police ethics training* are:

- to enable the students to recognise moral problems and moral or ethical dilemmas;
- to train the students in the process of moral reasoning and decision-making;
- to emphasise and develop the virtues necessary for the profession of policing, hence developing the students' moral character; and
- to develop the moral habits of the students.

The development of police ethics, including education and training, will not achieve its purpose unless all organizational processes, especially the behaviour of police managers and the top management of the organization, support and encourage the ethical conduct of all its members.

An ethical environment

If police officers experience inconsistent behaviour from their supervisors, preferential treatment of some officers and/or citizens, solidarity with, and cover-ups for, the officers who violate the standards of their profession, they will sooner or later become cynical regarding the value and appropriateness of ethical conduct in their organization. One cannot expect a cynical police officer to be motivated to adhere to the rules of ethical behaviour (Pagon, 1993).

Research shows the importance of *moral climate* in organizations for the behaviour of individual members. Experiments in schools and prisons (Kohlberg, 1984) have revealed that changing organizational processes such as policies and procedures can create a positive moral atmosphere that then contributes to improvements in individual moral development and moral judgment, as well as to reductions in cheating, stealing and similar anti-social acts. Investigations of organizational effects on moral conduct in business firms appear to support these observations. Firms demonstrating exemplary business practice attest to the value of creating a positive moral atmosphere for encouraging ethical behaviour and maintaining the firm's reputation. Conversely, the organizational environment can also promote unethical and criminal conduct in business firms (Cohen, 1995). Researchers have also demonstrated that organizational factors such as reward systems, cultural norms and codes of conduct can significantly decrease the prevalence of unethical behaviour in organizational contexts (Brass *et al.*, 1998).

---

[5] A moral problem is generally regarded as a challenge to which there is an appropriate response which may be difficult to achieve. In other words, we know what is the right thing to do: the difficulty is in doing it. A moral dilemma, on the other hand, gives us a choice between two (or more) choices of action, both of which could be argued for on moral grounds.

Cohen (*idem*) defines moral climate as the 'shared perceptions of prevailing organizational norms for addressing issues with a moral component'. These issues include:

- identifying moral problems;
- choosing criteria for resolving moral conflicts; and
- evaluating the moral correctness of outcomes that ensue from organizational decisions.

Since climate is a function of how employees collectively perceive and interpret these and other elements of the work setting, climate can be thought of as an intervening variable. As such it provides the necessary perceptual link between organizational processes and employee behaviour. According to Cohen, there are five dimensions that interact to determine the moral climate in an organization:

- *goal emphasis* (prevailing norms for selecting organization goals);
- *means emphasis* (prevailing norms for determining how organizational goals should be attained);
- *reward orientation* (prevailing norms regarding how performance is rewarded);
- *task support* (prevailing norms regarding how resources are located to perform specific tasks); and
- *socio-emotional support* (prevailing norms regarding the type of relationships expected in the firm).

The importance of trust

Organizational actors are embedded within a network of relationships. These ongoing social relationships provide the constraints and opportunities that may help to explain both ethical and unethical behaviour in organizations (Brass *et al.*, 1998). McAllister (1995) distinguishes two main dimensions of trust between organizational members:

- *cognition-based trust*, which relies on appraisals of others' professional competence and reliability; and
- *affect-based or emotion-based trust*, which is present when people feel safe to share their private feelings and personal difficulties, knowing that the other party will respond constructively and caringly.

Emotion-based trust has been found to be more effective in fostering ethical behaviour. It incorporates the virtue of benevolence, which refers to an altruistic concern for the welfare of others and is devoid of egocentric motives (Mayer *et al.*, 1995). In police settings, we could extend this notion to include trust between the police and the community.

Summary

It is important to note that all of the factors described above interact with each other in predicting ethical or unethical behaviour. Let us take trust as an example. In an organization with a strong moral climate, composed of individuals of good character and with dense social networks, it is safe to assume that a high level of trust will promote ethical behaviour. In such organizations people who trust others (both cognitively and emotionally), and feel trusted by them, will be reluctant to violate this trust by engaging in unethical behaviour.

On the other hand, if the moral climate is low, social networks are loose, with a lot of structural holes and many cliques, it is very likely that a high level of trust within a deviant clique will promote unethical behaviour. In this case, people who trust other clique members and feel trusted by them will be reluctant to violate this trust by giving up their own unethical behaviour or even by reporting on other members' unethical behaviour.

Trust, in other words, like loyalty, can work either way.

Therefore, to set a climate conducive to ethical behaviour in the police organization, police managers have to consider all of the above factors. They have to:

- foster the character development and moral habits of police officers by educating and training them in police ethics;
- establish a highly moral climate through the appropriate use of goals, means, rewards and support;
- facilitate development of strong and dense social networks, extending into the community;
- prevent cliques and conspiracies; and
- establish both cognitive-based and affect-based trust among all organizational members and between the police and the public.

In doing so, the managers will not only facilitate the ethical behaviour of their officers; they will also prevent or at least lessen the strength of the infamous police sub-culture, so typical of paramilitary policing.

In trying to achieve the above goals, police managers will soon discover that, firstly, setting their own example is of the utmost importance and secondly, that ethics does not only apply to police officers' dealings with the community but also to their own dealings with their subordinates. Police officers' human rights are as important as those of other citizens.

INTEGRITY

I agree with Sykes (1993) that the quality of policing in a democratic society relies on the quality of the people doing the work. This is why I believe that in policing we should strive to achieve the virtue of integrity in all police officers and supervisors, including top management.

Leadership theorists and researchers have found that integrity is a central trait of effective business leaders, while interpersonal and group relationship theorists have identified integrity as a central determinant of trust in organizations (Becker, 1998). Delattre (1996) and Vecchio (1997) agree that integrity is also central to the mission of policing. To Delattre, integrity is not only the highest achievement there can be in a human life but also the most difficult. So, what exactly is integrity?

Delattre (1996) defines integrity as 'the settled disposition, the resolve and determination, the established habit of doing right where there is no one to make you do it but yourself' (p. 325). He believes that integrity is 'irreplaceable as the foundation of good friendship, good marriages, good parenthood, good sportsmanship, good citizenship, and good public service' (ibid.).

Vecchio (1997) defines a person of integrity as somebody who has a reasonably coherent and relatively stable set of core moral values and virtues, to which he or she is freely and genuinely committed, and which are reflected in his or her acts and speech. So, the person's words and actions should be of one piece.

Becker (1998) subscribes to the objectivist view of integrity, namely that integrity is loyalty, in action, to rational principles (general truths) and values: 'That is, integrity is the principle of being principled, practising what one preaches regardless of emotional or social pressure, and not allowing any irrational consideration to overwhelm one's rational convictions' (p. 158).

Integrity in policing, then, means that police officers genuinely accept the values and moral standards of policing as they are espoused. The officers possess the virtues of their profession. They consistently act, out of their own will, in accordance with those values, standards and virtues, even in the face of external pressures.

Of course, not all police officers have integrity. Benjamin (1990) describes five psychological types lacking in the quality:

- The first is the *moral chameleon*, a person who is over anxious to accommodate others. Unable to withstand social pressure, he or she is thus willing quickly to abandon or modify previously avowed principles.
- The second is the *moral opportunist*, whose values are also ever changing, based on his or her own short-term self-interest.
- The third is the *moral hypocrite*, a person who has one set of virtues for public consumption and another set for actual use as a moral code.
- The fourth is the *morally weak-willed* who has a reasonably coherent set of core virtues, but is usually lacking in the courage to act on them.
- The final type is the *moral self-deceiver*, a person who thinks of himself or herself as acting on a set of core principles, while, in fact, he or she does not.

Of course, 'it is not a breach of integrity, but a moral obligation, to change one's views if one finds that some idea he holds is wrong. It is a breach of integrity to know that one is right and then proceed (usually with the help of some rationalization) to defy the right in practice' (Peikoff, 1991 p. 260; cited in Becker, 1998).

Why do some people lack integrity? Why is it so hard to achieve it? Based on a review of objectivist literature, Becker (1998) offers the three most common reasons.

Firstly, not everyone is rational. Integrity requires a discipline of purpose and the ability to maintain a long-range course of action, selecting corresponding goals and pursuing them fervently, carefully choosing the means to one's ends and making full use of one's knowledge.

Secondly, a person may lack integrity because of desires that are inconsistent with moral values. If a person, when under temptation, fails to call upon his or her rational mind, acting upon the whim of the moment instead, that person will indeed lack integrity. The same is true when an irrational fear drives behaviour. Similarly, an individual's integrity will be called into question if he or she does not put rational principles into practice simply out of inertia.

Thirdly, probably the most common reason a person may lack integrity is that he or she succumbs to social pressure. This may come from numerous sources (e.g., co-workers, bosses, or clients) and take many forms (e.g., physical intimidation or verbal and nonverbal disapproval). A person with high integrity will not allow popularity to take priority over rational convictions.

CONCLUSION

From the above discussion, it should be obvious that integrity can only be achieved if a person strives to achieve it. Appropriate education and training in police ethics, a good moral climate in the police organization, appropriate social networks (both within the organization and within the community), trust and support, can all both motivate police officers to strive for integrity and help them achieve it. I believe that, once achieved, integrity of police officers is one of the most important steps toward the professionalisation of policing, and one of the most powerful antidotes to police corruption, brutality, neglect of human rights and other forms of police deviance.

Police ethics provides a compass to both police officers and their managers. It specifies the core imperatives, values and virtues of policing. It delineates the process of moral reasoning and decision-making. It sets the standards of ethical conduct. And it defines both the means and the content of police ethics education and training. Police scholars and practitioners have to co-operate in developing police ethics. This is not an easy task for either group. Developing and implementing police ethics invokes changes in police organization. Police organizations and police officers, as we know, are very resistant to change. Those police scholars and practitioners entrusted with developing police ethics must, therefore, themselves be persons of integrity. We should not forget Newton's caution on flattery. The flatterer is a person who tells people what they want to hear, instead of what they should hear. Flattery, in Newton's words, 'is the major corruption available to the ethicist ... the only defence against flattery is personal integrity.' In developing and implementing police ethics, a lot of people will have to be told things they most definitely do not want to hear.

REFERENCES for *Chapter 9*

Becker, T. E. (1998), 'Integrity in Organizations: Beyond Honesty and Conscientiousness', *Academy of Management Review*, 23(1), 154-161.

Benjamin, M. (1990), *Splitting the Difference: Compromise and Integrity in Ethics and Politics*, Lawrence, KS: University Press of Kansas.

Brass, D. J., Butterfield, K. D., and Skaggs, B. C. (1998), 'Relationships and Unethical Behaviour: A Social Network Perspective', *Academy of Management Review*, 23(1), 14-31.

Cohen, D. V. (1995), 'Moral Climate in Business Firms: A Framework for Empirical Research', *Academy of Management Journal*, Special Issue: Best Paper Proceedings, 386-395.

Delattre, E. J. (1996), *Character and Cops: Ethics in Policing* (3rd edition), Washington D.C.: AEI Press.

Fry, L. W. and Berkes, L. J. (1983), 'The Paramilitary Police Model: An Organizational Misfit', *Human Organization*, 42(3), 225-234.

Hahn, P. H. (1998), *Emerging Criminal Justice: Three Pillars for a Proactive Justice System*, Thousand Oaks: Sage Publications.
Kohlberg, L. (1984), *The Psychology of Moral Development: Moral Stages and the Life Cycle*, Vol. 2, San Francisco: Harper and Row.
Mayer, R. C., Davis, J. H., and Schoorman, F. D. (1995), 'An Integrative Model of Organizational Trust', *Academy of Management Review*, 20(3), 709-734.
McAllister, D. J. (1995), Affect-based and Cognition-based Trust as Foundations for Interpersonal Cooperation in Organizations', *Academy of Management Journal*, 38, 24-59.
Murphy, P. V. (1996), 'Foreword', in: Delattre, E. J. *Character and Cops: Ethics in Policing* (3rd edition), Washington D.C.: AEI Press, xiii-xvi.
Newton, L. H. (1998), 'Doing Good and Avoiding Evil: Principles and Reasoning of Applied Ethics', Internet: http://funrsc.fairfield.edu/~cnaser/dgea/good-evil.html.
Pagon, M. (1993), 'Policijski cinizem: vzroki, zna•ilnosti in posledice' [Police Cynicism: Antecedents, Characteristics, and Consequences], *Revija Policija*, 13(4-5), 389-403.
Pagon, M. (1998), 'Organizational, Managerial, and Human Resource Aspects of Policing at the Turn of the Century', in: Pagon, Milan (ed.), *Policing in Central and Eastern Europe: Organizational, Managerial and Human Resource Aspects*, Ljubljana: College of Police and Security Studies, 3-14.
Pagon, M. (2000), 'Policijska etika kot zvrst uporabne etike' [Police Ethics as a Branch of Applied Ethics], *Varstvoslovje*, 2(2), 158-167.
Pagon, M. (2000a), 'Police Ethics and Integrity', in: Pagon, M. (Ed.), *Policing in Central and Eastern Europe: Ethics, Integrity, and Human Rights*, Ljubljana: College of Police and Security Studies, 3-14.
Ruch, W. V. and Crawford, M. L. (1991), *Business Communication*, New York: Macmillan.
Sykes, G. W. (1993), 'Why Police Ethics?', Internet: http://web2.airmail.net/slf/oct93/why.html.
Vicchio, S. J. (1997), 'Ethics and Police Integrity', *Law Enforcement Bulletin*, Internet: http://www.fbi.gov/leb/july972.htm.

CHAPTER 10

A Framework for Police Ethics Training

Neil Richards with Robert Adlam

This chapter is based on a paper presented by Neil Richards at a seminar on 'Police Ethics' in Tallinn, Estonia, 6-7 May 2003, held under the auspices of the Council of Europe.

On many occasions and in various contexts (e.g. Richards, 1985; 1993; Adlam, 2000; Richards and Adlam, 2003) we have sought to bring into the foreground the 'ethical' in policing—especially by insisting that the very *raison d'être* of the police institution is decidedly moral in nature. Thus, we understand the police as constituted to achieve morally worthwhile ends, such as safety, social peace and justice, through morally acceptable means. It follows that the police role is deeply moral in its essential character.

In the context of late modern societies the role of the professional police officer is complex and demanding. The European Code of Police Ethics attempts to define professional policing and what it is to be in the role of a professional police officer by providing an extensive set of principles or ethical rules (Council of Europe, 2001).

Ethical training is needed to bring out the universality of this dimension of police work, and to foster the continuing development of the appropriate knowledge, attitudes and skills amongst police officers and, where appropriate, support staff.

As a practical activity, the business of policing is surely best learned through the activity of policing. After all, this is the theatre in which a police officer will, as part of a process of life-long learning, gain most of his or her professional knowledge. It remains the case, however, that formal training at all stages of a police officer's career has an important role to play in his or her development. It enables new skills and knowledge to be acquired, enhanced, maintained and refreshed in keeping with the ever-changing complexities of the modern world. In addition, it acts as a counter to the development of inappropriate attitudes and patterns of behaviour to which prolonged work as a police officer may give rise: and we stress the word 'may.'

In this chapter, we shall explore the particular needs and aspects of police ethics training at various levels in the police organization.

POLICE ETHICS IN RECRUIT TRAINING

This is the fundamental and critical phase of ethical training. Recruits are predominantly young people at the beginning of their policing lives who are still relatively impressionable and eager for the challenges ahead. In broad terms one can assume that they are well selected for a police role. The ultimate mission of police in a democracy is, as we have underlined elsewhere (Richards and Adlam,

2003), to uphold the rule of law. Its meaning and implications are absolutely vital for the police. It is the ultimate basis of true order in a democracy. The problem is that this may well seem a somewhat abstract notion that lacks inspiration for recruits.

The task of the trainer is to show how a police career dedicated to such a notion could be the most challenging and fulfilling career, or indeed vocation, that a young person could wish for. The principle that nobody is above the rule of law, least of all the police who are appointed to preserve it; that no persons may be deprived of their fundamental liberty save in accordance with procedures prescribed by law; and that the protection of the law extends even to those who have broken it; is difficult to grasp even by mature and sophisticated minds.

This relatively stark notion can be readily complemented by all the other primary police objectives, together with the practical and ethical implications that flow from them, which show policing to be full of challenge and variety. However, it is essential for trainers to convey the importance and significance of upholding the rule of law, and they should be steeped in its meaning and be able to communicate it vividly. It lies at the very heart of the professional police role, with its emphasis upon legality as an absolute characteristic of correct police action.

If this is a relatively difficult task for instructors, there is another that is fortunately far easier, but in our experience, little utilised. In many countries, including the United Kingdom, a prospective police officer is only legally recognised as such once he or she has taken an oath of office. It is usually sworn before a judge or magistrate and is, at its best, the occasion for solemn ceremony and quiet celebration. Such an oath, as well as having great legal importance because of the powers it confirms for the person so sworn, also has great personal meaning for the man or woman undertaking the oath. It is a rite of passage that marks the assumption of a professional police role and has life (or identity) transforming significance.

It changes the person's status as a citizen. It empowers them to uphold the rule of law on behalf of their fellow citizens with the expectation that they are ethically 'fit' to do so and that they can be trusted with such a role. We have yet to meet a police officer, no matter how long in service, who does not remember taking his or her oath of office. Indeed, in the course of our work we have sometimes encountered police officers who tell us that it serves as the main framework through which they try to live out their professional lives. In many countries this oath represents a large part of the declared ethics of office and is characterised by solemnity and worthwhile *gravitas*. The oath, which has such significance in the lives of recruits, provides excellent material for highlighting the ethical character of policing and its requirements. Much ethical training can be made to hang on it.

Another important tool in the context of police ethics training is a national code of police ethics. This has been highlighted by, for example, Kleinig (1990) in his analysis of the various 'ingredients' that warranted a place on any police ethics training programme. The European Code of Police Ethics recommends that member states create such codes (Council of Europe, 2001: Paragraph 63). We cannot exaggerate the importance of such codes. Where they exist they provide an authoritative basis for the purposes of police, the value that attaches to those purposes and the morally acceptable means by which they should be achieved.

Given the complexity of modern life, the multiple demands that are often made on police and the current cultural mood that dismisses 'authority', it is not surprising that police officers sometimes lose their way: they wonder what they should be doing, what their essential task is and whether or not 'principles' really matter. We have witnessed this many times over the three decades we have taught at Bramshill. Armed with a national police code of ethics, a trainer is much better placed to raise the standard of the ideals of policing in an open, democratic society. Reference to such a code should be the 'lone star' of all police training (and at all levels).

This is the stage, too, when it is appropriate to introduce the European Convention On Human Rights (ECHR) and the European Code of Police Ethics. In their practical training, which includes the realities of policing, recruits begin to encounter some of the appalling aspects of human conduct both of a criminal nature and in terms of human degradation. Many recruits experience a degree of shock. Some behaviour is so terrible that it is deeply repugnant to decent people and great strength of will is needed if improper police conduct is to be avoided. Self-control under extreme provocation is one of the cardinal virtues of police officers, and preservation of their essential decency needs to be reinforced by training. This links closely with practical training in the proportionate use of force, and is part of its ethical underpinning. If legality, because it confers legitimacy and hence authority upon police actions, is the hallmark of good policing, its handmaiden is a fundamental respect for human dignity as a value. This standard runs through the articles of the Convention like a golden thread, and it needs to be instilled into the minds of police recruits. This would mark the beginning of a training theme that, with increasing levels of sophistication, would reach through to training at the highest level.

Training at all levels should 'take full account of the need to challenge and combat racism and xenophobia' (Paragraph 30, The European Code of Police Ethics). It is part of the police mission to combat racism and xenophobia whenever and wherever they occur. This area is one of the most difficult and demanding for police trainers. Indeed, there is persuasive evidence to suggest that poor or insensitive training can make matters worse. Unfortunately, racist and xenophobic attitudes share something of the same characteristics as indoctrinated beliefs. They have a tendency to be held unshakably, so that no amount of empirical demonstration or rational argument serves to dislodge them. They can be perversely inconsistent and resilient. Just as the price of freedom is eternal vigilance, so in this area the need to combat racism and xenophobia must be an enduring one—and a wide range of imaginative tactics needs to be employed in order to be successful.

A closely related requirement is the need to encourage officers to carry out their duties in a manner which does not alienate the public; and to equip them with the social skills necessary for the effective policing of a multi-cultural (or multi-ethnic) community, especially under stress and in situations that typically cause difficulty (ACPO, 1992: Appendix A).

Questions should be asked about the ethical significance for police performance of ignorance of the social arrangements, including, in particular, religious and cultural arrangements, of society's various groups. In these areas, more often than not, police errors are the result not so much of wilful intention but of unwitting ignorance. Corruption, too, needs to be touched upon, but not too heavily. We should emphasise however, that recruits need to be warned about the more deviant elements within the police culture—particularly about their strategies and tactics in corrupting others—as well as the preventative measures.

All these concerns involve the development of sound judgment, which is at the heart of police discretion. The exercise of police discretion has been authoritatively defined as ' ... the art of suiting action to particular circumstances. It is the police officer's daily task' (Scarman, 1981). A police officer is not a mechanical implementer of the rule of law. He or she is expected to 'fit' the law and common sense ethics to particular circumstances. This is a capacity officers need to 'grow' with their careers, and it is never too early to begin to train in it. Nonetheless, it stretches the imagination and ingenuity of trainers to the utmost. Here we are talking of nothing less than the development of wise judgement.

As we draw this section to a close we think it important to include one other item in the content of ethics training that has tended to be overlooked. In the main, the people who become police officers have, at the beginning of their careers, an impressively wrought moral system. Like most people, they admire justice, fairness, honesty and compassion; they are concerned to protect the weak and prevent suffering. They are, most typically, commendably virtuous people. This was acknowledged by, for example, Woodcock (1992). However, because the content of a person's moral system tends to remain unexamined, we think it important to undertake a form of 'moral consciousness raising'. Over the course of the years we worked at Bramshill Police College we created numerous educational structures to do this (e.g. Adlam, 2000). We think it important to remind recruits of the ways in which the 'ethical' is a major part of their psychosocial being. And we think it important to take the first steps in 'strengthening' this facet of their psychosocial development.

A full, varied and imaginative range of training methods should be used, and great care taken to ensure that the particular methods and topics are well suited to people with little experience of policing. Suitable methods should include: reading; lectures with plenty of opportunity for questions; the posing of ethical dilemmas, with some suggestion as to how to address them (e.g. Villiers, 1997); films; group discussions; structured learning experiences; case studies; and role-playing. Here we think it appropriate to draw attention to Kleinig and Leland Smith's (1997) excellent collection of papers detailing a number of educational approaches to police ethics training.

Properly used all these methods can contribute to successful training. We have found that role playing, which is widely used in training for some aspects of police work, such as giving evidence in court, can be invaluable in teaching the interpersonal skills and styles of conduct needed in ethically demanding situations.

POLICE ETHICS IN INTERMEDIATE AND SPECIALIST TRAINING

The functions and responsibilities of each rank call for a distinctive training programme in police ethics. In particular, officers at management level need to be equipped to understand the importance of commanding, supervising, managing and leading more junior officers in a manner that reinforces the police ethics training they will have received up to that point.

Ethics training at this level is able to draw upon the increasing experience of officers to broaden and deepen their understanding of their role, including its ethical implications. Ideally, they should be provided with new 'maps' that highlight their existing experience in new ways, make new links within their experience, and enable them to capitalise on their existing expertise and knowledge. Because of their supervisory, management and command roles, it will be necessary to look again at the critical functions of policing as mentioned in the section on initial training.

Policing styles

Police in the middle ranks play a critical part in setting police styles and monitoring their use. This is another dimension of the wise exercise of discretion, that is, police judgement. Officers need to be encouraged to be flexible and open minded in their thinking, to see the police service as the community may see it, and above all to consider carefully the level and style of response that may be required in different situations, particularly where they involve people with different cultural backgrounds. Great flexibility and delicacy of touch is required when handling such issues, and officers should be encouraged to refine their capacity to do so.

Part of flexibility in selecting the right style for a policing purpose is that of securing the co-operation of the public, and especially that of non-police agencies. There is a continual need to involve the community in long and short term measures designed to reduce crime, and this means dealing with representatives of the community, including local authorities and Non-Governmental Organizations (NGOs). Training in an appreciation of the functions, responsibilities, different organizational philosophies and ideals of other agencies, with a focus on the ethical dilemmas that arise as a result of these differences and likely conflicts of interest, is important at this level.

The police 'family'

The employment of different and appropriate styles is no less important inside the police organization than it is outside. When someone joins a police service in a democratic state, they are gradually inducted into what might be called the 'police family'. The shift system, which provides 24-hour cover for 365 days a year, necessarily involves police officers working unsociable hours that cut into social arrangements with those outside the police, and the role itself, regrettably, tends to distance police officers from other citizens. The upshot is the formation of a working culture which is unusually cohesive in comparison with most other human groups, with a tendency to be insular. There grows up, very largely unconsciously, a strong outlook of 'them and us'. In terms of their essential role, this 'police identity' tends to have positive outcomes but there are also negative ones. Police officers need to be aware of what has happened to them in this process if they are to take full advantage of their professional identity and avoid its pitfalls. We have found that anthropology, with its understandings of roles, rituals, symbols and performance, is rich in insights for this context.

Loyalty and cynicism

A consideration of police loyalty pays considerable dividends. Loyalty is the social cement that binds police officers to each other. Therefore, the building of such loyalty by both informal and formal processes is generally to the advantage of civil society. Its downside is misguided, misplaced, and corrupted police loyalty. Loyalty is, as we understand it, a derivative and secondary moral virtue. It depends for its validity upon the core virtues of honesty, benevolence, fairness and non-malevolence, and it is, therefore, highly conditional. In the business of everyday living this is easily lost sight of and, because it is a virtue that is vitally important to police officers, its workings need to be made transparent and its proper relationship with integrity explored and understood.

If police loyalty is not unproblematic, police cynicism, as Ker Muir (1977) brilliantly demonstrated, is totally corrosive. The trainer has the very real challenge of countering any tendency to cynicism. We have already highlighted the negative nature of many police encounters with the public, and the need for officers to rise above the feelings that these tend to engender. For a police officer to succumb to cynicism—having little faith in human sincerity or goodness—is to risk both personal and professional disablement. It deflates the sense of purpose and achievement that good policing offers. Police leadership and management has a very important part to play in countering police cynicism. The challenge is to help their staff to find a continuing compassion and tolerance even for the most degraded of human beings: for how else is their legal and ethical probity to be assured?

Police ethics in specialist intermediate training

Traffic officers face, perhaps, the most difficult and demanding of policing challenges in their encounters with both perpetrators and victims of sudden and violent death and destruction. They deserve more consideration in terms of this aspect of their experience than they usually receive, whether in training or by police management.

The ethical challenges and stresses that arise in criminal investigation are, perhaps, more widely acknowledged. Police investigators have to construct a plausible narrative that explains how a crime was committed, by whom, where and when. They are pledged to do so in a manner that takes full account of the criminal law and its procedures, which are in place to uphold the freedom of the individual from unwarranted and illegal interference by the state. Their work is conveniently summarised as being in continual conflict, potential or otherwise, with the ECHR articles 5, 6 and 8, and other rights may also be breached as a result of it.

Training in this area, fraught as it is with ethical considerations, needs to be particularly rigorous and exacting. The dual nature of the task and the full range both of properly achieved and improperly achieved outcomes need to be clearly understood. There are four principal combinations of these:

- good outcomes achieved by proper means;
- good outcomes achieved by improper means;
- bad outcomes achieved by proper means; and
- bad outcomes achieved by improper means.

All have ethical aspects. In our experience, the second option is an especially fruitful source for the discussion of practical ethical dilemmas amongst working detectives.[1]

Senior police investigators have a clear responsibility for ensuring the integrity of the process that they manage. The top down pressure to get results is often at the heart of police malpractice, and police officers with supervisory and management responsibilities need to be made fully aware of this hazard and fully armed to resist it.

Training methods

Because police activity at this level is so much about supervising, managing and monitoring performance, as well as commanding and leading, the stock of training techniques mentioned so far needs to be supplemented. How far it is supplemented will depend upon training budgets, but money invested in learning at this level is inevitably money well spent. Middle ranking officers provide so much of the substance, energy and expertise necessary to run a police organization that without their co-operation and understanding the policies and ideals formulated at the top have little chance of being implemented on the ground.

Situational analysis, or the comparison in classroom or syndicate of the practical dilemmas arising in police work, is a valuable training method, so long as it draws fully upon the experience of participants and the analysis applied is both friendly and critical. A more elaborate but undoubtedly beneficial approach depends upon work-based learning mixed with the training environment. One of the regularly repeated criticisms of much training is that the artificial character of the training environment does not relate well to the workplace and its culture. Consequently, there is a poor transfer of learning from training to the workplace. One way of overcoming this is to devise projects that involve trainees in applying the learning that they have gained in training to the workplace and then reporting back on the results to re-conventions of their classmates. This can often be tied to real workplace achievements, which, if costed, show the true efficiency of the method. The point is that experienced supervisors and managers are challenged to show what difference their newly acquired learning has made to them in practice.

With police investigators, simulations that reflect every aspect of their work are likely to be the most effective training tools. When exposed to the sympathetic but critical attention of their peers, simulations bring about powerful learning and understanding for many officers. In particular, the techniques of monitoring the investigative process for its effectiveness and integrity need to be focused upon since these are key to effective supervision and management in this area.

POLICE ETHICS IN HIGHER TRAINING AND EXECUTIVE DEVELOPMENT

Officers at the senior management level and executive level clearly play a vital part in ensuring that ethics training is effective. They have a particular responsibility for ensuring:

- that the ethos of a police force is right;
- that good performance means just that;
- that it is characterised by a high order of ethical probity;
- that ethical standards are honoured both in letter and deed; and
- that supervising officers of lower rank discharge their duties in a satisfactory manner.

Above all, senior officers must ensure that the right policies as regards police ethics are adopted and practised throughout their force and that in-force training is well designed to carry those policies forward.

There are, in our experience, two major conditions that tend to undermine the ethical resolution of police officers, apart, that is, from a straightforward commitment to criminal activity. The first involves law that is ambiguous, indeterminate or lacking in full public support. Under these circumstances, and given that a police officer is part of the public, the chances of him or her being tempted to 'turn a blind eye' for monetary considerations is considerably enhanced. The other instance is that of the mature and often effective officer, who, because of a radical change to his or her lifestyle without the funds to support it and little real chance of further promotion, seeks to 'supplement' their income through corrupt practice. To counteract these tendencies is clearly one of the more demanding requirements of senior police leadership and management.

Business ethics and political awareness

At the senior management level, police activities necessarily become more strategic. Policy necessarily starts at a high level of generality at the top of a police organization, and it needs to be adapted to the very real experience and circumstances that it meets on the way down. To discern the difference between the mischievous corruption of policy and its proper implementation is part of the exacting business of senior managers. They also have to concern themselves with the management proper to any large scale organization—objectives, planning, budgetary control, recruitment, promotion, training, for example—and ensure the integrity of all these mechanisms. In essence, police officers in positions of strategic command will need to address the rapidly developing area of business ethics. They also need to develop, if they have not already begun to do so, that understanding of the background to, and pressures of, political leadership which is essential if they are to function as both ethical and effective public service managers in a democratic society.

Senior police managers need, after full and proper consultation, to assess the ways in which a community's policing needs can be assessed and competing claims balanced, keeping a close eye on the balance to be struck between enforcing the law and keeping the peace, and having studied the relative advantages and impacts of different policing styles and their implications for properly ethical policing. To do this they will need to have a comprehensive and practical grasp of the working of democracy at both local and national levels, a full awareness of cultural relativism and equality before the law, and be aware of the practices of other police agencies and problems of a legal or quasi-legal and ethical nature dealt with by other such agencies.

Training should allow the opportunity for officers to explore new and different ways in which familiar operational problems, past solutions to which may have elicited an adverse response, might in future be resolved. Such training might use case studies based on real incidents that have recently occurred and might in effect constitute a step by step critical reappraisal of past action: a sort of critical debriefing. If a climate can be created in which officers are prepared to lend their own command experiences to such processes, so much the better.

The special additional need for officers at these ranks is for training in the supervision of large scale, or otherwise sensitive, operations that unless well handled may alienate the community from the police. The management and supervisory skills needed will not otherwise differ essentially from those required at lower ranks, the main skills being: to know who to assign to what duties; to appreciate when personal involvement is needed to ensure that operations are professionally conducted; and to ensure that subordinates never lose sight of the implications of their actions for the ethical integrity of the police.

Executive development

In recent years it has come to be recognised in both the private and public sectors that chief executives and their colleagues can also benefit from professional development. To this end the first author of this paper was responsible at Bramshill for establishing the Chief Police Officers' Development Programme. This comprised executive seminars and coaching, mentoring, consultancy, executive sets, master classes, bespoke conferences focussing on current critical issues, and specific courses to address knowledge and/or skills shortages identified by chief officers and their top teams, inspectors of constabulary or needs analyses. We mention this because we think it is something relatively new and it was greeted with great appreciation by chief officers themselves. In particular, one aspect of the programme, which managed to secure the trust of participants as to confidentiality, effected the sharing of the experience of large scale operations with major challenges and dilemmas of a critical sort at the chief officer level.

CONCLUSION

We are confident that the essential groundwork has now been completed, establishing the foundations upon which police ethics training should be based (e.g. Kleinig, 1996; *Explanatory Memorandum*, Council of Europe, 2001). We are also confident that, through our own formal and informal processes of action research concerning the teaching of 'police ethics', we are in a position to commend the framework that we have outlined in the foregoing paragraphs.

Training in police ethics should be progressive throughout a police officer's career; relate to the actual functions and responsibilities of the job; wherever possible be thoroughly related to other topics on courses and exercises; be highlighted whenever training in any other topic or speciality is undertaken; and be given immediately on any officer's assumption of his or her new responsibilities, and thereafter at regular intervals. Ethical training must begin with what is already there, in terms of the previous moral development of the individual. It needs to be linked to the philosophy of policing by consent and the social doctrine underpinning the policing of a safe, just and tolerant society.

REFERENCES for *Chapter 10*

ACPO, (1992), *Getting Things Right.* Available from the National Police Library, Bramshill.

Adlam, R. (2000), *Culture Change: an Attempt to Teach Ethics to Police Leaders and Managers in a Traditional Institution and Changing Social Context,* Doctoral dissertation, Department of Educational Studies, University of Surrey, Guildford, Surrey.

Council of Europe, (2001), *'European Code of Police Ethics'*, Strasbourg: Council of Europe Publications.

Ker Muir, W. (1977), *'Police: Street Corner Politicians'*, Chicago: University of Chicago Press.

Kleinig, J. (1990), 'Teaching and Learning Police Ethics: Competing and Complementary Approaches', *Journal of Criminal Justice*, vol. 18, pp. 1-18.

Kleinig, J. (1996), *'The Ethics of Policing'*, Cambridge: Cambridge University Press.

Kleinig, J. and Leland Smith, M. (eds.) (1997), *'Teaching Criminal Justice Ethics: Strategic Issues'*, Cincinnati, Ohio: Anderson Publishing Company.

Richards, N. (1985), 'A Plea for Applied Ethics' in R. Thackrah (ed.) (1985), *'Contemporary Policing'*, London: Sphere Reference.

Richards, R. (1993), 'A Plea for Applied Ethics' (second edition) in R. Thomas, (ed.) (1993), *Government Ethics,* Cambridge: CSPE.

Richards, N. and Adlam, R. (2003), 'Policing's Noble Cause: Democracy, Ethics and the Rule of Law', *Merengue*, October 2003 (publication available from the National Police Library).

Scarman, Lord (1981), *Brixton Disorders, 10-12 April 1981: Report of an Inquiry,* (Cmnd. 8427), London: HMSO.

Villiers, P. (1997) *Better Police Ethics*, London: Kogan Page.

Woodcock, Sir John (1992), 'Trust in the Police: The Search for Truth', International Police Exhibition and Conference (IPEC), Seminar reprints, London: Major Exhibitions and Conferences Ltd.

---

[1] *Editorial comment:* It is, of course, impossible to convey in a chapter of this sort the full richness and vitality of police ethics training at its best, of which both the authors of this chapter and the editors of this book as a whole have on occasion had full experience. It is, in our opinion, a profound mistake to believe that ethics training need be platitudinous, hollow or dull. Equally, it is a profound mistake to assume that the incidence of humour in syndicate discussion must be an indication that there is an absence of learning. Ethics teaching at its worst is often described as 'preaching'—the implication being that such an activity is of no use. We suspect that the best preachers do not actually 'preach', in the pejorative sense of the word, at all. The good ethics tutor, like the good preacher, needs to engage with the group and address real issues in an atmosphere of authenticity.

CHAPTER 11

A Tale of Two Cultures: Comparing the Police and Academia

David Canter

Who is a wise man? He who also learns from fools. (*The Talmud*)

One of the developments in policing that is significant in creating a more just society is the increasing openness of police forces to academic work and their embracing of scientific approaches to crime management. These increasing interactions require cross-cultural understanding that is not always present. It is therefore of value to explore the contrasts between the culture of the police and of academics. It is argued that these two cultures differ in:

- their approach to the nature of knowledge;
- what are considered appropriate forms of action; and
- the objectives that motivate individuals within these contexts.

These differences are generated by the overall missions of the different institutions and are usually consonant with them. However, academics can benefit from recognising and adjusting to some of the perspectives of the police: and the police increasingly need academic and scientific inputs. Thus, whilst both cultures have something to offer there is great benefit in them getting to understand each other so that they can work together more productively. It is out of the interaction between these cultures, as a sort of miscegenation, that more effective policing will emerge.

LITTLE BLACK BAGS

In his delightful novel *The Long Good-Bye* Raymond Chandler records the conversation between two hardened detectives:

> 'You two characters been seeing any psychiatrists lately?'
>
> 'Hell,' Ohls said, 'hadn't you heard? We got them in our hair all the time these days. We've got two of them on the staff. This ain't police business any more. It's getting to be a branch of the medical racket. They're in and out of jail, the courts, the interrogation rooms. They write reports 15 pages long on why some punk of a juvenile held up a liquor store or raped a schoolgirl or peddled tea to the senior class. Ten years from now guys like Marty and me will be doing Rorschach tests and word associations instead of chin-ups and target practice. When we go out on a case we'll carry little black bags with portable lie detectors and bottles of truth serum. Too bad we didn't grab the four hard monkeys that poured it on Big Willie Magoon. We might have been able to unmaladjust them and make them love their mothers.'
>
> (Chandler, 1959 p. 275-6)

Chandler was characterising police in Los Angeles in the 1950s: a time and place when psychology and psychiatry were represented in the public mind by the Rorschach inkblot test and the search for psychological complexes through Jungian word association. It was also a time when the polygraph 'lie detector' and the use of sodium pantothenate as a 'truth drug' were still fashionable and acceptable in some courts. But if we up-date the technology and broaden the science base to include DNA, latent fingerprint examination and the many other developments in science that police services are embracing now, there is much in this conversation that captures the views of police officers today. Most notably is the conceptualisation of developments in science and technology as a bag of tricks to be taken along to a case. Ohls does not say, 'We'll all be reading Freud and Jung instead of the police procedures manual'. He draws the processes of police training, like chin-up exercises and target practice, into the use of particular procedures drawn from the black bag of the physician.

The fictional conversation rings true to me because of how it reflects conversations I have had as a psychologist discussing research developments with the police. Not very long ago I suggested to people organizing training courses for senior police officers that they ought to provide a basic introduction to scientific concepts and methods, including behavioural science, as a fundamental component of the educational process. My suggestion was dismissed out of hand as being far too academic. I was assured that what they needed were practical, operationally oriented training sessions that would be of obvious and immediate value in their day-to-day work. This was a reaction little different from that reported many years earlier by Holdaway (1989) who spoke of the police as absorbed by crime fighting, arrests and 'their insatiable need for action'.

The 'man of action' persona reflected in this view is also the spirit of Ohls' comments. He does not need the entire debate and analysis of the circumstances of the crime: he just needs to get to the baddie and sort him out. Such a style of dealing with the world makes for good fictional drama. Heroes combat villains and good prevails. Indeed, there can be no other line of work (with the possible exception of doctors and nurses in emergency settings) that is so frequently portrayed in the mass media. It must be the case that many police officers, especially detectives, see their activities as reflections of the dramas that nightly fill the TV screens. Indeed some commentators have named 'syndromes' such as the 'John Wayne' or 'Dirty Harry' syndrome that characterise a particular stance taken by police officers, and have argued that there is a distinct phase in officers' careers when they see themselves as 'TV cops'—although not, perhaps unfortunately, in the style of PC George Dixon of Dock Green. They and the public they serve see their job as essentially one of action, not of contemplation. This is true to such an extent that a fictional detective's interest in opera (like Morse) or playing the violin (like Holmes) is a way of showing how out of the ordinary he is in having a contemplative side to his nature.

Yet much of what present-day police officers are called to do includes strategic considerations, especially once they get above the rank of sergeant. Even with the huge resources that go into a murder enquiry in the UK it is no longer possible to 'leave no stone unturned' as Senior Investigating Officers (SIOs) like to claim. Some assignment of priorities is necessary. In effect, this requires the specification of some form of hypotheses about the murder, then following them up. Often these hypotheses will require testing, or be developed from forensic evidence and interaction with forensic scientists as varied as pathologists, toxicologists, entomologists and even investigative psychologists. Treating these advisors as merely technicians who are giving readings off a piece of equipment can lead to misunderstandings and frustrations on all sides.

The need for a scientific perspective on large enquiries was identified by Byford (1981) in his review of the Yorkshire Ripper enquiry. Byford's point was that the exploration of the issues and testing out of ideas in a complex investigation would benefit considerably from a scientific perspective. He even suggested that a scientist should be assigned to each major enquiry to provide such a perspective, a role that came to be known as the 'Byford scientist'. Yet it is interesting how police forces interpreted this challenging idea. The role became one of liaison officer with the forensic scientists and the scientific perspective became interpreted as the need for computer systems to store the massive amount of information collected. What was proposed as a change in the way of thinking became just another piece of technology to take out of the black bag. It is therefore not surprising that 20 years later Macpherson (1999) identified similar weaknesses, in the Stephen Lawrence enquiry.

This need for police interaction with the academic/scientific perspective goes far beyond major murder enquiries and has been developing over many years. Drummond (1976, p. 40) pointed out that ' the police are far more open with others than was the case a decade ago' and interaction has since increased greatly. Partnership strategies with various agencies in the local community are part of this increased openness. They also require a more abstract understanding of the processes that underlie the problems being tackled than was the case when it was considered just a matter of putting a bobby on the beat. Furthermore, the requirement of setting priorities for dealing with volume crime cannot be intelligently based on a casual glance at the weekly crime figures. Issues like the management of crowds and other public order matters cannot be dealt with as just working out procedures for subordinate officers to follow. As Drury (2003) and his colleagues have shown, some understanding of the psychology of crowds is essential if they are to managed effectively, but this means engaging with social science debates that have been ongoing for 150 years.

The difficulty of interaction between what I am characterising as, on the one hand, the academic/scientific culture and, on the other, the culture of the police is not merely a matter of vocabulary or engrained habits. It is a set of fundamental differences in thought processes, typical modes of action and the central objectives that shape the institutions in which these cultures thrive. They therefore have implications for all aspects of the lives of the people involved.

My point is to emphasise the importance of the interaction between the different cultures. For whilst there have been many academic studies of police cultures over recent years there has been a tendency for their apparent objectivity to hide a somewhat supercilious attitudes towards the rough-neck cops. There are good reasons why police culture is different from scientific culture, and there are certainly strengths and weaknesses in both. Therefore understanding these cultural differences helps to improve the ways in which the different perspectives may complement each other.

Recognising that the culture of the police is an integrated aspect of the ways in which police officers see themselves and the attitudes they hold, also sheds light on such contentious and apparently varied issues as how racism survives in the police, and why police forces have such difficulty in taking full advantage of new technologies. In addition, it helps to explain why academics who want to help the police so often get it wrong. In order to develop our understanding further a closer look at the differences in these cultures will be worthwhile.

WAYS OF KNOWING

Perhaps the most fundamental distinction between the police and academic communities is in what each regards as knowledge. Their histories and training, as well as the difference in context between science and the law, define what is known in different ways. Like all such distinctions there are overlaps and variations within the different cultures: but the broad difference that undoubtedly exists nonetheless provides different bases for subsequent actions.

Data versus evidence

It was the Senior Investigating Officer of Operation Trinity, Superintendent Vince McFadden (reported in Canter, 1995) who first pointed out to me that what the police search for is evidence, something that can be used to prove a case in court, whereas what scientists want is data, material that they can work with, and on which they can test their hypotheses. This distinction has many ramifications for the different approaches to the information available and what can be done with it.

From the police point of view, the power of evidence is that it leads to conviction or acquittal in court, and its relevance is determined by the case in hand. It is in the possession of one side of an argument or another and serves one or the other's ends. In the way that it must be protected and defended, there is almost a sacred quality to evidence. Evidence is finite and fills the scales of justice until its very weight tips the balance one way or the other.

Data is very different from all this. It is the raw material out of which science is fashioned. The data itself may have varying degrees of reliability. It does not enshrine validity itself. That comes from the arguments that are developed from it. There can never really be enough data, because data itself generates the possibilities for further questions. Its quality is, of course, important but not crucial. If the data is suspect then its support for a particular hypothesis is lukewarm and future data may help develop the argument further. There is therefore a less respectful view towards data than there is towards evidence. Data is, after all, what your theory makes of it. Evidence makes or breaks the case.

When it comes to transactions between scientists and police officers over the information available from an investigation, these differences in perspective take their toll. In my experience the police are reluctant to make information available to scientists unless what can be done with it will help to turn it into evidence. The material that is collected as part of general stocktaking, for Home Office statistics and the like, is not regarded with anything like the same seriousness as the material collected for investigative purposes. There are still police officers who cannot see the point in studying information derived from a number of solved cases, believing that the central problem of each case is to find the evidence that will lead to a conviction for that crime alone.

One instance of this difference in approach was brought home to me when I was advising a murder enquiry in which a shoe print was available. Investigators went to considerable trouble to see if they could find anyone who had bought shoes like those for which they had a print. Hundreds of house-to-house enquiries were conducted, like the Prince trying to find his Cinderella. The focus was on the shoe print as evidence that would tie a particular individual to the crime scene. However, along the way the police collected data for which a market research company would have paid real money. In their enquiries they had the information on which they could have built up a statistical profile of the sort of people who bought such shoes. This profile would not have been of evidential value but it might have been useful for assigning priorities to suspects. Unfortunately the information was never systematically collected and stored so it was not possible to test out the utility of any such profile that might have been generated.

The police collect vast amounts of information in the many forms that feed central records. Only a very small proportion of it is drawn upon to develop our understanding of crime and criminality. Recognising this, scientists are developing ways of making more effective use of the information collected by the police. Canter and Alison (2003) have argued that this is a central challenge for developing a science that is relevant to police investigations. But there is also a feedback from this. As police begin to see what can be done with all the information they collect, they put more emphasis on careful collection even though they do not necessarily know in advance the use to which it will be put.

Evidence and information from the victims of rape

A clear example of this is the great improvement there has been in the way statements are taken from rape victims, now that it is understood that the statement is not merely a record of the crime that had occurred to be used as evidence in court. Understanding that the statement can provide data which can be drawn on to guide the investigation beyond the presentation of evidence, has made police interviewers much more aware of the need to record the nuances of what the victim reports. This in turn means that these statements can be used much more effectively for general research purposes. One further consequence of this more thorough recording of all the surrounding aspects of an offence, when investigating burglary as much as rape, is that the victims feel they have been taken seriously and been given the opportunity to give a full account of what they have experienced.

Process versus product

If information is only of significance in relation to the case at hand, the significance of knowledge for the police is in its contextual consequences. This contrasts with the interest that academics have in the process by which the results were obtained, and the possibility of the wider application of the methodology that may have been developed.

An interesting illustration of this is reported in Canter (2003) in relation to the Yorkshire Ripper enquiry. As part of that enquiry a leading forensic scientist, Dr Stuart Kind, carried out a spatial analysis of the locations of the crimes attributed to the 'Yorkshire Ripper'. This analysis led to the specification of an area of Yorkshire in which the killer was likely to have been living. Around the time that Kind's report was presented to the enquiry a man was arrested who turned out to be the offender, Peter Sutcliffe. The arrest was the result of an alert police officer following up unexplained actions of Sutcliffe when he had been stopped for a minor crime. Dr Kind's analysis therefore played no role in helping to identify or arrest Sutcliffe and was not used as part of the evidence in court.

The lack of any direct contribution to the enquiry meant that Kind's work was ignored. However, the area he identified was precisely that in which Sutcliffe lived. If that information had been available earlier it could have been of considerable help to the investigation. Of even more importance was the fact that Kind had established an approach to looking at an offender's geography that could have been useful in subsequent investigations. But when I was asked, a couple of years after Kind had submitted his report, to advise the enquiry into the Railway Rapist, I was not told of Kind's work, which was not published in academic journals at that stage. Instead, I had to work out from first principles a process that was quite similar to Kind's. As it happens I was fortunate in providing this information to the enquiry before a suspect had been identified, and my contribution was eventually recognised as being of value in identifying the offender. This success drew attention to my work and helped me to develop the process further and contribute to other investigations.

I have learnt from this that in order to have any scientific process taken seriously by the police it is no use demonstrating that its principles are sound and empirical data have validated those principles. It has to have been successful in use in an actual investigation. This naturally limits the uptake of many scientific developments, and those that are utilised owe more to the 'success stories' they are sold on than to the robustness of the science behind them. It also means that attempts to convince police officers that certain scientific processes are relevant to their activities often fall on stony ground unless they can be illustrated with gripping accounts of their effective use.

Trend versus case

There is considerable evidence that, without formal training, most people have difficulty in understanding probabilities. Gambling and such institutions as the National Lottery would have far less appeal if people understood what the odds really meant. This weakness manifests itself in police work when people purveying particular processes offer examples of the success of the process, without putting that example into the context of the general trend of successes and failures. So, for example, a case in which a 'lie detector' has proven useful will be mentioned without any understanding of the significance of findings that in a high proportion of cases it does not help to demonstrate guilt. Indeed, the idea that psycho-physiological indices of emotional excitement may be, on average, better indicators of innocence than they ever are of guilt (Kleiner, 1999) is difficult for people to understand if they are focusing on cases where such a process has 'worked'. Similarly, procedures that have great potential for the police may be quickly dropped because of one 'failure' despite the trends that indicate their overall effectiveness.

Trade versus profession

One fruitful way of characterising the differences in approach to the nature of knowledge in the police compared with that among scientists is to see police officers as typically plying a trade. They know the details of the procedures they must follow to achieve certain ends, whether it be, for instance, a legal arrest, preparation of evidence for court or the management of a public demonstration. But they have little command of the principles behind the procedures they are following; or an understanding of the empirical trends on which such procedures can be based.

The contrast is with the professional perspective that recognises all decisions as part of an evolving body of knowledge. The actions of any professional are a contribution to the development of that knowledge base, which is why research is so highly prized by all professional bodies. Any given example is understood as an illustration of a possible class of examples. It is a point within a trend that may be understood or may still be enigmatic. It is data out of which further understanding may emerge if it is put together with other examples.

The mechanisms of prejudice

Of particular interest here is the way the focus on the mechanics of a procedure, against the background of discussions about particular cases, provides the seeds for prejudicial attitudes that in their extreme are racist and/or sexist. The essence of a professional perspective, that comes from seeing any given example in a broader context, is to be able to take an objective stance that distances someone's personal views from the judgement of the case at hand.

Simplifying thought processes characterises one case as typical of a whole class of poorly defined events. These uninformed views are then bolstered by similar anecdotes, as when examples of particular ethnic minority groups involved in given crimes are taken as definitions of the nature of those groups. This sharing of individual cases provides a framework in which racism is seen as a logical conclusion and is extremely difficult to change by 'diversity training'. What generates the 'institutional racism' to which Macpherson (1999) drew attention, is not therefore the entrance of many people with racist attitudes into the police service, but a way of looking at the information available that supports a very limited understanding of the processes from which crime emerges. So long as many examples are presented to illustrate actions by individuals from ethnic minorities, and these examples are used to defend trends without a broader picture of the processes involved, then no matter what courses police officers attend, about what opinions are or are not acceptable, there will still be a drift towards racism that emerges from treating policing as a craft for coping with individual cases rather than a profession that draws on trends and a scientifically based understanding of crime.

There is another process that also fosters prejudicial attitudes: one that has been understood by psychologists for more than half a century. As the distinguished social psychologist Gordon Allport wrote in 1951:

> Attitudes serve a purpose in the life-economy of the individual. The California farmer who is prejudiced against Japanese-Americans has a definable attitude, but this attitude is not isolated in his life. Rather it may be for him a means of excusing his failures, maintaining his self- esteem, and enhancing his competitive position. (p. 373)

In other words, prejudice is sustained whenever there are real psychological benefits to holding prejudicial views. If they make the racist feel more significant, enable that person to cope more readily with anxieties and frustrations, or give the feeling that they are an accepted part of a group, then edicts and assessments will not weed out people who hold those views. Others who will be more careful in keeping those attitudes to themselves will replace any individual who is ejected from the police force because he or she has revealed racist attitudes. It is only by removing the reliance on individual cases, the focus on evidence and the development of an understanding of how trends operate and are revealed that the environment for prejudice can be destroyed.

WAYS OF ACTING

The approaches to the nature of knowledge that distinguish the two cultures are products of the different relationships to the legal process that distinguish science from police work. The training police officers receive is, inevitably, focused on the law and its workings. The practical constraints and demands that come from working as an arm of the law are not present for academics and scientists. This gives academics a fundamental commitment to intellectual freedom that is a luxury in which the police cannot indulge. There is as a consequence a shaping of the processes by which they go about their activities that further distinguishes between their different cultures and interferes with their effective co-operation.

Refutation versus confirmation

Science is based in failures. It is by challenging hypotheses that they become more robust. Yet such challenges go against the well-documented human tendency to seek out confirmation for any suppositions we make (Wason, 1960). It is because of this natural 'confirmation bias' that the training of scientists gives such emphasis to mastering procedures for setting up tests of hypotheses so that they can be refuted. There are, of course, parallels in police work, most notably determining whether a suspect has an alibi that would, in effect, refute the hypothesis of guilt. Yet the resources involved in police work and the emphasis on the case currently the focus of attention means that there is a reluctance to risk exploring possibilities that may turn out to be without substance; and a tendency to look for support for any suggestions that emerge.

The risks involved in offering a suggestion that may prove to be invalid are managed in science by starting with small-scale experiments that are not part of the main stream of activity. As these prove fruitful they are developed further. However, there is always the risk that an experiment will fail.

For men and women of action there is a considerable loss of face in putting in process systems or action plans that turn out to be unproductive. The way of thinking that relates directly to the search for evidence to support a particular viewpoint also is brought to bear when new strategies or procedures are put in place. It is rare indeed, for example, for a consultant to be asked to provide a system that is then piloted to determine the conditions under which it fails and to use this to develop the system further. Instead, individuals become identified with particular approaches and their career development is based on the success or failure of what they recommend. There is therefore considerable pressure to seek out evidence for the effectiveness of what has been introduced, rather than treating it as a pilot scheme that may need further development.

Publication versus secrecy

One of the main ways in which scientific findings gain their robustness is through the process of submitting the work for publication and having it reviewed by peers. Whilst there are disadvantages to this system, most notably an inherent conservatism and a tendency for current scientific fashions to dominate, it provides a basis for checking the validity of the conclusions of research. There are a number of well-documented failures of secret research that informed policy making, the failures being due to the lack of overt scrutiny of the research findings.

Yet in my early contact with senior police officers they expressed puzzlement as to why I should want to publish my research. Some even claimed it was just to have the pride of seeing my name in print. They understood nothing of the career imperative to publish and less of the moral imperative of putting back into the public domain something of value that was made possible with support from the public purse. The importance of sustaining the development of scientific understanding through contributing to the scientific literature seemed alien to them.

A number of people have commented on the 'defensiveness' of police culture. Holdaway (1989) refers to the secrecy, lack of trust and feeling of a need to 'watch your back' that is found in many interviews with police officers. Some of this comes from the understandable concern to maintain security over sensitive information that is part and parcel of the investigation of criminal activities. Hiding information from those who may destroy evidence or evade detection or capture is a wholly appropriate part of police activities. This becomes a dominant way of dealing with the world that makes contact with academics often quite fraught.

Anarchic versus hierarchical

It is interesting to consider the implications of action plans that are aimed, at least ostensibly, at refutation in an atmosphere of open debate and publication of results. I would suggest one implication is that anyone with the intellectual skills can challenge anyone else. Authority is only as powerful as the most recent successful experiment. Furthermore, knowledge can be gained from published sources by anyone who can understand it: and can then be acted upon. This all produces an unstructured network of contacts and influences that are extremely difficult to manage. The world of scientists is thus anarchic in some fundamental sense of the way in which the discipline is managed and evolves.

As Drummond (1976) and many others have pointed out, 'police departments are almost universally structured to conform to the military hierarchical model of organization' (p. 19). There is at least a notion of the strong chain of command that is necessary for organized action in response to incidents and crimes as they happen. Ranks are important in determining authority. Therefore, as in all hierarchical organizations, information flows as water does: more readily from the top down than in the other direction.

In their dealings with academics the police have concern as to what form of control there may exist over information or the actions of individuals: but at the same time they tend not to understand that their contacts with a student or junior member of staff may be unknown to others more senior in the organization.

Academics, by contrast, make the mistake of assuming that because something has been authorised by senior police officers there will inevitably be support for it from the rank and file.

The public expects an enormous amount of discretion from even the most junior police officer. He or she is looked on as the representative of the forces of law and order at the particular point in time that the public comes into contact with them. Police officers quickly learn that they have to wield this discretion with confidence if they are to be taken seriously. This engenders a network of contacts that are far closer to the anarchy with which I have characterised academia than is often appreciated. The crucial difference, though, is that the processes of publication and peer commentary ameliorate academic anarchy. In contrast, the myth that police officers are actually operating under the control of a strict chain of command combines with the inherent culture of secrecy to generate conditions in which bad practice can be perpetrated for generations without anyone knowing about it.

This complex organizational process is one of the reasons why developments in policing tend to move in fits and starts, often after a serious bloodletting, such as the Yorkshire Ripper or Stephen Lawrence enquiries. Whereas academic life has unfolded with only minor changes over the half-millennium that universities and scientific laboratories have been in general existence, there have been very considerable changes in the fundamental processes that characterise police work over the century-and-a-half that police forces have played a role in public life.

KEY OBJECTIVES

I have tried to be even-handed in my accounts of police and academic cultures, probably with less success than I would like. It has certainly not been my intention to imply that there are fundamental flaws in police culture that are the cause of many failings. Rather, I have been trying to identify what characterises the different cultures and to show the implications of these characteristics beyond their immediate spheres of relevance. The crucial point is that these characteristics are derived from the primary objectives of the different institutions. It is the management of the knock-on effects of achieving these objectives that is the challenge that emerges when scientists and the police are brought into co-operation with each other.

Knowledge versus conviction

The central difference in objectives can be distilled down to that between the search for a conviction and the desire to contribute to knowledge. These differences are doubtless being eroded as the police become more involved in public order issues and desire to respond generally to community concerns. Applied scientists are also keen to have their findings acted on, although that often becomes confused with consultancy activity that takes them outside of a strictly academic environment. Yet the approach to knowledge and the patterns of activity are still largely dominated by these differences in objectives.

The important point here is that these different objectives are what the organizations are there for. As citizens we no more want our police to spend their time unpicking the subtleties of bodily decay or the criminal's psyche than we want our physicists to seek out wrong-doing and ensure that a conviction is achieved. But these different objectives point the practitioners in different directions: the police officer to the uniqueness of the crime at hand; the academic to the broader debate within the discipline.

Career versus posterity

One intriguing consequence of these different key objectives is in the way individuals within the different contexts consider their own personal objectives. This relates back, in some ways, to the distinction drawn earlier between craft and profession. Until very recently academics evaluated their scholarly pursuits in terms of how they felt they could contribute to knowledge. There is a subtle arrogance here. People stay within academia, on lower salaries and with less social status than their abilities may be able to gain for them in commerce or industry, in part because they wish to be at least a footnote in history. They think they have something to offer intellectual life that will be recognised by posterity. Changes in the management of universities are undermining the possibility of indulging in such high-flown aspirations, but they are still an acceptable part of academic culture.

By contrast, it is more common for police officers to consider the way in which their current activities may directly further their career progress. In part these considerations are probably brought about by the many more levels in the organizational hierarchy that are typically available to ambitious police officers. These days many academics in their thirties are just pleased to obtain a full-time, permanent job. Also, police officers may retire after fewer years of service than academics, so the more capable ones look to how their current job can open the way to post-retirement employment.

These differences in personal objectives map onto the issues mentioned earlier, of a culture of secrecy and a focus on particular cases. For ambitious police officers, solving the current case themselves, or making a significant arrest, can create very direct career prospects. There are therefore pressures to hold onto information relevant to that case that will be of direct benefit to the individual officer. If, on the other hand, those police officers are at a stage in their career when academic recognition may be of some utility, they can be very forthcoming and open to academic collaboration.

Academics often ignore these dynamics at their peril, thinking that the benefits of the sharing of information on which science is supposed to be based will be immediately recognised by their police contacts. For the academic, contributing to knowledge leads to respect from colleagues and sometimes even to promotion. For the police officer such openness to those outside the police is fraught with dangers and does not necessarily offer any direct career benefits.

Of interest also is the way in which scientists who find their way into the police service in various jobs quickly absorb the ethos of secrecy and the use of information for personal career development. Some learn that association with particular high profile investigations offers the possibility of success stories that can outweigh any contributions to knowledge those individuals may make. There is certainly a curious sort of kudos that comes with the assignment of a 'man of action' image to someone who is thought of as a scholar, almost an 'Indiana Jones' syndrome. But, like most such images it is inevitably more mirage than reality.

Politics versus ideology

One further consequence of the very different contexts of police and academic work is the pressures to which they are prone. Crime and policing are so much on the political agenda, and police forces, appropriately, need to respond so directly to pressures from elected politicians, that an awareness of current political concerns is essential for effectiveness in the higher echelons of the police—if not at all levels. Traditionally academics, and especially scientists, have been spared these concerns. This does not mean they are immune from any form of social pressure. Peer review provides a coercive process that requires academics to be aware at least of the current academic orthodoxy in their discipline, and in most cases to take it into account.

Police officers are less likely to be aware of the fashions within the arcane debates of science than scientists are to know about the issues reported regularly in newspapers. Political imperatives also change more rapidly than do scientific ideologies. These different contexts offer further bases for confusions and misunderstanding when embarking on collaboration.

Long-term versus short-term

Overall, the objectives of the police tend to be couched in the here and now. Problems appear quickly on the horizon and charge towards police forces that have to be able to respond instantly. Academic life has a more leisurely pace. Journal articles can take months, often years, to be published and research projects of any note rarely take fewer than a couple of years to complete. There are therefore rather different rhythms in the two different cultures and getting them synchronised can be difficult, although certainly not impossible.

CONCLUSION

As a member of the public I want action from the police. The constant public refrain for more Bobbies on the beat is a product of the belief that crime is prevented and solved by the hands-on acts of on-the-spot police officers. Yet there are many pressures that are making this less and less effective, however much the public and tabloid press still believes it is of operational value. The police are under pressures from many different directions to take a more strategic approach to their activities. There is consequently an inherent conflict between what populist politicians demand of the police and what is needed to manage the modern police service.

On the other hand, academics have to respond to the demands of their discipline whilst being able to show, at least to their students if not to their peers, that what they are doing has some 'real-world' relevance. Agencies that fund research are also under increasing political pressure to demonstrate that the work they support has some value to society. As a recent EPSRC initiative shows[1], tackling crime offers great potential for scientific innovation, provided that it can be integrated with the work of the police.

The academic/scientific community and the police service need each other. The pressures coming from both contexts for greater co-operation are healthy and will be productive if each draws on their own strengths and recognises the special qualities of the other. For example, if information is collected both with an eye to its evidential value (and therefore the care with which it must be obtained and recorded) and its scientific value (and therefore the need to collect it over time and across carefully recorded samples) then it will provide a firmer base for all the uses to which it can be put.

One interesting consequence of this treating of information as both evidence and data is that those who provide the information, whether they be victims, witnesses, experts or suspects, will see that they are being taken seriously and their experiences have the potential of contributing to the improvement of society for all. But that improvement also requires a more effective sharing of information and the results of its analysis. It requires the respect for the sensitivity of information to be tempered with the value of serious publication. Overall, the ability to respond immediately to a dangerous incident or recent crime, for which the police are often so effective, needs to be balanced with the longer-term perspective that comes from academic study of these incidents. It is by harnessing the benefits that come from the complementarity of the two cultures that a more just society will evolve.

REFERENCES for *Chapter 11*

Allport, G.W. (1951), 'Prejudice: A Problem in Psychological and Social Causation', in T. Parsons and E. A. Shils (eds), *Towards a General Theory of Action*, New York: Harper and Row, p. 366- 87.

Byford, L. (1981), *The Yorkshire Ripper Case: Review of the Police Investigation*, London: HMSO.

Canter, D. (1995), *Criminal Shadows*, London: Harper Collins.

Canter, D. (2003), *Mapping Murder*, London: Virgin Books.

Canter, D. and Alison, L.J. (2003), 'Converting Evidence into Data: The Use of Law Enforcement Archives as Unobtrusive Measurement', *The Qualitative Report*, June 8, (2) [online journal].

Chandler, R. (1959), *The Long Good-Bye*, London: Penguin Books.

Drummond, D. S. (1976), *Police Culture*, London: Sage Publications.

Drury, J, Stott, C. and Farsides, T. (2003), 'The Role of Police Perceptions and Practices in the Development of "Public Disorder"', *Journal of Applied Social Psychology*, 33(7): 1480-1500.

Holdaway, S. (1989), 'Discovering Structure: Studies of the Police Occupational Culture', in M. Wetheritt (ed.), *Police Research: Some Future Prospects*, Aldershot: Avebury.

Kleiner, M. (1999), 'The Psychophysiology of Deception and the Orienting Response', in D. Canter and L. Alison, (eds.), *Interviewing and Deception*, Aldershot: Ashgate, pp. 183–208.

Macpherson, W. (1999), *The Stephen Lawrence Enquiry*, London: The Stationery Office, cm 4262-I.

Wason, P.C. (1960), 'On the Failure to Eliminate Hypotheses in a Conceptual Task', *Quarterly Journal of Experimental Psychology*, 12, pp. 129–140.

---

[1] Of particular note is a recent initiative from the major funder of scientific research in the UK, the Engineering and Physics Research Council (EPSRC). They have many millions of pounds specifically earmarked for 'Technologies in Crime Prevention and Detection'. This is to develop the science and technology that will reduce crime and enhance detection and conviction. Grant applications from scientists have to show that there are direct links with law enforcement agencies to ensure that the results of the research funded by the EPSRC will have direct applications.

CHAPTER 12

Combating Noble Cause Corruption

Seumas Miller

In this chapter Professor Miller discusses the phenomenon known as noble cause corruption. In the first section he addresses corruption in general; in the second section, the use of harmful methods in policing; and in the third section, the nature of so-called noble cause corruption in policing.

THE CONCEPT OF CORRUPTION: A PHILOSOPHICAL ANALYSIS

The nature of corruption, its causes and effects, and how to combat it, are issues that are increasingly on the national and international agendas of politicians and other policymakers.[1] For example, the World Bank has relatively recently come around to the view that economic development is closely linked to corruption reduction.[2] By contrast, the theoretical notion of corruption has not received much attention. Existing conceptual work on the subject consists of little more than the presentation of brief definitions of corruption as a preliminary to extended accounts of the causes and effects of corruption and the ways to combat it.[3] Moreover, most of these definitions are unsatisfactory in fairly obvious ways.

Consider one of the most popular of these definitions, namely, 'Corruption is the abuse of power by a public official for private gain'.[4] No doubt the abuse of public offices for private gain is paradigmatic of corruption. But when police fabricate evidence out of a misplaced sense of justice this is corruption of a public office, but not for private gain. And when a punter bribes a boxer to 'throw' a fight this is corruption for private gain, but it does not necessarily involve any public office holder; the roles of boxer and punter are not necessarily public offices. Indeed, there is a whole range of different forms of corruption outside the public sphere. Consider corruption in relation to the role of a father. Suppose a father persuades his naïve, but nubile, 13-year-old daughter to provide sexual favours to

---

1. See Seumas Miller, Peter Roberts and Edward Spence. *Corruption and Anti-Corruption: A Study in Applied Philosophy* (N.J.: Prentice Hall, 2004) for a detailed treatment of many of these issues.
2. See *Helping Countries Combat Corruption: The Role of the World Bank* (Washington DC: World Bank, 1997).
3. For example, Robert Klitgaard, Ronald Maclean-Abaroa and H Lindsey Parris in *Corrupt Cities: A Practical Guide to Cure and Prevention* (Oakland, Calif.: ICS Press, 2000) p. 2 define corruption as 'misuse of office for personal gain'. For a recent review of the general literature on corruption see Jonathan Hopkins, 'States, Markets and Corruption: A Review of Some Recent Literature', *Review of International Political Economy*, 2002.
4. For one of the most influential statements of the abuse of public office for private gain definitions see Joseph Nye, 'Corruption and Political Development: A Cost-benefit Analysis', *American Political Science Review*, Vol. 61, No. 2, 1967, pp. 417-27.

middle aged businessmen in exchange for payments to him and gifts for his daughter; this is corruption, but it is not abuse of a public office.

In the light of the failure of such analytical style definitions it is tempting to try to sidestep the problem of providing a theoretical account of the concept of corruption by simply identifying corruption with specific legal and/or moral offences.

However, attempts to identify corruption with specific legal/moral offences are unlikely to succeed. Perhaps the most plausible candidate is bribery; this is regarded by some people as the quintessential form of corruption.[5] However, corruption is exemplified by a very wide and diverse array of phenomena of which bribery is only one kind. Paradigm cases include the following:

- a national leader channels public monies into his personal bank account;
- a political party secures a majority vote by arranging for ballot boxes to be stuffed with false voting papers;
- a respected researcher's success relies on plagiarising the work of others;
- a police officer fabricates evidence in order to secure convictions;
- a number of police officers close ranks and refuse to testify against a colleague that they know to be corrupt; and
- the government minister for law and order directs the police commissioner to have police aggressively confront and disrupt lawful street demonstrations in order to create a manageable level of public disorder from which the government will derive political benefit in a forthcoming election.

It is self-evident that none of these corrupt practices is an instance of bribery. Further, it is far from obvious that the way forward at this point is simply to add a few additional offences to the initial 'list' consisting of the single offence of bribery. Candidates would include fraud, nepotism, fabricating evidence, perverting the course of justice and so on. However, there is bound to be disagreement in relation to any such list. For example, law enforcement practitioners in Australia and elsewhere often distinguish between fraud on the one hand, and corruption on the other. Most important, any such list needs to be justified by recourse to some principle or principles. Ultimately, naming a set of offences that might be regarded as instances of corruption does not obviate the need for a philosophical analysis of the concept of corruption.

As it happens, there is at least one further salient strategy for demarcating the boundaries of corrupt acts. Implicit in much of the literature is the view that corruption is essentially a legal offence in the economic sphere.[6] Accordingly, one could seek to identify corruption with economic crimes, such as bribery, fraud, and insider trading. To some extent this kind of view reflects the dominance of economically focused material in the corpus of academic literature on corruption. It also reflects the preponderance of proposed economic solutions to the problem of

---

5 The definitive account of bribery is by John T Noonan, *Bribes* (New York: Macmillan, 1984).

6 This is implicit in much of Susan Rose-Ackerman's influential work: *Corruption and Government: Causes, Consequences and Reform* (Cambridge: Cambridge University Press, 1999).

corruption. After all, if it is essentially an economic phenomenon, is it not plausible that the remedies will be economic ones?[7]

The first point to be made here concerns the proposition that corruption is necessarily a legal offence. Many examples are not necessarily unlawful. That paradigm of corruption, bribery, is a case in point. Prior to 1977 it was not unlawful for US companies to offer bribes to secure foreign contracts.[8] So corruption is not necessarily unlawful. This is because it is not at bottom simply a matter of law; rather it is fundamentally a matter of morality.

The second point concerns the (allegedly) necessarily economic character of corruption. An academic who plagiarises the work of others is not committing an economic crime or misdemeanour, and might be committing plagiarism simply in order to increase his or her academic status; there may be not be any financial benefit sought or gained. As is well known, academics are more strongly motivated by status than by wealth. A police officer who fabricates evidence against a person he or she believes to be guilty of paedophilia is not committing an economic crime. The officer may do so because he or she believes the accused to be guilty, and does not want the offender to go unpunished. Economics is not necessarily involved as an element of the officer's crime or as a motivation. As is also well known, when police do wrong they are often motivated by a misplaced sense of justice, rather than by financial reward. Again, a person in authority who abuses his or her power by meting out cruel and unjust treatment to those subject to their authority, and who does so out of sadistic pleasure, is not engaging in an economic crime, and is not motivated by economic considerations. Many of those who occupy positions of authority are motivated by a desire to exercise power, rather than by a desire for financial reward.

Economic corruption is an important form of corruption; however, it not the only one. Indeed, there are as many forms of corruption as there are human institutions that might become corrupted. Further, economic gain is not the only motivation.

It is only one species of immorality. Consider an otherwise gentle husband who in a fit of anger strikes his adulterous wife and kills her. The husband has committed an act that is morally wrong; he has killed his wife. But his action is not necessarily an act of corruption. His wife has not been corrupted. And as for him, perhaps he is so filled with remorse that he undergoes a process of moral regeneration, rather than one of corruption.

Human rights violations also are wrong but not necessarily corrupt. There is often a close and mutually reinforcing nexus between corruption and human rights violations.[9] Consider the endemic corruption and large-scale human rights abuse that have taken place in authoritarian regimes such as those of Idi Amin in Uganda and Suharto in Indonesia. And there is increasing empirical evidence of an admittedly complex causal connection between corruption and the infringement of

---

7 See Rose-Ackerman op.cit. for this kind of view. See Barry Hindess, 'Good Government and Corruption' in Peter Larmour and Nick Wolanin (ed.), *Corruption and Anti-Corruption* (Canberra: Asia Pacific Press, 2001) (ed.), for this kind of critique.

8 See 'The Foreign Corrupt Practices Act of 1977', *Public Law*, 95-213 (5305), 19 December 1977, United States Code 78a, Section 103.

9 See Zoe Pearson, 'An International Human Rights Approach to Corruption' in Larmour and Wolanin (eds.), *op. cit.*

subsistence rights; evidence, that is, of a causal relation between corruption and poverty.

Defining a corrupt action—three guiding intuitions

1. If we are to provide a serviceable notion of a corrupt action that does not collapse into the more general notion of an immoral action, we need firstly to focus our attention on the moral effects of actions; specifically the moral effects of actions on persons and institutions. Presumably, if an action is corrupt then it corrupts something or someone. I take it that an action is corrupt only if it has a *corrupting effect* on a person's moral character, or a corrupting effect on an institution, or institutional process or role.
2. My second guiding intuition is that if an action is corrupt then the agent who performed it is to some extent, or in some sense, *blameworthy*; corrupt acts are not simply acts that have untoward effects of which the agent could not possibly have been aware.
3. My third guiding intuition is that if an action is corrupt then the person or persons who are corrupted (including members of institutions) are to some extent or in some sense *participants* in this process of corruption. Persons who become corrupted have to some extent allowed themselves to be corrupted. This participation would typically be willing, e.g. a police officer who accepts a bribe from an offender for refraining from investigating the offender. At the very least 'participation' would take the form of culpable negligence, e.g. in safety inspection. (The existence of children and non-rational adults makes me stop short of saying that all who are corrupted are necessarily culpable for so allowing themselves to be corrupted.)

Defining a corrupt action: a working hypothesis

By my lights, a corrupt action is an action that contributes to the despoiling of the moral character of a person or to the undermining of a morally legitimate institutional process or role.[10]

The corruption of an institution does not assume its previous purity. A police officer who fabricates evidence in the context of a police service whose members have always fabricated evidence is still guilty of corruption. His or her act has a negative moral effect on the institutional process of evidence gathering and presentation as that process ought to be in that institution at that time.

The despoiling of moral character or the undermining of institutional processes or roles would typically require a pattern of actions and not merely a single one. However, there are some cases in which a one-off action would be sufficient to corrupt an instance of an institutional process. Consider a specific act of 'testi-lying' in court by a police officer that has the consequence that a person is convicted of a crime he or she did not commit. Suppose the police officer does this once and only once. Nevertheless, that particular testimony is false, and the court process has been undermined. This is corruption.

---

[10] This kind of analysis has ancient origins. See Hindess, *op. cit.* for a recent discussion.

Immorality and illegality

Morally illegitimate institutions cannot in my view be corrupted, since they are already so. Marriage across the colour bar was unlawful in apartheid South Africa: but a police officer who refused to arrest a black man married to a white woman did not engage in an act of corruption. A legally required but morally unacceptable institutional procedure cannot be corrupted. Indeed, the legal prohibition on marriage across the colour bar is in itself a corruption of the institution of marriage. By contrast, another officer's practice of arresting and charging mixed-race married couples was corrupt; it was undermining the institution of marriage as it ought to be.

In the light of the diverse range of corrupt actions and the generic nature of the concept of corruption, it is unlikely that any precise definition is possible. Nor is it likely that the field of corrupt actions can be neatly circumscribed by recourse to a set of self-evident criteria. The wide diversity of corrupt actions has at least two further implications. Firstly, it implies that acts of corruption have a correspondingly large set of moral deficiencies. Secondly, there is implicit a need for a correspondingly wide and diverse range of anti-corruption measures to combat corruption in its different forms. Accordingly, anti-corruption measures against corrupt police might need to differ from those to be taken against corrupt business people; and measures against police engaged in noble cause corruption might need to differ from those to be taken against corrupt police motivated by greed.

HARMFUL METHODS IN POLICING

Commissions of inquiry into police corruption, including the Mollen Commission into the New York Police Department (1994), and the Royal Commission into the NSW Police Service (1997),[11] have uncovered corruption of a profoundly disturbing kind. Police officers have been involved in perjury, fabricating evidence, protecting paedophile rings, taking drug money and selling drugs. However, unacceptably high levels of police corruption have been a persistent historical tendency in police services throughout the world. Corruption in policing is neither new nor especially surprising.[12]

There are a number of features of police-work which combine to provide an explanation for this tendency. Police officers are exposed to an extraordinarily high level of temptation in areas such as the investigation of drug trafficking and gambling. They have very considerable powers, including the power to take a person's liberty away from them, and it is well known that power tends to corrupt. Officers have high levels of discretionary authority, often exercised in circumstances in which close supervision is not possible and they have ongoing interaction with corrupt persons who have an interest in compromising and corrupting police.

---

[11] The commission's original remit (1994) was to inquire into the nature and extent of corruption, with a single commissioner (Wood), a judge. The first two volumes addressed, respectively, corruption and reform; the third held the appendices; the fourth concerned corruption associated with paedophilia and related matters, and resulted from a broadening of the scope of the inquiry (and the addition of a second commissioner.

[12] Much of the content of this section is based upon my 'Corruption and Anti-Corruption in the Profession of Policing' *Professional Ethics*, Vol. 6 Nos. 3 and 4 1998, pp. 83-107.

However, there is a structural feature of police work that has not received the amount of attention it warrants, and which contributes to the moral vulnerability of police. This concerns the relationship between means and ends in policing.

Egon Bittner (1975), in stressing the importance of coercion, draws our attention to a fundamental feature of policing, namely, its inescapable use of what in normal circumstances would be regarded as morally unacceptable activity. The use of coercive force, including in the last analysis deadly force, is in itself obviously harmful.[13] Accordingly, in normal circumstances it is morally unacceptable. It would be morally wrong, for example, for me as a private citizen to take someone by force to my house for questioning or because I felt like some company. Use of coercive force, especially deadly force, requires special moral justification precisely because it is harmful, and therefore—under normal circumstances—morally wrong.[14]

The same point holds for some of the other methods used by policing, including deception, cooperating with informers who are criminals and intrusive surveillance.

It might be suggested that such methods could be wholly abandoned in favour of the morally unproblematic methods already heavily relied upon, such as rational discourse, appeal to moral sentiment, reliance on upright citizens for information, and so on. Doubtless, *in many instances* the use of morally problematic methods could be avoided. And certainly overuse of these methods is a sign of bad police-work, and perhaps of the partial breakdown of police-community trust so necessary to police-work. However, the point is that the morally problematic methods could not simply be *replaced*. For one thing, the violations of moral rights which the police exist to protect are sometimes perpetrated by persons who are unmoved by rationality, appeal to moral sentiment, and so on. Indeed, such persons, far from being moved by well-intentioned police overtures, may seek to influence or corrupt police officers for the purpose of preventing them from doing their moral and lawful duty. For another thing, the relevant members of the community may for one reason or another be unwilling or unable to provide the necessary information or evidence, and police may need to rely on persons of bad character or methods such as intrusive surveillance.

So the use of methods which in normal circumstances are considered to be immoral is necessary in order to realise the fundamental end of policing, namely the protection of moral rights.[15] An armed bank robber might have to be threatened with the use of force if he is to give himself up. A drug dealer might have to be told lies if a drug ring is to be smashed. A blind eye might have to be turned to the

[13] For an account of the moral justification of police use of deadly force see Seumas Miller, 'Shootings by Police in Victoria: The Ethical Issues' in Tony Coady, Steve James, Seumas Miller and Michael O'Keefe (eds.), *Violence and Police Culture* (Melbourne: Melbourne University Press, 2000), pp. 205-218.

[14] At this point there is a possible dispute among philosophers as to whether the justified use of many such harmful methods should be described as morally justified infringement of rights or simply as morally justified use of harmful methods. On the latter account, there is no infringement of a moral right. I do not wish to enter into this kind of debate. Hence I will speak of harmful methods the use of which is immoral or an infringement of rights *under normal circumstances*.

[15] I argue for this teleological rights-based conception of policing in Seumas Miller and John Blackler, *Ethical Issues in Policing: Contemporary Problems and Perspectives* (Aldershot: Ashgate, 2003) , Chapter 1. For a teleological account of social institutions in general, see also Seumas Miller, *Social Action: A Teleological Account* (New York: Cambridge University Press, 2001), Chapter 6.

minor illegal activity of an informant if the flow of important information he or she provides in relation to serious crimes is to continue. A paedophile might have to be surveilled if evidence for conviction is to be secured. And so on.

The paradox whereby police necessarily make routine use of methods which are normally morally wrong to secure morally worthy ends sets up a dangerous moral dynamic. The danger is that police will come to think that the ends always justify the means; to accept the inevitability and the desirability of so-called 'noble cause corruption'. From noble cause corruption they can in turn graduate to straightforward corruption: corruption motivated by greed and personal gain.

NOBLE CAUSE CORRUPTION

The notion of noble cause corruption receives classic expression in the film *Dirty Harry*.[16] Detective Harry Callaghan is trying to achieve a morally good end. He is trying to find a kidnapped girl whose life is in imminent danger. In the circumstances the only way he can determine where the girl is in order to save her, is by inflicting significant pain on the kidnapper who is otherwise refusing to reveal her whereabouts.

The image of Harry Callaghan inflicting non-lethal pain on a murderous psychopath is emotionally, and indeed ethically, compelling. However, the question that needs to be asked is whether fabricating evidence, beating up suspects, 'verballing' suspects, committing perjury, and so on to obtain convictions is in the same moral category as Harry's action. The answer is in the negative.

For one thing, Harry Callaghan's predicament is a romantic fiction or at best a highly unusual combination of circumstances. Most instances of police fabrication of evidence, and even excessive use of force, have not been used to save the life of someone in imminent danger, nor have they been the only means available to secure a conviction. For another thing, the ongoing recourse to such methods not only violates the rights of suspects; it tends to have the effect of corrupting police officers. To this extent the moral harm that results from such methods not only harms suspects, it can eventually destroy the moral character of those police officers deploying these methods.

The dangers attendant upon noble cause corruption demand that we provide a principled account of the difference between justifiable use of normally immoral methods and noble cause corruption. We can do so as follows.

Firstly, any use of normally immoral methods has to be provided with an adequate ethical basis. Consider coercive force. This is ethically justified in relation to the apprehension of offenders under certain conditions, if it is necessary, restricted to the minimum level required and not disproportionate to the offence that has been committed.

Secondly, the relevant ethical principles need to be clearly articulated and communally sanctioned. This is achieved by enshrining them in the law. When police officers act in accordance with the legally enshrined ethical principles governing the use of harmful methods they achieve three things at one and the

---

[16] See Carl B Klockars, 'The *Dirty Harry* Problem' reprinted in A S Blumberg and E Niederhoffer (eds.) , *The Ambivalent Force: Perspectives on the Police* (New York: Holt, Rinehart and Winston, 1976).

same time. They do what is morally right; their actions are lawful; and they act in accordance with the will of the community.

Balancing the rights of victims and suspects

There is a need to strike a balance between the rights of victims and suspects. Suspects have moral rights: to life, not to be tortured, and not to be subjected to psychological techniques such as brainwashing. More generally, suspects have a right to procedural justice: including a presumption of innocence and a fair trial.

On the other hand, the police and the criminal justice system do not exist for the sole purpose, or even for the principal purpose, of protecting the rights of suspects. They exist largely for the purpose of protecting the rights of victims and to ensure that punishment is administered to offenders. Accordingly, if the police believe on the basis of evidence that a particular person is guilty of a serious crime then they are obliged to do their utmost to arrest and charge the suspect, and provide sufficient evidence to enable his or her successful prosecution.

There is inevitably a certain tension between these two moral requirements of the police.[17] Further, there is the possibility discussed above that harmful methods devised for apprehending and convicting offenders will in fact be deployed in a manner that harms the innocent. Perhaps in policing infringing the rights of the innocent is at times unavoidable, especially as new technology becomes available, which may be used, for example, to invade privacy.

Discretionary ethical judgment

Individual police officers have a significant measure of legal authority.[18] The officer is legally empowered to intervene—including stopping, searching, detaining and 'apprehending without a warrant any person whom he, with reasonable cause suspects of having committed any such offence or crime'[19]—at all levels of society.

Moreover the law has to be interpreted and applied in concrete circumstances. There is a need for the exercise of discretion by police in interpretation and application of the law. And the law does not exhaustively prescribe. Accordingly, a number of police responses might be possible in a given situation, and all of them might be consistent with the law. Further, upholding and enforcing the law is only one of the ends of policing, others include maintaining social calm and the preservation of life. When these various ends come into conflict, there is a need for the exercise of police discretion, and in particular of discretionary *ethical* judgment. The judgments in question are typically ethical since they involve a conflict between ethical or moral ends or between such ends and harmful means. For example, deciding whether to arrest an Aboriginal youth who is committing an offence may be the wrong decision if such an attempt would lead to a situation of large-scale public disorder. There is a clear moral duty to arrest offenders. But there is also a clear moral duty to prevent public disorder.

---

17 I discuss these issues in greater detail in Seumas Miller and John Blackler *Ethical Issues in Policing: Contemporary Problems and Perspectives* (Aldershot: Ashgate, 2003) Chapter 2.

18 On general issues of autonomy and accountability in policing see my 'Authority, Discretion and Accountability in Policing' in C. Sampford *et al.* (eds.) *Public Sector Ethics* (Routledge: 1998). See also David Moore and Roger Wettenhall (eds.) *Keeping the Peace: Police Accountability and Oversight* (University of Canberra, 1994).

19 *NSW Crimes Act,* no. 40 section 352, sub-section 2(a) (1990).

The unavoidability of the exercise of discretionary ethical judgment in policing means that it will never be sufficient for police simply to learn, and act in accordance with, the legally enshrined ethical principles governing the use of harmful methods.

The problem of noble cause corruption

Difficult as these two above-mentioned problems are, they do not go to the heart of the moral problem of noble cause corruption. This latter problem arises in policing when moral considerations pull in two different directions, and especially when the law thwarts, rather than facilitates, morally desirable outcomes.[20] But here we need to distinguish types of case.

Assume that a police officer breaks a morally unacceptable law, but acts in accordance with the law as it ought to be. For example, suppose a police officer refuses to arrest a black person who is infringing the infamous pass laws in apartheid South Africa. Such a police officer is not engaged in noble cause corruption; for breaking a morally unacceptable law is not engaging in corruption, and therefore not engaging in noble cause corruption.

A second kind of case involves a police officer breaking a law which, although not morally unacceptable, is nevertheless flawed in that it does not adequately reflect the ethical balance that needs to be struck between the rights of suspects and those of victims. For example, assume that a law only allows a suspect to be detained for questioning for a limited period of time: a period that is wholly inadequate for certain kinds of criminal investigations. The law is not necessarily immoral but it ought to be changed. A police officer who detains a suspect for slightly longer than this period has technically breached the law; but the officer has not violated a suspect's rights in any profound sense. Once again, the term corruption is too strong. This is not a case of noble cause corruption; though it is a case of unlawful, and perhaps unethical, conduct.

A third kind of case involves a police officer violating a suspect's legally enshrined moral rights by, for example, using the third degree, fabricating evidence or committing perjury. Here the police officer has not only acted illegally, but also corruptly. If he or she engages in this kind of corrupt activity in order to achieve morally desirable outcomes, such as the conviction of known perpetrators of serious crimes, then the officer is engaged in noble cause corruption. Let us examine this kind of case further.

Noble cause corruption is clearly not morally justified if there is some lawful means to achieve the morally desirable outcome. But are there cases in which the only way to achieve a morally obligatory outcome is to act immorally? Genuinely morally problematic cases are hard to find, but not impossible. Consider the following scenario based on a real life situation. It was provided to me by Father Jim Boland, Senior Chaplain in the New South Wales Police Service. I outline it with his permission.

---

[20] Some of the material in this section is drawn from my 'Noble Cause Corruption in Policing', *African Security Review* 8 http://www.iss.co.za/Pubs/ASR/8No3/NobleCauseCorruption.html. However, since then I have changed my view in relation to the habitual nature of corruption. I now no longer believe that corrupt acts are *necessarily* habitual, though in fact most are.

Case study—noble cause corruption

A young officer, Joe, seeks advice from the police chaplain. Joe is working with an experienced detective, Mick. Mick is also Joe's brother in law and looked up to by Joe as a good detective who gets results. Joe and Mick are working on a case involving a known drug dealer and paedophile. Joe describes his problem thus:

> Father—he has got a mile of form, including getting kids hooked on drugs, physical and sexual assault on minors, and more. Anyway, surveillance informed Mick that the drug dealer had just made a buy. As me and Mick approached the drug dealer's penthouse flat we noticed a parcel come flying out the window of the drug dealer's flat onto the street. The parcel was full of heroin. The drug dealer was in the house, but we found no drugs inside. Mick thought it would be more of a sure thing if we found the evidence in the flat rather than on the street—especially given the number of windows in the building. The defence would find it more difficult to deny possession. Last night Mick tells me that he was interviewed and signed a statement that we both found the parcel of heroin under the sink in the flat. He said all I had to do was to go along with the story in court and everything will be sweet, no worries. What should I do, Father—perjury is a serious criminal offence.

In this scenario there are two putative instances of noble cause corruption. The first one is Mick intentionally unlawfully fabricating, or at least 'loading up', the evidence and committing perjury in order to secure a conviction. This instance of noble cause corruption is not morally sustainable. For there is a presumption against breaking communally sanctioned ethical principles enshrined in the law, and this has not been offset by the moral considerations in play here. Indeed, it is by no means clear that in this situation Mick's unlawful acts are even necessary in order for the drug-dealer to be convicted; presumably a more considered plan of action could result in his conviction. Moreover, achieving the good end of securing conviction is outweighed by the damage done by undermining other important moral ends, namely, due process of law and respect for a suspect's moral rights.[21]

Nor is there anything to suggest that this is a one-off unlawful act by Mick, and that he had provided himself with what he took to be a specific and overriding moral justification for committing it on this particular occasion. Indeed, the impression is that Mick loads up suspects and commits perjury as a matter of routine. Further, there is nothing to suggest that police powers in this area are hopelessly inadequate; that police and others have failed in their endeavours to reform the law; and that therefore police officers have no option but to violate due process law, if they are to uphold substantive law. (If an increase in police powers were morally justified then the appropriate response of the police ought to be to argue and lobby for this increase; not engage in unlawful conduct.)

There is a second possible example of noble cause corruption in our scenario that is more morally troublesome. This is Joe committing perjury in order to prevent a host of harmful consequences to Mick, Joe and their families. If Joe does not commit perjury, Mick will be convicted of a criminal act and their careers will be ruined. Moreover, the friendship of Mick and Joe will be at an end, and their respective families will suffer great unhappiness. The second example is a candidate

[21] For a good discussion of this issue see Howard Cohen 'Overstepping Police Authority' *Criminal Justice Ethics* Summer/Fall 1987 p. 57f.

for justified, or at least excusable, unlawful behaviour on the grounds of extenuating circumstances. Let us assume that were Joe to commit perjury, his action would be morally justified, or at least morally excusable. The question to be asked now is whether it is an act of noble cause corruption.

Certainly, such an act of perjury is unlawful. But here we need to distinguish a number of different categories. Some acts are unlawful, but their commission does not harm any innocent person. Arguably, such acts are not necessarily immoral. The drug-dealer will be harmed in that he will go to prison, but he is not innocent; he is a known drug dealer and paedophile who deserves to go to prison.

But the fact that the drug dealer is guilty of serious crimes does not settle the issue. Consider Joe's actions. Some acts are unlawful, but their commission does not infringe anyone's moral rights. Joe's act will certainly infringe the drug-dealer's moral rights, including the right to a fair trial based on admissible evidence. Moreover, perjury undermines a central plank of due process law; without truthful testimony, the whole system of criminal justice would founder: perjury is a species of institutional corruption. Considered in itself, the act is a serious moral wrong, and an act of corruption.

Unfortunately, as we have already seen, the moral costs of his not committing perjury are also very high—perhaps higher than those involved in perjury. We can conclude that Joe faces a genuine moral dilemma; he will do moral harm whatever he does.[22]

Moral negligence

Corrupt actions, including acts of noble cause corruption, are typically habitual rather than case-specific. Given a presumption against infringing communally sanctioned and legally enshrined ethical principles, this failure to engage in moral decision-making on a case by case basis is surely morally culpable by virtue of being, at the very least, morally negligent. Acts of noble cause corruption have not been communally sanctioned; they are actions justified, if they are justified at all, only by some set of moral principles held by the individual police officer or group of officers. Further, this set of alleged ethical principles is typically not objectively valid; it is not a set that ought to be enshrined in the law. Rather, these allegedly ethical principles are in fact typically spurious; they are the kind of principle used to justify actions of the sort that Mick commits, viz. loading up suspects and perjury.

Accordingly, there is a strong possibility of, and perhaps tendency to, moral arrogance, moral insularity and the application of unethical principles, inherent in noble cause corruption.Noble cause corruption is both dangerous in its own right and likely to be at least in part self-serving. In short, while acts of noble cause corruption are by definition not motivated by individual (or narrow collective) self-interest, in so far as they are habitual actions, they are likely to be indirectly linked to, and in part sustained by, self-interest. Indeed, this conceptual claim of an indirect connection between noble cause corruption and self-interest seems to be supported by empirical studies. Police who start off engaging in noble cause corruption often end up engaging in common or garden, out and out corruption.[23]

---

[22] Delattre op. cit. in effect makes this distinction between instances of noble cause corruption and genuine moral dilemmas.

[23] See Justice James Wood, *Final Report: Royal Commission into Corruption in the New South Wales Police Service* (Sydney: NSW Government, 1998).

CONCLUSION

Corruption of any sort is incompatible with the establishment and maintenance of a safe, just and tolerant society. A society that is policed by venal and corrupt police officers can be neither just nor safe. For even those who have bribed the police cannot be sure of their services, which remain open to the next highest bidder. On the other hand, a police service which decides that the criminal justice system is itself corrupt, and that the police must avoid, bend or break the rules in order to address criminality effectively, is of equal danger to the citizen, although the motives of the police are of a different order.

The paradox of tolerance

There is a paradox about the word tolerance itself that needs to be examined and resolved. We expect the police to be intolerant of crime and disorder. On occasion, we believe it appropriate for them to use condemnatory moral language: for in a sense, they are speaking for the public themselves. Let us suppose that the innocent and helpless have been slain in order to carry out a robbery, and a police officer is using the mass media in appealing for information. Under those circumstances, he may be entitled to speak of the wickedness of the act, the negative impact upon his own feelings at the scene of the crime, and the need to apprehend its perpetrators before they can do further harm. *'What sort of people could do this?'* he says—and we agree. But anyone who is apprehended in connection with the crime must be treated with full respect for their human rights, including the presumption of innocence before conviction; and the police officer must not allow his intolerance of a wicked act to prejudice his behaviour towards its perpetrators, whether before or after conviction.

We do not expect police officers to be moral automatons, unsusceptible to the feelings of ordinary people. Indeed, part of the genius of policing by consent is that its operatives *are* ordinary men and women, recruited from the public whom they serve. But they are ordinary men and women with extra responsibilities: and whilst we expect them to carry out their duties, on occasion, with that extra element of commitment that is created by moral outrage—for they would be less than human if they did not—we do not expect that outrage to lead to institutionalised intolerance. Police officers, like nurses, doctors and priests, may have strong feelings about the attitudes, values and behaviour of those whom they serve. But those feelings cannot be allowed to prejudice behaviour in such a way as to corrupt the wider process of which their duties are a part.

REFERENCES for *Chapter 12*

Bittner, Egon (1975), *The Functions of the Police in Modern Society: A Review of Background Factors, Current Practices and Possible Role Models*, New York: Jason Aronson.

Commission to Investigate Allegations of Police Corruption and the Anti-Corruption Procedures of the Police Department (Mollen Commission), *Commission Report*, New York: City of New York, 1994.

Wood, J R T (1997), *Final Report of the Royal Commission into the NSW Police Service* (4 vols.) Sydney: RCNSWPS.

CHAPTER 13

Creating a Safer *and* More Tolerant Society: The Means is Already to Hand

Robert R Sullivan

The author presents a lively and challenging perspective of British society and its values. In his view, the way to make Britain both a safer and more tolerant society is already clear. It is not a question of whether change will occur, but when.

It is best to start in midstream by noting that Britain is already a reasonably safe, just and tolerant society. No doubt Britain could be made *more* safe, just and tolerant, but by the same token changes in its institutional arrangements could make Britain *less* so. Or, to continue in the same random fashion, making Britain more safe might be achieved by making it less just and less tolerant. Or making Britain more tolerant—let us say of political asylum seekers—might make Britain less safe in respect to terrorism. The point, in any case, is that we need to be careful in fixing a society that is not broken.

But first a nod to Nietzsche: we cannot discuss such values as *safety, justice and toleration* without taking up a perspective on them (Nietzsche, 1967, III 12). There is no such thing as 'the state' as such. Every modern state is accompanied by a directional adjective, therefore *fascist* Italy, *communist* Russia, or *Islamist* Iran. For its part, Britain embraces a complex history and also comprises a society of persons who embody often conflicting values and so a warning about simplification is in order here as well. There is no Britain as such and so gaining a perspective on it will not be an easy task.

Once these warnings are posted, we also need to note that in recent decades Britain has become a more *liberal* society, and liberal in some conflicting senses of that term. Margaret Thatcher launched a social revolution designed to overturn the values of the previous welfare society that had characterised industrial Britain. Property ceased to be collectively or state owned and tended to become private (or privatised), the explosion of automobile ownership being the chief example—to the demise of the state-owned railway system. In other words, Britain became a market society as never before, and the official and common sense understanding of safety, justice and toleration changed greatly.

But Britain also became liberal in the American sense of that term, seeking above all, and sometimes disproportionately, to secure the rights of individuals and collectivities. As a result, the value here called *tolerance* not only increased its market value but also changed its meaning from mere tolerance toward inclusivity. There was a time, perhaps as recently as 50 years ago, when the British state would not have traded much of the currency of *safety* to gain an increase in its stock of *tolerance,* but since the MacPherson report on the murder of Stephen Lawrence, the British state has admitted its deficit in the area of tolerance and made efforts to catch up. Arguably, the British Government has succeeded remarkably well, raising the question whether it has not become too politically correct.

But still, Britain is unlikely to pursue any of the three values named in the title of this chapter if that is to be done at too great a cost to the others. Like the famous trinity of life, liberty and property, the values *safety, justice and tolerance* may not lend themselves to trade-offs with a self-conscious and outspoken populace. They are jealous gods. This is what it means to say that Britain is a complex society. Adjustments, maybe, but no wholesale changes. But before we even speak of adjustments, let us take a look at each of these liberal gods in turn.

SAFETY

Thomas Hobbes posited a society of atomised individuals who could create binding social arrangements only by consent ([1693] 1991, Ch. VIV). He called this naturally atomised condition the *state of nature,* or war of all men against all men. It was a condition that provided no safety whatsoever and is thus an ideal starting point for the present discussion. In the state of nature, or in a condition of no safety at all, a person is justified in using whatever lethal force is available to him or her, presumably also in advance of any actual threat. So in a condition of anarchy, Hobbes' solution is kill-or-be-killed, shoot first and ask questions later, or feel justified in acting pre-emptively. Let us not quibble over the details but rather posit such a condition as a convenient starting point for grasping the mechanics of liberal society.

John Locke was and still is a more interesting liberal philosopher than Hobbes because he posited the attainment of the elusive Hobbesian value of safety and thus made room for a discussion of justice. Locke confirms what Hobbes had already told us and what common sense tells us, namely, that safety takes priority over justice and that without safety there will be no justice to speak of. How exactly Locke does this is of great interest because it tells us that crime is something of an advance on war. By this I mean that Locke (1962, Chapters II, III) also has something called the *state of nature,* but it is nothing like that condition in Hobbes' writing. The Lockean state of nature is rather a situation in which the danger of criminal attack is of prime importance. Given that there was no formal policing in Locke's seventeenth century vision of society, he assigned the policing power to every law-abiding individual, and such a power amounted to the right to kill a thief, the assumption being that the act of theft on a dark London street in the last decade of that century was likely to include the threat of murder: 'Yer money or yer life, mate'.

Now a key question arises and quite naturally: if Locke or someone else actually creates a police force, does it follow that the individual citizen has forfeited the right of self-defence? The question looks absurd at first glance. 'Of course not,' is the most natural reply. The police are seldom present at crime scenes and so in the circumstances Locke describes, an individual accosted by a thief would be fully within his or her rights in exercising self-defence. But let us in any case put a paper clip on this problem, because it will come back to bother us before long. Let us now move on to our third and last position.

A century after Locke, Jeremy Bentham advanced the debate about the place of safety by putting forth the notion that the force used in self-defence should be proportionate to the threat. Bentham actually didn't raise the issue so directly, he rather associated *proportionality* with punishment, but we can easily make the jump and associate it with self-defence (1988, Chapter IV). Bentham was an enlightenment thinker, borrowing from Cesare Beccaria (1986), the Italian utilitarian, and his passion was not just for discovering the mechanisms of liberal society but also for making such a society itself a mechanism. Bentham's most famous version of his passion for mechanism was his panopticon prison, based on the idea of a manipulation of forces to achieve maximum efficiency. A framework for the issue of safety then follows:

Hobbes	Kill or be killed
Locke	Use lethal force in response to a real threat
Bentham	Use proportionate force in response to a real threat

Now back to the issue of safety, brought to the attention of the British public in 2003 by the refusal of parole to Tony Martin, a Norfolk farmer who had shot and killed one intruder to his property and injured another. On the popular daytime television show *Kilroy* of 16 May 2003, no one said that a homeowner should anticipate burglars and kill them in advance. So there was implied popular agreement that Britain is not now a Hobbesian war-of-all. A few persons said that the force should be strictly proportionate and so there was some support for the enlightenment position of Bentham, but it was noteworthy that the persons who supported this position were few and generally well-fed. They were thus easy to marginalise as well-meaning liberals who could be safely disregarded. The overwhelming majority of the audience thought homeowners defending their property against intruding burglars ought to be allowed to use *dis*proportionate force: enough to frighten the burglars from the property if they had no weapons and enough to kill them if they indicated any weapon.

Why should Britain in 2003 be not much further advanced than Britons were in 1693? The answer I would briefly explore is that thieves are more advanced. Britons felt threatened in 2003 because burglars were perceived to be more in number and more dangerous. Burglary is a booming activity in contemporary Britain. But are burglars more dangerous than ever? That is hard to say. Certainly they are less dangerous than eighteenth century thieves, who routinely threatened people with knives, but thieves and burglars are not the same people. So why are Britons today so jumpy about crime, specifically burglary? The answer I would suggest is precisely the one that is most evident to even the most casual viewer: *television.* Britain is a well-integrated country that has had a genuinely national press for a century, and now possesses a set of television shows that work to nationalise the perception of crime, increase the fear factor in the British public and decrease confidence in the police.

A number of specific issues emerge from these shows. The first is a widespread belief that Britain is awash in crime and that safety has never been lower. To any claim that crime figures for a specific crime category or area are down, a standard response is that the figures are suspect because the books are being cooked, the definitions of crime rigged or the crime displaced. The police themselves are often the first persons to say such things, partly because they themselves are awash in crime reports. One can understand such complaints in

Merseyside (Liverpool) or Avon-Somerset (Bristol), but when they also come from Dorset and Kent police officers, it becomes more understandable that the feeling of British housewives is that crime is everywhere and is threatening home and hearth.

The second issue from these TV shows is that the police are unresponsive. Repeatedly the complaint is heard that when the police are called after a burglary they decline to send a team to investigate but rather limit themselves to taking information on the telephone and giving the complainer an insurance number. So cynical has the public become here that it is now believed that people burgle their own homes in order to claim the easy insurance benefits. So the breakdown in police responsiveness is seen as being itself criminogenic. It leads to an increase in insurance fraud. The interesting aspect of this second issue is that it reinforces the first. If the police are unresponsive to reports of burglary, it is because they are thought to be overwhelmed, and thus police behaviour tends to reinforce the popular belief that Britain is awash in crime.

In fact, the lack of police responsiveness is indicative of another and very different problem. If the British police are ever going to make a difference to crime, then they have to shift resources from one side of the action agenda to the other. They will need to put the bulk of their resources into being pro-active in preventing crime, rather than in reacting to what has already occurred. If the police seek to increase public confidence by reacting to every crime, then they will be drawing resources away from other areas but not achieving much, even in the way of public confidence. The more authentic ideal of the police is to invest in pro-active crime detection, to trust that such action brings down the crime rate and then to hope that public confidence will grow. Note that this formula kills two birds with one stone.

Measuring police performance against a variety of targets

There seems little point in improving police performance in one area if there is a corresponding decline in performance elsewhere—or if it requires a disproportionate investment of resources. Can the Police Service use its resources in a co-ordinated fashion, in order to achieve progress in a number of areas? Indeed it can; and here is the favourite contemporary example. Increase camera surveillance of motorways, hooking the cameras into computers that provide automatic number plate recognition. Two effects are achieved. Conventional drivers slow down and drive more carefully, reducing the high accident rate. Criminals, who often have defective papers or outstanding summonses or are using stolen cars, are either caught or forced from the motorways onto slower secondary roads, thus reducing the crime rate. Values are increased in detection, crime reduction, public safety and public confidence and, if bonus points are given out by those in charge of performance monitoring, in resource usage as well. That's genius policing!

Safety first?

A final note on the British police before leaving the issue of safety. At the end of the day, the police are bureaucrats and as such they respond to Home Office directives telling them what to do. Ten years ago the New York City Police Commissioner told his police department to concentrate upon reducing crime and to ignore public confidence. The police stopped enforcing traffic laws, thus showing no concern with safety in that area. Crime fell. This success caused public confidence to soar and politicians like Mayor Giuliani were delighted.

British politicians are exactly the same as American politicians in caring about public confidence. The difference was that a few New York politicians were willing to let public confidence take care of itself while British politicians are always looking over their shoulders and insisting that public confidence be maintained while taking measures to reduce the crime rate, increase the detection rate, ensure the safety of children on streets and use resources in a reasonable manner. New York's mayor proved to be a risk-taker where David Blunkett is not.

JUSTICE

In modern Anglo-Saxon liberal societies, the issue of justice in what is commonly called the criminal *justice* system is dealt with most interestingly by the nineteenth-century philosopher John Stuart Mill. Mill argues that the only allowable punishment of an authentic liberal society is the denial of its chief value, which is liberty (1989, Ch. I 13). But why should liberty ever be denied to anyone? Because they have done *harm to other persons.* In Mill's formulation, *harm to self* should never be criminalised, which means that suicide—or more accurately, attempted suicide—should not be made a crime. Hurt and harm are two different things. Thus I might hurt you with a slap to the face, but if I haven't harmed you, then no criminal penalties should be attached. The criminalisation of smoking might be considered in a liberal society, but only on grounds of the harm that smoke does to persons other than the smoker, never on grounds of the smoker's own health. Criminal penalties might be attached to the failure of motorcyclists to wear helmets, but only on the grounds that their hospitalisation would do harm to the financial interests of other persons, namely taxpayers: never on grounds of the motorcyclists' own health and safety.

Mill's argument is pragmatic, utilitarian and romantic all at once. For Mill, society is invariably conformist and intolerant of genius, which always appears in isolated cases and needs to be protected precisely because the greatest benefits to society always originate in such corners. It is, therefore, very much in the interests of a free society to draw tightly the limits of criminal law so that free speech and free activities are given maximum protection.

I have begun this section on *justice* with consideration of John Stuart Mill's famous harm doctrine not only because it dominates Anglo-Saxon criminal law but also because it is completely inadequate for the problems of modern criminal justice. In putting all its chips on *harm,* Mill sets the stage for the claim that crimes must have real victims, or else they are not crimes at all.

Victimless crimes?

Fraud

The activity of *fraud* is the classic example of a so-called victimless crime. Defrauding an individual person is of course significantly harmful. But if I cheat on my Inland Revenue forms and systematically fail to disclose significant earnings or hide them by illicit means, then I have stolen from all other citizens in such a way that it will not be noticed by any one of them. If my fraudulent activity results in a benefit of £10,000 but is spread over 60 million Britons, it amounts to a theft of less that two-tenths of a penny per person, and that theft must be spread out over a calendar or fiscal year. Such an amount is far below the harm radar. I have committed a victimless crime.

Fraud as it has been discussed above is a status offence. It distinguishes itself from theft proper because it does not have a clearly identifiable victim. I may say that Jones defrauded Smith of £10,000, but what I really mean is that Jones stole Smith's money in a very clever way. To keep this discussion clean, we do well to treat fraud (as I have described it above) as a theft without an identifiable victim.

The drugs argument

A comparable but more complex crime involves the sale of drugs. The British Government does not prosecute the personal use of small amounts of drugs because any discussion of harm is related to the self and if suicide is allowed by liberal values, then the more gradual harm to the self involved in casual drug usage ought also to be allowed. Sales to strangers in the open drug market are prosecuted because the real or potential harm is to persons other than that of the drug dealer, but we have a problem because the supposed victim is giving his or her consent. We revert to the first example above. If any personal use of small amounts of drugs is not prosecuted, then why should sales of those drugs to the same persons be prosecuted? There is a failure in logic here.

We might argue that the problem with drugs is that the victim is several steps separated from the crime of selling or using drugs. Large proportions of drug users tend to be persons who for one reason or another are dysfunctional. Drug usage relieves their pain, frustration and boredom, but it also makes them more dysfunctional, especially in the economic sense. They therefore begin resorting to street crime to gain the means to support their habits and for convenience we might call them a first category of victim. The second category is more conventional in being shop-owners and businesses that are victimised by theft, old persons carrying home their groceries and having them snatched, homeowners being burgled, car owners having their cars vandalised and stolen, and individuals being robbed of items of personal property like mobile telephones. Even if a person is not a direct victim of crime because he or she takes precautions, he or she is harmed tangentially by being forced to give out extra money for alarm systems, locks and the like. The harm to society as a whole is great.

The problem with victimisation is very different from that with fraud. In fraud cases, the victims do not clamour for justice: either because they do not know they have been victimised, or because their victimisation is so small that they are indifferent to questions of justice. In drug cases, the second category of victims described above clamours for justice from the first category. This is to say that the person who has been burgled, robbed, or compelled to put out large sums of money for alarm systems is enraged or annoyed and wants vengeance against the first category of victims. It very rarely occurs to the second category of victim that the first is also a rather complicated mix of perpetrator and victim. It almost never occurs to the shop-owner to demand vengeance against the wholesale drug dealers who started the problem in the first place.

The problem of organized crime

At this point we begin to sense the shape of a contemporary problem, which is the sheer complexity of criminal activities in modern society or, to put matters in more familiar terms, the problem of organized crime. We all know to varying degrees that modern society has become immensely complex, so much so that it is very hard to trace lines of responsibility and causation through it. Drug crime is sufficiently complicated at the wholesale level to confuse thoroughly the British public, with the result that justice is seldom done. The police know very well that if they are going to combat street crime effectively they must do so by devoting their resources not to that immediate problem, which is symptomatic, but rather to the more causal problem of wholesale drug dealing. This is extremely difficult to do with localised forces operating in places like Suffolk, Hampshire and Manchester. Precisely because those forces are under popular pressure to devote their resources to reducing street crime, new and more anonymous policing operations must be created and kept out of the public's gaze. The chief among these is the National Crime Squad, a force whose chief remit is to combat wholesale drug crime.

What is immediately apparent is that if justice is going to be done in a complex society with organized crime, then complex and remotely organized policing operations must be created. The problem of safety proved to be very elusive, but now we see that the problem of justice is every bit as elusive. It is always satisfying to the public when a notorious paedophile gets what's coming to him or a venal politician is caught out and convicted, but there is little satisfaction when an unknown drug wholesaler in Austria gets arrested and tried in Austrian courts on the basis of evidence gathered and made effective by MI5 working with the National Crime Squad. Yet this is where justice most strongly begs to be done.

TOLERATION

The Stephen Lawrence case raises the issue of institutional racism: or, putting it another way, of systematic intolerance. Stephen Lawrence, a young black man, was murdered by some young white men, pretty obviously for reasons of intolerance. But the real issue of intolerance in the criminal justice system began after the murder, not during it. The police investigation was lacklustre at best and so it did not manage to come to closure rapidly, preventing justice from being done. Very rapidly the issue ceased to be the murder and became the police performance. Charges of racism were levelled at the Metropolitan Police and the case became a national political issue on that basis. The question was: were the police systematically racist? An investigation was conducted. The chief finding was that the British police were indeed institutionally racist, a variation on the theme of *systematic* intolerance.

Insiders and outsiders

This was a case of nonfeasance, in which the police passively condoned the murder of a British citizen because of his skin colour. As a result, there was a rash of *mea culpas* to the effect that there was institutional racism in various police forces and, as a follow-up, the creation of diversity courses to change the attitudes of British police officers at all levels. On the face of it, these courses are beyond reproach, but it is precisely this that makes them most questionable. They aim to change the attitudes of insiders toward outsiders and hope as a result that the insiders will treat the outsiders better and more effectively. If the British police can be brought to understand how relationships work in black or Pakistani families or in homosexual communities, then they will become more tolerant and better police officers.

It is impossible to argue that this approach is mistaken, but it can be maintained that it is systematically flawed and ought to be scrapped for a more effective approach. Let us do this by trying an actual experiment. It has been agreed that the Royal Ulster Constabulary that used to police Northern Ireland was a compromised police force, both because it was too military in character and because it was dominated by Protestant officers. Setting aside the military question, the way to reform the intolerance of Protestant officers would have been to mount a series of courses that gave them greater insight into the workings of the Catholic community. It would be pleasant to say that this would have changed the knowledge base of Protestant officers about a distant outsider group, but in fact Protestants are a minority in Ireland as a whole and being a minority they already know a good deal about the majority. All that Protestant officers have to do is take a Sunday drive across the border and visit persons and places in the Irish Republic. That way they can achieve all the information and understanding they need.

But even if the Ulster Protestants had been made sensitive, a decisive flaw would have remained. The Protestants would have stayed in place as sensitive *insiders*, the Catholics would have been kept in their place as now understood *outsiders*. There would have been tolerance, but a question would have been raised about tolerance itself. A far more satisfactory solution would be to make the outsiders into insiders, for then the issue of intolerance would disappear naturally, and so too would the value of tolerance. There is no way that black and white American soldiers in the same tank can remain intolerant of each other. Their lives depend on their working together and they do in fact work together as a team. They may not like each other as individuals, but these are individual rather than group reactions. Social integration eliminates the issue of tolerance.

Therefore the new Police Service of Northern Ireland (PSNI) decided to be really new by mandating that henceforth 50 percent of its officers be Catholic. This is of course problematic with recruitment, because to make 50 percent of the service Catholic, each recruiting class might have to be 60 percent Catholic or more, and competent fit Catholics might not be so forthcoming in adequate numbers. One solution is just to draft batches of Catholics and let it go at that. Such a recruitment policy was followed in 1922, when the original Garda was made up almost entirely of IRA personnel and the original Royal Ulster Constabulary of Black-and-Tans. The concept behind this procedure is that of the press-gang, or the military draft. The problem is that such a procedure does not fit very well with the emphatic individualism of contemporary liberalism. Thus the Catholics will have to be voluntary recruits.

What the PSNI is doing is not being emulated by other British forces, however. Quite the opposite. Recruitment policies have remained passive, with the result that very few blacks and South Asians have been recruited. But even this formulation is not quite correct. An unstructured recruitment has meant a large influx of females, so that the average probationer class passing through Harrogate or Bramshill is about 50 percent white male, 40 percent white female and ten percent South Asian and black. The white males and females band together easily, so that the South Asians and blacks are marginalised. The result should be predictable: the blacks and South Asians will continue to feel marginalised and leave the forces in large numbers before they have put in five years. The other choice is to stay in for 25 or 30 years and adapt.

There will be a great future for diversity and sensitivity courses and they should work, but they are a little like scotch tape holding together otherwise separate parts of an unintegrated society.

ADJUSTMENTS

There is no need to shift much the judgments asserted in the first paragraph of this chapter. Britain is a pretty well adjusted society, measured in terms of safety, justice and tolerance. Therefore it might be asked why this chapter was even written, but the answer to that should by now be clear. Britain can become a safer and more just society as well as one that can forget about the issue of toleration—if the police create programmes of change based on concepts aired here. There is nothing original in this. Every idea has been thought about by numerous chief constables and criminologists, and there is even a good deal of agreement on them. It is not a question of whether Britain will change, but when.

The British police are a bureaucracy and as such are inclined in normal circumstances to be reactive. Thus they are likely to respond to public opinion and practise much more reactive policing than is desirable if the elusive drug problem is to be dealt with—and to do much more justice to the practitioners of retail crime than to the dealers in wholesale crime, and lastly they are likely to practise adaptive behaviour in respect to social problems of intolerance than to solve those problems. Fair enough, but a writer on the British police does not have to go along with such patterns. In fact the writer's mandate ought to be to state the options clearly and then let the powers that be decide what to do.

REFERENCES for *Chapter 13*

Beccaria, C ([1764] 1986), *Crime and Punishment*, Indianapolis: Hackett Publishing Company.

Bentham, J ([1781] 1988), *Introduction to the Principles of Morals and Legislation*, Buffalo: Prometheus Books.

Hobbes, T ([1693] 1991), *Leviathan*, Cambridge: Cambridge University Press.

Locke, J ([1680-1690] 1962), *Two Treatises of Government*, London: J M Dent and Sons.

Mill, J Stuart ([1869] 1989), *On Liberty*, Cambridge: Cambridge University Press.

Nietzsche, F ([1887] 1967), *On the Genealogy of Morals*, Walter Kaufmann (trans.), New York: Vintage Books.

CHAPTER 14

The Emerging Model of Public Safety Policing

Robert Panzarella

This chapter argues that for some 200 years the mandates and roles of police have been in a constant state of change and that a new mandate and role are emerging now. The distinction between mandates and roles, in simplified terms, is the distinction between what police are meant to do versus what they actually do. Mandates are the functions of police as described in enabling legislation and in police agency documents; roles are the actual activities of police, whether included in the mandates or not. The concept of roles is that police fulfil certain functions in society, assuming that police do not exist, as some works of art might, for their own sake. Somewhat different perspectives have been developed, such as Manning's (1997) view of police as a dramatological expression of governmental control in which various rhetorical devices like 'professionalism' conceal the ambiguity and minor mayhem of social regulation. In dramatological terms, all the world is a stage and even police are merely actors thereon. It is all a show, however serious. But, more for the sake of simplicity than out of conviction, this chapter is set within the staid framework of police mandates and roles, which, upon examination, are in themselves sufficiently numerous and conflicting to occupy a chapter in a book and unsettle an orderly mind.

The evolution of police encompasses the development and adaptation of police organizations but more fundamentally the development and adaptation of the very idea of police in changing social, legal and technological environments. The historical struggle of police to adapt to these environments, which themselves are churning in a dynamic evolutionary process, is an unfinished tale. An evolutionary perspective on police may reveal not only how police have evolved thus far but also the direction in which they are now evolving. This paper points to clues suggesting that police are continuing to adapt, willy-nilly, to changes in the social, legal and technological environment. Out of this process is emerging a new kind of policing, which optimistically may be called 'public safety policing.'

We begin by re-examining briefly the origins of the 'paramilitary' model of police organizations. This will be followed by consideration of the subsequent models that have had the greatest impact on policing, namely, the crime solving model and the business models of policing. A short sketch of other models will illustrate how policing has been modified continually by social developments, critical events and new ideas. Finally, the partnership model for policing in Britain and the new military model of police in the United States will be described as the immediate precursors of an emerging new kind of policing which, hopefully restrained by democratic sensibilities, will be called the 'public safety model' of policing.

ORIGINS OF THE PARAMILITARY MODEL OF POLICE ORGANIZATIONS

Continental origins

When looking for the origins of modern policing in Britain and the United States, the ancient English systems of watchmen, shire reeves, justices, constables, etc. are less relevant than the paramilitary police forces developed on the European continent and in Ireland (see Fosdick, 1969, and Palmer, 1988). Although the French *gens d'armes* at their origins in 1544 were a rural police force with a restricted mandate to control soldiers, they gradually assumed broader roles and eventually became a nationwide paramilitary force with an explicit civilian crime fighting mandate following reforms in 1720. The separate police of Paris were placed under a single *Lieutenant de Police* in 1667; they included a uniformed semi-military armed civil force which encompassed patrol units and investigative branches as well as units attending to a multitude of urban government tasks ranging from street lighting and garbage collection to supervision of markets and food supplies. For about a decade following the French Revolution the Paris police changed their predominant role and became almost exclusively a political police force; but they were reformed and resumed ordinary crime fighting and the wide range of other activities after 1800. A major overhaul of the Paris patrol forces occurred six months before London's Metropolitan Police began their duties in 1829.

Following the French models, in some cases imposed by Napoleonic conquest and in other cases freely adopted, paramilitary police forces were established in Belgium in 1795, in Luxembourg in 1798, in the Low Countries in 1810-11, in Prussia and Austria in 1812, in Italy in 1814, and in Russia in 1815.

The London Metropolitan Police (1829)

Sir Robert Peel adapted the paramilitary model of policing considerably, but we should argue that whilst his force was civil in its appearance and to some extent in its tactics, it was paramilitary in organization and discipline. Peel's Bow Street Runners existed to prevent disorders and certain crimes rather than to apprehend people. One of the main obstacles to creating a civil paramilitary police force in England had been the English hatred of the French institutions of police which concentrated on surveillance, informers and inquiries. Hence, Peel's police were not criminal investigators. The original 1829 General Instructions for the Metropolitan Police enjoined:

> It should be understood that the principal object to be attained is '*the Prevention of Crime*'.
>
> To this great end every effort of the Police is to be directed. The security of persons and property, the preservation of the public tranquility, and all the other objects of a Police Establishment, will thus be better effected than by the detection and punishment of the offender, after he has succeeded in committing the crime.
>
> (Italics in the original. Cited by Stead, 1985, pp. 40-1.)

Application of the London model in the United States

The source of the paramilitary model of policing for the United States was Peel's Metropolitan Police (Fosdick, 1920; Smith, 1949). The Industrial Revolution had the same effects in America as in England. Cities were subjected to spontaneous mob disorders in which property was destroyed and set afire and people were injured and sometimes killed. Several major riots specifically targeted blacks and their property. It was primarily to control mobs that a new police force was needed. Mob disorders led Philadelphia to establish a police force in 1838. In the same year Boston deliberately copied the London model. Riots in New York, in which there had been fatalities, led to protracted debates about the need for a police force and a delegation was sent to London to study the new police force there. The New York State legislature authorised the establishment of a force for New York City in 1844 but the city continued to debate until the next year before reorganizing the existing day and night watchmen groups into a unified police force

The new American police forces were resistant to many aspects of a paramilitary model. Unlike in Peel's force, in the American forces entrance standards were low, training was scant, supervision was minimal, discipline was virtually unknown, prior military experience was neither a prerequisite nor a guarantee of rank, and only the police of Boston were willing to wear any sort of uniform.

The military style became important when organized labour began calling strikes and demanding unionisation of workers. Factory owners funded local police units to be deployed against demonstrating workers, but they also hired private forces such as Pinkertons to crush labour movements. In Pennsylvania the mining companies prevailed upon the state government to establish the Coal and Mining Police to put down a strike, similar to the mine owners' influence on the development of police forces in Wales. When labour unions finally achieved legal status and strikes were also declared to be legal, the need for military style police forces declined. But when an established organization loses its original purpose, whether by historical accident or by its own effectiveness, rather than cease to exist an organization finds new things to do. The military style police forces found new vitality by gradually expanding their role to cover a broader range of criminal activity and public order problems. An archetype of this process was how the Coal and Mining Police evolved into the present Pennsylvania State Police (Johnson, 1981). American policing in general has held onto its military form while changing its purposes and activities.

HISTORICAL DEVELOPMENT OF MODELS OF POLICING

There is no fixed answer to the question: What do police do? From time to time and from place to place the answers have changed. The changing models of British policing have been chronicled, for example, in Critchley's *A History of Police in England and Wales* (1978) and in Emsley's *The English Police: A Political and Social History* (1991). As far as American policing is concerned, a historical approach to the answer is encapsulated in Fogelson's (1977) *Big-City Police.* A sociological approach is exemplified in James Q. Wilson's (1973) *Varieties of Police Behaviors.* Wilson's analysis of police styles may also be viewed as a slice of history, revealing what police were doing in the 1950s and reminding one that different models may coexist in the same police department at the same time. The two on which we shall concentrate here are the crime solving model and the business model.

The crime solving model

In 1842 the Metropolitan Police established its own detective unit, consisting of two inspectors and six sergeants. This was in response to a brutal murder in which the murderer had fled and had to be tracked down (Howe, 1965). Mayne took a special interest in this unit and promoted its growth. This headquarters unit grew very slowly until it was increased to 40 in 1869. In 1862 about 200 officers were made plainclothes investigators in divisional units, which was changed to ten detectives per divisional unit in 1869.

The shift from crime prevention to crime solving accelerated with the expansion of the London Metropolitan Police model of policing to the rest of England and Wales. Smaller communities could not afford to maintain a large police force for the purpose of crime prevention patrol; and it was Rowan himself who declared that 'a rural police was to prevent crime by detecting offenders rather than to prevent it by their actual presence in every village' (*The Times*, 15 October 1850, p. 5, cited in Emsley, 1991 p. 41). Detective units were established in police departments where police detectives quickly won the same bad reputation as private detectives, but at least they provided services without charging fees. Detectives have rarely fitted comfortably into the military style police departments. They have openly maintained the work styles of individual entrepreneurs rather than the operational interconnectedness of a military unit.

The business model

Directly in response to the political model of policing, a business model developed in the United States at the turn into the twentieth century. It was not particularly a model of policing but rather one of all government. Under the name of 'the progressive movement' upper class Americans sought to eradicate corruption and promote efficiency in all levels and agencies of government. The proponents were themselves successful business people. They believed in the new management and public administration sciences.

The management model was itself derived from the military, having an emphasis on leadership invested in a single individual at the top, staff planning, standardised procedures, a clear chain of command and strict accountability. In government affairs, the ideals of bureaucracy reflected these same principles as private sector management. In regard to policing, the explicit intent of the progressives' business model was to destroy the political model. They wanted to eliminate partisan political control of police.

Although police retained some of the veneer of a military organization, they in fact became a civil bureaucracy with the military embellishments retained mostly for role calls and parades. Like businesses, police developed large staff units, specialised units, standard procedures, an official emphasis on paperwork, and a clear command structure. The business model also facilitated the greater utilisation of technology, thereby also fostering the development of the police science model of policing. The implementation of a civil service removed some of the political influence on hiring and promotional systems.

In Britain the Conservative government under Prime Minister Thatcher implemented a business model in the 1970s and 1980s. Unlike the American progressive movement, the British model originated in the government itself.

Other models of policing in Britain and the United States

Besides the paramilitary model, the crime solving model and the business model, there have been many other models of, or influences upon, British and American policing that have flourished for a while and left their mark.

Public order and decorum

In Victorian England and to a lesser extent in the United States police began to play a much broader role in maintaining order in public places. Besides conspicuous use of patrols to discourage criminal acts, police began to regulate matters hitherto ignored, especially matters which might have some vague connection to crime (Palmer, 1988). During the same period legislators also began to criminalise some actions that had been ignored as personal problems or tolerable nuisances.

Political involvement

In the ethnically defined neighbourhoods of nineteenth-century America, police became the political machine as well as the order maintenance force. As the frontline agents of the political machine, the police found their mission expanded to cover a broad range of urban problems such as licensing authorities, election officials, neighbourhood watchmen, health inspectors, building inspectors, providers of soup kitchens and shelters for the homeless, and so on.

The first political involvement of British police was when Police Sergeant William Popay went undercover and infiltrated the National Political Union, where he acted as an *agent provocateur*, even advocating assassinations (Howe, 1965). By accident a Union leader discovered Popay's true identity. Although Popay believed that he had been acting with the knowledge and approval of his superiors, the resulting public outcry led to his dismissal. Still, undercover Metropolitan Police were used to infiltrate the Chartist movement in the 1830s and 1840s. In the 1850s and 1860s uniformed police constables could be seen openly taking notes at political meetings. Political surveillance activities became a constant feature of British policing as the police turned their attention to various groups. These included: refugees from the continent in the 1840s; American based Fenian Irish terrorists starting in 1867; possible anarchists at the end of the century; suffragettes and socialists before World War I; foreigners during that war; and Bolsheviks and fascists in the decade before World War II. But these surveillance activities were in the interests of the central government and provided no rewards for the police officers. Thus, although both British and American police were enmeshed in politics, it was in quite different ways.

Police science

Developments like August Volmer's creation of the criminology program at the Berkeley campus of the University of California, J Edgar Hoover's establishment of the FBI crime laboratory in Washington DC, and police athletic activities for youth were embodiments of the police science idea. The model failed largely due to funding limitations but also because police were unable to do much about the social causes of crime. However, the technological aspects of the police science model have remained a staple ingredient of crime solving.

Professionalism

Fogelson (1977) has described how the notion of professionalism led police administrators to claim that crime is what constitutes police business. Apart from redefining police business in a narrow way, the leading police administrators seemed to give scant attention to what police officers actually did on the frontlines. Like the police science model, the professional model produced some changes, mostly in administration and personnel matters, then spluttered to a halt.

Harassment

While professional police administrators were focusing on the internal organization of police departments, some academic sociologists began to look at what officers on patrol were actually doing. In the 1950s the pioneering studies of Westley (1970), Skolnick (1975) and Bittner (1990) exposed a real but unacknowledged model of policing which is aptly described as a harassment model. Order maintenance and crime control were merged in this sort of policing, and law enforcement was opportunistic. The police officer was essentially an independent agent in charge of controlling an area as he or she pleased, with the power of the law and other police available as support if needed. The principal tactics were harassment and curbstone justice as needed. It became clear that police officers operated mostly as individuals without direct supervision and with minimal direction from superiors. The harassment model illustrates the development of a role with only a vague matching mandate, i.e. maintain order and control crime.

Britain's police in wartime: the model citizen

Amid wartime rubble and human tragedies, constables as individuals assumed a very broad role as model citizens in their neighbourhood beats. It was a time when everyone accepted new and deepened obligations of citizenship and community, and police were expected to be the model citizens. The return of peace brought a return to a narrower police role focused once again on public order and crime control. The same ideology was felt and expressed in American policing at the time, but to a lesser degree.

Law enforcement

The civil rights movement of the 1950s in the United States forced a new law enforcement model on policing, ready or not. When white southern police officers in Birmingham, Alabama confronted old black ladies who insisted on sitting in the front of buses in seats reserved for whites, it was too much of a challenge for traditional policing to survive. These were officers who had grown up in a middle-class southern world where old black women had been their caring nannies, cooks and household helps. It was hard to define these old ladies as public enemies or to use force against them. The officers felt a need to justify their actions by saying that they were just enforcing the law as neutral agents, not being personal. Thus was born a different idea of police as 'law enforcement officers.' Police administrators quickly chirped in that the role of the police was merely to enforce the law, not to question it nor to make up their own laws, and that police would simply enforce laws until the laws themselves were changed.

Police administrators at first denied the existence of discretion. However, the American Bar Association study of police practices (1973) as well as the sociological studies of police in the late 1950s demonstrated that police did in fact exercise a great deal of discretion in choosing which laws to enforce and with how much vigour they were going to act. Faced with the evidence, the administrators admitted that discretion was a reality and defended it as a practical necessity. The shift was reflected in successive editions of the virtual handbook of American police administration, *Municipal Police Administration* (see the discussion of police discretion in the sixth edition, Eastman, 1969 pp. 13-14).

Wilson's models of policing: the service model

When James Q Wilson (1973) made his study of police styles, he found the law-enforcement model side by side with the order maintenance model, the crime control model and a 'service' model. The service model harped on the false but flattering idea that the police were the only people available 24 hours a day to resolve problems of all kinds. People locked out of their houses, people battered by bad weather, and even people with their cats in trees could call upon police for assistance. This model of the police job was limited by the fact that few recruits have any background in service jobs, few have the skills or the interest to help people in dealing with problems unrelated to crime, and crime itself seemed to increase so much in the 1970s and 1980s that most other things fell off the police agenda. Few frontline police officers accepted this model.

Problem solving

An expanded model for policing returned with the realisation that crime itself could not be dealt with effectively one incident at a time. This new model was created largely by Herman Goldstein (1990) under the heading of 'problem-oriented' policing. Problem solving policing aims at reducing crime by identifying and resolving proximate sources of repetitive crimes (see Eck and Spelman, 1987). It makes considerable use of broad criminological concepts, such as the ideas of defensible space pioneered by Oscar Newman (1973). The problem solving model in the United States was anticipated in some respects by the 'unit beat' model developed in England in the mid-1960s, which linked individual police officers to particular beats, encouraging closer community ties and a holistic approach to peacekeeping.

This model suffers from the following drawbacks: police have limited jurisdiction; officers are usually outsiders in high crime neighbourhoods; they tend to lack training in urban problem solving; other agencies are essential but often unco-operative; and there is a tendency to throw out the baby with the bathwater, e.g. solving the problem of crime in a public housing complex by imploding the complex.

Wilson and Kelling (1982) espoused the ideology that police should reduce crime by maintaining maximum order in public places, using problem solving, legal and harassment strategies as needed. 'Broken windows' became the symbol of a high crime neighbourhood out of control. In practice, their philosophy of 'zero tolerance' for minor offences can be applied only in limited areas or for limited periods of time, and so ends up being a cloak for discriminatory law enforcement. This is not so much a new model of policing as a reversion to the older model of crime control and harassment based on a hazy nostalgia for a period of low reported crime rates. Two decades later even Wilson could only suggest that the 'broken windows' notion was an interesting one even if there was, and still is, no evidence to support it (Harcourt, 2001).

Community policing
Conceivably the emphasis on 'community policing' in the United States for the past two decades could be considered a new model of policing (Oliver, 1998). However, it has covered such a broad array of ideologies and practices, some new but mostly old, that it is impossible to specify much about what it means (see Manning, 1984). The common thread in community policing programmes has been at least a rhetorical emphasis on policing as a function of the whole community with police as the driving force. In practice, the principal role of the community in most community policing programmes is to provide information to police. Information is then used to implement problem solving policing or at least to make police more aware of neighbourhood concerns when engaged in traditional patrol activities.

CURRENT MODELS OF POLICING IN BRITAIN AND THE UNITED STATES

The partnership model in Britain
The principal theme in the history of policing in Britain has been the continuous development of central government control over police forces. This is epitomised in a number of parliamentary acts from the 1829 Act establishing the London Metropolitan Police to the Crime and Disorder Act of 1998 which incorporated a new model of policing. Co-operation between various government authorities, including police, was viewed as the key to a safe society. The Act did not assume that police would have to be the lead player in any project.

The idea that crime and disorder can be managed effectively only through collaboration between various government agencies is also one of the basic tenets of 'community solving' policing in the United States. However, in the United States there is no effective mechanism for making it happen. Hence, although this model of policing through partnerships is in the forefront in Britain, it is unlikely to make rapid headway in the United States.

The special operations military model in the United States
Kraska (2001) and others have argued that American police are becoming more rather than less paramilitary.

The accelerated militarisation of police in the United States was already well under way before the terrorist attacks on the Pentagon and the World Trade Center on 11 September 2001, but the pace quickened after that. Local police have been asked to detain and question people without charges but with ethnic backgrounds matching the enemy.

In New York City a judge issued an injunction against police interrogating people in custody about their political beliefs and affiliations and their attitudes towards the current government administration, in the same way as foreign military prisoners from Afghanistan and Iraq were being interrogated in American custody (*New York Times*, 2003).

The American military itself has adopted a business model that makes it more responsive to civilian sentiments than are most American police. The military have objected to their being used for border control, drug interdictions and other law enforcement operations. The police are interested in only the special operations aspects of the military, not the full range of the modern establishment with its mission constraints, controls, proficiency demands and rigorous personnel practices. Furthermore, technology transfers from the military to the private sector, including private security, have been as great as the transfers to police. As a result of these factors, the new military model of police in the United States may have a weaker grip on the future than the public security model to be described here.

HOW MODELS CHANGE

Innovations and evolutions

Models of policing do not supercede one another neatly or entirely. Since Peel's revolution, all other models have built on top of the paramilitary model.

It is possible to conceptualise police models in terms of Kuhn's (1996) distinction in the history of science between relatively minor changes and fundamental reinventions amounting to new paradigms. Wadman and Allison (2004) have suggested that 'the development of American police is filled with paradigm shifts' (p. xi). Peel's military model was certainly a paradigm shift for British and American policing. If other models are considered from the point of view of lasting consequences, the crime solving model, the police science model if considered separately and the business model have altered the course of policing most notably.

Implementation

The models which endure are those which permeate the entire police organization and the broad array of police forces. Those that do not thrive are implemented only locally, or those which, although officially espoused by many police forces, are relegated to special units only or even to only a few individuals in a police force. When models are squeezed into special units it is because either their implementation requires skills which most police officers do not have (e.g. police science, problem solving policing) or the large majority of police officers do not accept the model (e.g. Wilson's service model, community policing).

Implementation of a police model usually requires forceful drive from someone with some kind of authority. Exceptions have probably been the harassment model and the wartime model citizen, both of which had only the authority of the street level police officer to support them. Police leadership was the primary driving force for several models, including the crime solving model, which Mayne especially relished; the public order and decorum model; and the police science model, especially pushed by August Vollmer and J Edgar Hoover in the United States and by Sir Henry Edward and a number of chief constables in England (see Emsley, 1991, p. 143). Leadership was also the impetus behind the professional model championed by Orlando W Wilson and William H Parker; and the special operations military model pushed by mid-level commanding officers of special units in the United States. The principal driving force has been above or outside the police in the cases of Peel's paramilitary model, the political models, the business models, the problem solving model, community policing in the United States driven by federal government funding and the government sponsored partnership model in Britain. One way or another, there have been some identifiable driving forces behind most models of policing.

A rhetoric for change

Changes in the police role have usually been justified in rhetoric, whether or not a mandate existed for them. However, the great changes in policing have occurred with virtually no regard for the public and even despite widespread public disapproval. Peel's model was not the only one to disregard public opinion. The scientific model also encountered general opposition. The idea that police would build archives of data on individuals—physiognomic measurements, then photographs, fingerprints, biographical data, habits of individuals, etc.—raised the spectre of tyranny through technology then as computer databanks and DNA databanks do now (Manwaring-White, 1983). But this did not deter police, who rationalised then as now that only criminals would object.

Likewise, later models of policing paid little heed to the public. The professional model evoked a chorus of public disapproval, among other things for its claim that police should be free of outside control and subject only to self-determination, self-scrutiny and self-discipline. There was also objection that the professional model was a thinly veiled instrument of discrimination, since it would block admission to police by the underclass. But police administrators proceeded to implement this as if it were in the public interest. Similarly, the problem solving model simply assumed that the public would want police to be the ones to take charge of the broad array of neighbourhood problems which might have some connection to crime or disorder. In the problem solving model, sometimes efforts are made to involve the public in implementation of police plans, but they are not asked about the specific goals of police operations or about the appropriateness of police tactics. In the spirit of the professional model, these matters are considered police business, not matters for the public to decide.

POLICE AND PRIVATE SECURITY

Private security is a bigger industry than policing in the United States, and it is still one of the fastest growing. Both in size and in the scope of activities private security has been expanding since the 1960s (Shearing and Stenning, 1983). Private enterprise is the primary supplier of protection to commercial establishments. Business people depend more on private security personnel and privately provided technology than on police. Private enterprise has also been the mainstay of residential crime protection. Police have usually explained their failures in this area by pointing out that these crimes generally occur off the street, out of sight of patrol officers.

Semi-public places such as shopping malls depend almost entirely on private security, beginning with the design of such places and continuing through to the emergency response procedures of the security managers. These places are characterised by very large crowds of people, abundant merchandise on display, vast amounts of cash at hand, but low personal and property crime rates. These semi-public places, like private spaces, do depend on police to respond to crime after it has been committed, and they do find it helpful to have some moonlighting or retired police officers on staff when they want a police response, have traffic or parking problems, or want some special service. Nonetheless, police have a limited, mostly reactive role in providing protection for the public in these areas.

Private enterprise has been less successful in providing personal security to individuals in such completely public places as streets, parks and outdoor markets. Among motorists cellular phones are increasingly common as a security device. So too are satellite based monitoring systems both as security for car passengers who have satellite emergency communications and for the security of a vehicle when left parked. Even with these developments, most people remain dependent upon police to provide personal safety in completely public places they pass through or in outdoor areas where they tarry.

At least until recently, private security has been more open than police to low profile technology for use in everyday contexts. This has meant mostly the use of surveillance cameras, alarms, entry and area defences, scanning equipment, biometric identification systems, global positioning, cell phones and computer based information systems about people and property. For routine security police have relied more on traditional security through a human presence. However, they have been attracted to more high profile technology for non-routine occurrences, such as the military-style armoured vehicles acquired by American police departments during the urban riots of the 1960s and 1970s and the military-style assault gear of all sorts popular with American police officers in the current 'war on crime', the 'war on drugs' and the 'war on terrorism.' Less popular have been the applications of technology to routine crime prevention.

The emergence of a public safety model of policing is much more evident in England than in the United States, and we would suggest that there are a number of reasons for this. Contributory factors would include the following:

- the new economic realities which have forced cost considerations into British policing;
- cost conscious use of private firms to provide consultation and services to police;
- greater interest in science and technology on the part of British police administrators;
- political leadership insisting on multi-agency approaches to problems of crime and disorder;
- a prolonged history of domestic terrorism which can be contained only by a public safety approach;
- increasing population diversity; and
- greater accountability to local authorities and the public.

In the United States, on the other hand, the emergence of a public safety model is an outcome of increasing military and private security influences on traditional policing.

THE PUBLIC SAFETY MODEL

The public safety model of policing has three outstanding characteristics:

- emphasis on the safety of people through risk reduction, including crime prevention;
- increased reliance on technology for routine policing; and
- increased co-operative relationships between police, other agencies and the public.

A major strength of the public safety model is that it breathes new life into old bones. To start with, it revivifies the paramilitary model. For decades students of policing have been saying that the paramilitary model is antiquated and unsuited to the needs of contemporary policing. Indeed, this might be true if the military had remained the same. The classic military model of masses of soldiers moving in orderly formations under the command of generals with diligent staffs and clear chains of command has very little to do with the usual operations of police. But the evolution of military special forces with small self-directing units, individual soldier specialisations, rapid mobility, integration of different forces in operations and even collaboration of military and civilian organizations in mission task forces provides a different paradigm for a new sort of paramilitary model. It is not the classic military model but rather some features of the modern military that are attractive to police today. Although police are most attracted to the tactical operational aspects, the modern military also can provide a new and different model of socially sensitive ideology, complex and flexible organizational structure, and rigorous personnel practices. The modern military offers more than police want, but the fascination with military special operations may create an opening for some additional influence. The public safety model of policing has the potential to preserve the basic paramilitary structure of policing while transforming it.

The primary goal: safety

As far as crime is concerned, the primary goal of the public safety model of policing is to prevent crime. This is similar to the original mandate of the London Metropolitan Police but contrasts with the subsequent primary goal of apprehending offenders. It is not necessarily a matter of one goal excluding the other, but of which goal is primary. The public safety model, like the problem solving one, is concerned with criminogenic situations more than with individual incidents. But it is particularly focused on anticipating these situations rather than reacting to incidents afterwards. In the public safety model a police officer might be apt to stop more people not because they are suspicious but because they are at risk.

The mentality behind public safety policing is very much like that of private security. One cannot imagine a private security director in a shopping mall engineering a situation to facilitate shoplifting, robbery or drug dealing in the mall in order to catch someone committing the crime; the security emphasis is on prevention, not on apprehension. Causing crimes in order to prevent crimes has become a popular part of American policing despite the failure of such tactics to impact on the overall problems of drugs, rape, robbery or whatever the crime. 'Stings' of various sorts are popular because of the emphasis on catching offenders rather than preventing the crimes. It remains unclear whether such apprehension tactics actually reduce crime, increase it or make no difference. The dubious impact of a fencing sting to combat burglary is a case in point (Langworthy, 1989).

Manning's dramatological view of police provides a more accurate view of such tactics than any crime fighting model.

Prevention is less alluring to action prone police officers and less newsworthy to publicity hungry police, prosecutors and politicians. In addition, crime-provoking tactics are a way for frustrated police to go beyond the rather limited and ineffectual tactics of traditional crime fighting. Police will say that no other tactics are so effective, meaning that no other traditional police tactics are so effective.

Consider the difference in goals in a situation such as the kidnapping of a business executive for ransom. The traditional criminal apprehension mentality will urge tactical responses aimed at freeing the hostage and capturing the kidnapper simultaneously. However, if the company has its own risk management team with private security specialists, its priority probably will be to secure the release of the hostage. They may choose not to involve police at all if they fear that the officers will place a strong emphasis on capturing the kidnapper. If they do choose to involve police (like the victim of a domestic robbery making a similar choice), they may want to insist upon tactics that pose no danger to the kidnapped person, although once they involve police they lose control. Their attitude is likely to be that any attempt to apprehend the criminal must come later, after the victim is entirely safe.

The interest of police in criminal apprehensions and convictions often imposes costs on victims (lost time, lost money, increased personal endangerment, etc.) which victims may find unacceptable. They tend to make an informal costs/benefits analysis which police more often omit in the single-minded pursuit of arrests and convictions. Victims sometimes judge that they are likely to be more victimised by the police than they were by the original criminal (Symonds, 1980). The organizational and personal interests of police often conflict with the interests of crime victims in reactive models of policing. To some degree such conflicts may still occur in a public safety model. However, to the extent that this model shifts the emphasis from arrests and convictions to preventing future crime and victimisation, the organizational goals of the police and the public may be more congruent. Clearly, the public safety model of policing is more than a tactical change; it is also a change in goals, roles, values and attitudes.

Creating an environment and culture conducive to public safety requires concern about other hazards and risks in addition to crime. The hazards and risks of motor vehicle and pedestrian traffic are an established part of policing, although concern has often been limited to cautioning or ticketing individuals for individual violations. Police need to take a larger role in traffic regulation and management both at the planning level and at the operational level. Similarly, they need to become more responsive to building, sanitation, environmental and other hazards. This does not mean that they should take over the functions or supervision of other regulatory agencies. Most police forces still preserve official channels and procedures for bringing matters to the attention of these other government agencies. A public safety model requires police to strengthen and utilise such links with other agencies even if their own role may be more co-operative than controlling.

Increased reliance on technology

The public safety model makes more use of technology and requires more technological competence of officers than does traditional policing. The most conspicuous technological developments have been in the areas of computer information systems and surveillance systems

Americans are sometimes surprised to learn that in some city centres in England there is comprehensive camera coverage of the area, so that a person or a vehicle can be followed (or traced backwards) throughout the city centre and along access routes. In keeping with the private security model, this is conspicuous monitoring, not hidden cameras, with conspicuous signs as well as the highly visible cameras themselves so that they function primarily as preventive tools and only secondarily, albeit quite effectively, as apprehension tools. They have reduced crime by two-thirds in these central city areas at the same time as the number of police officers assigned to the areas has been reduced to very few.

In the United States many police superiors are reluctant to initiate such a programme openly, although they do use some surveillance cameras covertly, especially to catch traffic violators. This use of cameras springs from the priority given to apprehension of offenders, e.g. use of cameras to record traffic violators, rather than to prevent offences. The covert use of surveillance cameras may have poisoned the waters to some extent, causing police to be less trusted than the private security people who monitor shopping malls and other semi-public places. Although some police administrators may fear a public outcry if they try to use more surveillance cameras, the growing pervasiveness of security cameras in and around apartment buildings, parking garages, residential enclaves and work places, as well as in semi-public places like shopping malls and even inside taxis continues to diminish the public's expectation of privacy in public places.

Global positioning technology has also found applications in policing. Private security has led the way with technology to locate stolen vehicles, provide drivers with traffic and route guidance as well as emergency assistance, and provide fleet owners with real time tracking of their vehicles and more effective routing systems. Police use thus far has concentrated on surveillance of vehicles to which transmitters have been attached secretly. Non-vehicular, personal global positioning systems have been used for tracking US Drug Enforcement Administration agents operating in Mexico. Computerised information systems and satellite tracking systems, such as package delivery companies use to monitor their vehicles continuously in the field, have great potential for enhancing operational command and routine control of police resources, and to impact upon the effectiveness of police responses. Some police forces have already implemented vehicle tracking systems but the vast majority have not. Officer resistance as well as costs have impeded this development.

The public safety model of policing also makes much greater use of computer information systems to enhance public safety. These are very useful for carrying out continuous 'crime analysis' of the sort usually done by police to monitor the occurrence of crime. Computerised data are much more amenable to searching for patterns in crimes on a timely basis, whether they be patterns in types of crime, offender characteristics, victim characteristics, *modus operandi,* places or times of occurrence or other aspects of crime. But beyond these data specifically related to past crimes, computer information systems can more fully and in more timely fashion keep track of public safety data with regard to traffic conditions, public events, neighbourhood resources and potential problems. It is possible to tie into other databases, e.g., a utility company's records of where there are neighbourhood residents on life-support systems.

The most striking development in forensic science has been the technology related to DNA analysis. Traditional policing has made use of forensic science, but to a very limited extent and in a deplorable fashion. Under-funded, under-equipped, under-staffed crime labs have been notorious for their ineptitude in handling and analysing physical evidence (Peterson, 1983), making it difficult to have confidence in their science or courtroom testimony. However, DNA testing technology, while not infallible, so constricts the interpretative range of the technician and involves so many points of comparative analysis that the probability of errors is dramatically reduced, bringing forensic science more in line with the ordinary standards of science. Furthermore, investigations based primarily on DNA are usually less intrusive or abusive and more conclusive. Investigations based on DNA evidence help to obviate the acquired dependency on the crime-solving tactics of deception, intimidation and blackmail.

In many places direct linkages between police and private security already exist. A growing number of police departments have set up their own websites, which have virtually unlimited potential for enhancing effectiveness. In some places certain types of crime victims, such as burglary victims, can already file their own reports with police via the internet.

Increased collaboration with other agencies and the public

Collaboration with other agencies and the public is not only a prerequisite for public safety policing but also possibly a source of it. In collaborative relationships it may be other agencies and the public who insist on a public safety emphasis, more than the police—who may be conditioned by their history and culture and constrained by their present organizational structure and technology to view matters more in terms of crime and crime solving. Other agencies may have a broader view. For example, an agency charged with responding to the needs of youth may take a wider view and seek a more comprehensive approach than a police force. Indeed, a police force might be accused of going beyond its role and mandate if it were to put forth a comprehensive programme on its own. But working in partnerships enables police, and others, to engage in broader, systemic problem-solving legitimately, and prods them to do it.

A public safety model of policing requires collaboration with private agencies as well as other public agencies. Police agencies have long recognised the advantages of co-operating with religious leaders in addressing problems of youth, the elderly, homeless people and so on. It is fairly common for police to have collaborative relationships with private security agencies that monitor alarm systems in business premises and residences and those that monitor anti-theft global positioning systems in vehicles. In return private security consulting firms have provided tools and skills to enable police to be more effective in protecting people, places and things. It is common for corporate headquarters, industrial complexes, utility facilities and transport enterprises to have full and immediate access to police response systems and for them to provide police with information for public safety and emergency planning. Many police forces are quite dependent on various private organizations to provide resources and participate in joint strategies to prevent man-made disasters and to respond to emergencies. In addition, private organizations have tended to be generous in transferring technology to police agencies. Collaboration is more than compliance or staying out of one another's way; it is mutual co-operation.

Finally, a public safety model of policing requires greater collaboration between police and the public. Police still do not favour direct involvement of the public in crime solving or thief catching. However, they may be more willing to share responsibility for more mundane tasks of public safety. In New York City's summer 2003 electrical blackout, when traffic signals went dark along with everything else, citizens took the initiative on their own. They took over most traffic control and gave assistance to individuals physically or psychologically unable to cope with the confusion and physical paralysis of everything from the city's lights and elevators to the subway system, while most police personnel massed in strategic locations and waited for something else to happen. Under the best of circumstances police alone would not have been able to handle the situations. Under even the best of routine circumstances, they cannot create the environmental and social conditions to minimise crime and other risks to public safety.

CONCLUSION

The mandates and roles of police continue to change, at times in response to new ideas about society or government, at other times in response to social unrest, new technology or extraordinary events, sometimes embossed by forceful personalities. There is no line of logic connecting all the changes, although each succeeding model of policing has its own logic. Similarly, there is no continuity in whose interests are being served, although each model of police serves someone's interest. One might like to believe that the models which produce 'the greatest benefit for the greatest number', as the philosophers Beccaria and Bentham proposed, are the models which spread farthest afield and last longest, but there are many things one might like to believe. One might argue that the police had their finest hour when World War II transformed their role into the police officer as model citizen. One might also argue that the ideal police model was the purely fictional one of the television character PC George Dixon: whose 434 episodes fashioned the image of the Bobby as the wise, helpful and efficient maintainer of the peace and who, even in American minds, stood not only for police but for England. But PC Dixon made more impact on the public than on the police.

One might object, rightly, that the Enlightenment ideal of 'the greatest good for the greatest number' assumed a homogeneous society. In a heterogeneous society it is a formula for oppression, for, as both Beccaria and John Stuart Mill (*On Liberty*) observed, the tyranny of the many can be more cruel than that of any despot. The problem in regard to policing is to develop a model that can create a safe society that is also just and tolerant. In the United States following the 11 September 2001 terrorist attacks, one sees a national government, acting with the assumed consent of the majority of the people, redefining the role of police in pursuit of a safe society but at the cost of a just and tolerant one. One reads of people arrested without charges, held secretly, confined and interrogated with methods not far from torture. One reads of confessions prompted by threats against prisoners' families, fuelled by ethnic stereotypes, with unprecedented pressure from national officials on local police forces to participate in these operations which were considered repugnant in a democratic society until that fateful day. Some police forces refused to co-operate, citing legal objections, but many citizens and police did set aside concerns about justice and tolerance in pursuit of safety. It remains to be seen whether one can have safety at the cost of justice and tolerance, or whether safety becomes all the more elusive without the other two.

A more positive aspect of the current anti-terrorism hysteria in the United States is the new appreciation of public safety as broadly defined. Although the new rhetoric of policing about creating a safe society may be especially aimed in the United States at reducing risks of terrorist acts, it requires a greater awareness of the total environment than traditional police concern with criminal apprehension: and a greater reliance on the public as participants in policing society. Decades ago, IRA terrorist acts in Britain also led to greater police powers and threatened to undermine traditional notions of justice and liberty. But with time and reflection, the responses of government, police and the public have developed into concern for public safety in a much broader sense and to a greater awareness that only the public can create a safe society.

British and American policing sometimes converge and sometimes go their separate ways. Sometimes they assume the same form but at different times in history, so that one could compare the early twentieth-century American progressive movement with the late twentieth-century Thatcher reforms in Britain, or the Victorian model of police as guardians of public order and decorum with a recent American model based on the theory of 'broken windows.' Despite such apparent randomness, there are indications that a new model of policing may be emerging in both Britain and the United States. In Britain the national government is promoting core components of a public safety model of policing. In the United States some of the core components are being promoted through the models of problem solving policing and community policing and some through national initiatives under the banner of 'homeland security.' The new model may be more evident, more refined and better articulated in Britain, but developments in American policing are aimed in the same direction, even if they are less thought out and seem to be overshooting the mark at this time.

In summary, the new model of policing may be aptly called a 'public safety model' of police. Its primary characteristics are:

- emphasis on reducing risks to public safety, including crime prevention;
- increased reliance on technology; and
- increased collaborative relationships with other organizations and with the public.

This new model includes a mandate for police to engage in a broader range of activities related to public safety. The way in which this new role is carried out will determine whether it forges a closer bond between police and the public or whether it alienates them. If the pursuit of a safe society is done though activities which also show concern for a just and tolerant society, then, to cite the Peel's Police Act of 1829, 'The security of persons and property, the preservation of the public tranquility, and all the other objects of a Police Establishment, will thus be better effected.'

REFERENCES for *Chapter 14*

Adlam, R and Villiers, P (2003), *Police Leadership in the Twenty-first Century: Philosophy, Doctrine And Developments*, Winchester: Waterside Press.

American Bar Association, (1973), *The Urban Police Function*, Chicago: The American Bar Association.

Bittner, E (1990), *Aspects of Police Work*, Boston: Northeastern University Press.

Blumberg, A S (1967), 'The Practice of Law as a Confidence Game,' *Law and Society Review*, Vol. 1, pp. 15-39.

Critchley, TA (1978), *A History of Police in England and Wales*, revised edition, London: Constable.

Eastman, GD (ed.) (1969), *Municipal Police Administration*, 6th ed., Washington DC: International City Management Association.

Eck, J E, and Spelman, W (1987), *Problem-solving: Problem-oriented Policing in Newport News*, Washington DC: Police Executive Research Forum.

Emsley, C (1991), *The English Police: A Political and Social History*, New York: St Martin's Press.

Fogelson, R M (1977), *Big-City Police*, Cambridge, MA: Harvard University Press.

Fosdick, R B (1920), *American Police Systems*, New York: The Century Company.

Fosdick, R B (1969), *European Police Systems*, Mountclair, NJ: Patterson Smith.

Goldstein, H (1990), *Problem-Oriented Policing*, New York: McGraw-Hill Publishing Company.

Harcourt, B E (2001), *The Illusion of Order: The False Promise of Broken Windows Policing*, Cambridge, MA: Harvard University Press.

Howe, Sir R (1965), *The Story of Scotland Yard*, London: Arthur Barker Ltd.

Johnson, D R (1981), *American Law Enforcement: A History*, Saint Louis, MI: Forum Press.

'Judge Criticizes Police Methods of Questioning War Protesters', *The New York Times*, 8 August 2003, pp. B1, B4.

Kraska, P B (ed.) (2001), *Militarizing the American Criminal Justice System: The Changing Roles of the Armed Forces and the Police*, Boston: Northeastern University Press.

Kuhn, T S (1996), *The Structure of Scientific Revolutions*, 3rd ed., Chicago: University of Chicago Press.

Langworthy, R H (1989), 'Do Stings Control Crime? An Evaluation of a Police Fencing Operation,' *Justice Quarterly*, Vol. 6, pp. 27-45.

Manning, P K (1984), 'Community Policing,' *American Journal of Police*, Vol. 3, pp. 205-27.

Manning, P K (1997), *Police Work*, 2nd ed., Prospect Heights, Illinois: Waveland Press.

Manwaring-White, S (1983), *The Policing Revolution: Police Technology, Democracy and Liberty in Britain*, Brighton: Harvester.

Newman, O (1973), *Defensible Space: Crime Prevention through Urban Design*, New York: Macmillan.

Oliver, W M (1998), *Community-Oriented Policing*, Upper Saddle River, New Jersey: Prentice Hall.

Palmer, S H (1988), *Police and Protest in England and Ireland 1780-1850*, Cambridge: Cambridge University Press.

Peterson, J L (1983), 'The Crime Lab,' C B Klockars (ed.), *Thinking About Police: Contemporary Readings*, pp. 184-98, New York: McGraw-Hill Book Company.

Shearing, C D and Stenning, P C (1983), 'Private Security: Implications for Social Control,' *Social Problems*, Vol. 30, pp. 493-506.

Skolnick, J H (1975), *Justice Without Trial: Law Enforcement in a Democratic Society*, 2nd ed., New York: Wiley.

Smith, B (1949), *Police Systems in the United States*, New York: Harper and Brothers, Publishers.

Stead, P J (1985), *The Police of Britain*, London: Collier Macmillan Publishers.

Symonds, M (1980), *The 'Second Injury' to Victims, Evaluation and Change*, special issue, pp. 36-8. Minneapolis: Minneapolis Medical Research Foundation.

Wadman, R C and Allison, W T, (2004), *To Protect and to Serve: A History of Police in America*, Upper Saddle River, New Jersey: Prentice Hall.

Westley, W A (1970), *Violence and the Police: A Sociological Study of Law, Custom and Morality*, Cambridge, MA: The Colonial Press.

Wilson, J Q (1973), *Varieties of Police Behaviors*, New York: Atheneum.

Wilson, J Q and Kelling, G L (1982), 'Broken Windows: The Police and Neighborhood Public Safety,' *Atlantic Monthly*, March, pp. 29-38.

CHAPTER 15

Fundamental Principles: Seven Conditions for a Safe, Just and Tolerant Society

Peter Villiers and Robert Adlam

In our view there are seven requisites for a safe, just and tolerant society each with its implications for policy. Although inter-dependent and not wholly distinct from each other, they can usefully be described separately. We present them first in summary and then in extended form, with comment on their implications for policing.

A safe, just and tolerant society is made possible if the following seven conditions are met:

- it is an open society;
- it practises pluralist democracy;
- it is governed by the rule of law;
- it upholds human rights and fundamental freedoms;
- it expresses an active and shared concept of citizenship. Its members cannot be so selfish, egotistic or simply self-absorbed as to be indifferent either towards the welfare of others or the common good. They have duties, responsibilities and obligations as well as rights, and go beyond tolerance to show care and compassion for others;
- in recognition of human fallibility and the continuing need to strive for virtue, it places an emphasis on education in the fullest sense (e.g. Benn and Peters, 1959) including education in the rights and responsibilities of citizenship. Education develops the capacity for informed and rational decision-making, and thereby reduces ignorance, prejudice and fear. The educated person is able to resist indoctrination and see through propaganda; and
- finally, a safe, just and tolerant society needs to recognise the necessary limits to toleration and to have a fair, impartial and effective means to control intolerable behaviour.

AN OPEN SOCIETY

'An open society'[1] is Karl Popper's phrase (2002), and we are pleased to acknowledge our continuing debt to the work of that outstanding thinker. It emphasises the need for informed choice by educated and responsible citizens who have access to the information that they need in order to play their proper part in the decision-making process. Popper believes that a closed society, such as a dictatorship, is of necessity less efficient than its democratic counterpart, and that it is only through what may appear on occasion as the confusion of democracy that proper choices can be made. An open society:

- encourages freedom of thought and expression, generally forbids censorship and questions the premature assumption of consensus;
- maintains a healthy scepticism for official propaganda; and
- protects the mechanisms whereby democracy itself is safeguarded: thus an elected assembly cannot vote itself into becoming a dictatorship.

The key to an open society is, therefore, that it maintains free institutions, and is thereby more effective in problem-solving than its totalitarian and authoritarian counterparts. As Magee puts it in his guide to Popper (1973):

> The common notion that the most efficient form of society, in theory at least, would be some form of dictatorship is on this view utterly mistaken. That the dozen or more countries in the world that have the highest living standards (not that this would be Popper's main criterion) are all democracies is not because democracy is a luxury which their wealth enables them to afford; on the contrary, the mass of their people were living in poverty when they achieved universal suffrage. The causal connection is the other way around. Democracy has played a vital role in bringing about and sustaining high living standards. Materially, as in other ways, a society is practically bound to be more successful if it has free institutions than if it does not.

A PLURALIST DEMOCRACY

Democratic rights are exercised not only through the mechanism of a parliament or assembly containing the elected representatives of the people, but also through a plethora of other means, including the pressures exercised both by formal and informal organizations, whether lobbying for a single issue or many; and through the expression of individual opinion alone. Protest and opposition can and should take place on the streets as well as in the representative chamber or by means of judicial review. Rioting is intolerable—although, judiciously controlled, it need not lead to insurrection. The vigorous expression of opposition, on the other hand, is both desirable as a constitutional ideal and of practical necessity in a working democracy.

Here, we think it appropriate to make reference to Richards' (2003) recent work for the Council of Europe. He reminds us that, overall, 'democracy is a great good'. Moreover, he points out that this claim may be vouched for by an appeal not to theory but to experience. Thus, most of those who have sampled any one of democracy's alternatives will need little convincing of its merits. Except where majorities become tyrannous, democracy tends to maximise individual political freedoms, such as freedom from slavery, freedom from abject want and poverty, and freedom of speech and expression—all of which are conditions of democracy's own flourishing. Free speech is far more likely to produce a general spread of true opinion than is any suppression of it, principally because all men and women are fallible. The faith of the democrat is that, through an open climate and forum for debate, good ideas will drive out bad. Furthermore, it is sometimes claimed that the exercise of reason and choice educates and improves the intelligence of the population.

A pluralist democracy accommodates the conflicting interests that, under other circumstances, have no other recourse but to violence, insurrection, riot and civil war. This further implies the peaceable transition of governments and, consequently, the avoidance of revolutions. Furthermore, democratic systems of government tend to promote the greater prosperity of the larger community, which is in itself a good.

Although the proper realisation of the rule of law is theoretically possible in constitutions other than democracies, the ethical consensus that constitutes the essential condition for its existence is hard to achieve outside them. One example of the ethical consensus that underpins the rule of law is the restraint shown time and again by people with intense grievances. They do not usually resort to the extreme levels of violence that are potentially available to them, because they accept the fundamental legitimacy of the system and believe that their grievances will at some point obtain redress.

THE RULE OF LAW

Despite Newman and Laugharne's précis (1985) we have noted in our long association with police that they tend to have an inadequate grasp of the signal importance of the rule of law. We must add to that generalisation, our certainty that the great majority of police officers are convinced of the importance of discretion, and rightly so: for in our view the proper use of discretion by the police is not only commensurate with the rule of law, but an indispensable adjunct to it. (By corollary, the improper use of discretion by police or other state officials is a body blow not only to those individual police officials and the force they represent, but also to the rule of law itself.)

Again, as Richards (2003) has underlined, the rule of law is probably 'the most civilised and least burdensome conception of the state yet to be devised'. It is a form of state in which no power can be exercised except according to procedures, principles and constraints contained in the law, and in which any citizen can find redress against any other person, however powerfully placed, and against the officers of the state itself, for any act which involves a breach of the law. In carrying out their duties, police need to respect human rights and freedoms and to avoid arbitrary or unlawful actions.

This is fundamental to the meaning of the rule of law and therefore to the whole meaning and purpose of police duty in a democracy. Above all, the rule of law requires that those who make, adjudicate and apply the law should be subject to the self-same law that they both apply and uphold. After all, as citizens out of uniform, this is exactly what they too would expect. This condition is the best and most secure guarantee that the public has against unlawful and arbitrary activities by the police; it is the 'gold standard' of professional policing for police officers themselves.

RESPECT FOR HUMAN RIGHTS AND FUNDAMENTAL FREEDOMS

The United Kingdom includes under the phrase 'human rights' at least some of the social and economic rights that are included in the Universal Declaration of Human Rights (1948), as well as the constitutional rights incorporated in the European Convention On Human Rights (1950), and which are especially concerned to protect the citizen's life, liberty and privacy against the real or potential depredations of the state. The state, in other words, has so-called positive obligations, as well as negative ones. It has an obligation to provide for the welfare of its citizens, as was recognised in the creation of the 'welfare state'—although it has since been recognised that state ownership or direction is not the only way to provide a necessary level of welfare for the populace. However, the aim remains, and no modern state will retreat to a minimalist position and cease to care for the education, housing and health of its citizens.

So far as the police are concerned, the key to human rights is a full understanding of the meaning of the principle of proportionality, and a proper application of this principle in practice: a theme to which we shall return.

ACTIVE CITIZENSHIP, BASED ON A RECOGNITION OF HUMAN FALLIBILITY

As Rousseau famously and pithily observed 'man is a mixture of both generous and selfish impulses'. In his celebration of the remarkable achievements in science, art, technology and social organization Bronowski (1983) rightly highlighted the positive gifts with which humanity is endowed. However, like Rousseau, he also hinted at the intransigence of human weakness. That we are creatures of limitations has been underlined by Warnock (1971) in his discussion on the object (or function) of morality. Warnock identifies five such limitations to which we are subject: sympathy, co-operation, rationality, imagination and information. We find it difficult to disagree with his analysis. The implication for the construction of a safe, just and tolerant society is clear. We need to combat these limitations through an array of methods. Paramount amongst these is the development of an educated and active citizenry.

As members of a democratic society we have responsibilities and duties as well as rights, as every state acknowledges. Our most threatening potential obligation is that of compulsory military service, to which all states, democratic and non-democratic alike, have resorted in time of general war: but there are other and less dramatic obligations that affect us in our everyday lives, such as taxation.

Our responsibilities as citizens stretch far beyond our legal obligations to the state, and extend to our relationship to the community that surrounds us and of which we are a part, and which requires our active support and participation in order to function properly. We may serve the community as lay magistrates, special constables, retained fire fighters, lay visitors to police stations, prisons or hospitals, or in a kaleidoscope of other ways, both formal and informal, all of which are essential in maintaining the positive link between citizen, community and state that is vital to an open society. Such service has, moreover, an independent value in reminding the trained, full-time, and professional servants of the state that theirs is not the only way to serve the common good.

This leads us to the question of the achievement of a multi-cultural society. Here we believe that there is no national consensus as to what needs to be done, and a clear need for a more open and honest debate on the subject, in which the police service can play its part.

Multi-culturalism and national allegiance are not by definition opposites. There is no reason, in principle, why any citizen should not be subject to more than one affiliation or source of loyalty, provided that fundamental priorities are recognised. We may be a cricketing enthusiast, Zoroastrian, water-colourist, divorcée and accountant, without necessarily causing any great difficulty either as to our conception of what we owe to the state or local community, or what that state or community owes to us—particularly if that larger community exercises a benign and judicious tolerance towards those of our activities or beliefs that may conflict with the practices or norms of the majority, but do not cause harm to others. But there are other loyalties that may cause greater divisions, and where in the end we shall have to decide whom we are, and where our fundamental allegiance lies.

THE NECESSARY LIMITS TO TOLERATION

The most significant power of the police is the monopoly of the use of legitimate force within the United Kingdom, including where necessary the application of lethal force. It is the police who have both authority and power to stop, control or prevent intolerable behaviour by some members of the public towards others. Traditionally, the British police refer to this as keeping the Queen's Peace. If that peace has already been disturbed, then it is the police who have both duty and power to investigate any such breach, and to put in place the process which will culminate in the bringing of the offender to justice.

When should that power be used? In John Stuart Mill's beguiling view, the only purpose for which the state is justified in interfering in the liberty of the individual is to prevent harm to others. As Robert Sullivan pointed out earlier in this volume, Mill's classic definition of liberal doctrine gives rise to problems. For example, the use of force cannot be justified on Millian grounds in regard to addressing so-called victimless or consensual crimes, as there is no immediate and tangible harm to others—and yet these crimes must be addressed. Moreover, there are areas of criminal activity of which ordinary members of the public are either unaware altogether, or which they regard as of very low priority for action, compared with their immediate concerns: but which, law enforcement officials will argue, are of strategic concern.

On practical grounds, many so-called victimless or consensual crimes may not need the use of force, in order for their perpetrators to be controlled. Riot police use or threaten force: fraud investigators scrutinise accounts and seize assets. Where force is needed, we would argue that the language of human rights gives us some possibility towards a moral clarification of the proper use of police powers. The citizen has certain rights, some absolute and some qualified, which the police official must respect. There is no possible justification under human rights doctrine, for the violation of absolute rights and fundamental freedoms, such as freedom from torture. Qualified rights may only be violated where the police action can be justified in accordance with the doctrine of human rights.

That doctrine may sound abstract—legality, necessity and proportionality are indeed abstractions—but they are easily charted in reality, as the police officer who contemplates the use of disproportionate force in arresting a burglar should know. The ordinary citizen, who has had no special training in the use of force, and may have been woken up in the middle of the night by strange and alarming sounds downstairs, may be given a greater latitude in the use of force by the jury than the trained and accountable officer of the law: and rightly so. For the concept of what is reasonable will vary according to the circumstances of the case.[2]

THE USE OF FORCE WITHIN THE CONTEXT OF THE SOCIAL CONTRACT

The inhabitants of certain states of the United States of America are permitted, under state law, the use of lethal force in the protection of their homes. That is not the case in the United Kingdom, where the use of force must be 'reasonable', and some citizens acting to protect their homes have been charged with murder: the Norfolk farmer, Tony Martin, being a conspicuous example .[3]

Why do British citizens accept that their ability to protect themselves, their possessions and their loved ones should be so severely circumscribed? We would suggest that there are two main reasons. Firstly, there is some sort of moral consensus, we believe, that the use of extreme force should be very severely circumscribed in society as a whole; and that there are no crimes which merit summary execution. Secondly, however, there is perhaps a more compelling reason, at least as far as the police are concerned. Citizens are prepared to cede certain duties to the police, including the use of lethal force—*provided that the police are perceived to be generally effective in the use of that ceded power.*

Let us put it as simply as we can. If the police protect us, our lives, welfare and property, then we have no need to shoot burglars or other violators of our well-being, even supposing we could bring ourselves to do so. If, for whatever reason, the police fail to provide the necessary level of protection, then we must ultimately question the continuation of the social contract that has failed in its essential purpose. In that sense, and to adapt the language of human rights in which we have so far placed such reliance, let us put our case thus. The police have a qualified and not an absolute right to a monopoly of the use of legitimate force within the United Kingdom. That right has been ceded to them and could be taken back. The inhabitants of a small, densely populated and generally peaceable society would no doubt be extremely reluctant to acquire personal firearms, train in their use, and open fire on burglars, rapists and muggers when their judgement told them that it was necessary to do so. But the situation is not inconceivable.

In depicting this conundrum, we believe that we have isolated its essential element. The use of force is, in some deep sense, both uncivilised and repugnant. On the whole, we should prefer the police to act on our behalf, to make the necessary legal and moral decisions in our place, and to live with the consequences of the deed. (What would be better still, of course, would be to prevent the need for the use or threat of force in the first place: a point to which we shall return under the concept of public safety policing.) In the United States, with its frontier traditions and right of the citizens to bear arms enshrined in the constitution, the private use of force may seem on occasion both necessary and even noble: but there is not the same association in the United Kingdom.[4] When we learn of an isolated farmer waiting up at night to protect his property against invaders, we may consider his life, in Hobbes' classic description of the life of man before the social contract was agreed, as being nasty, poor, solitary and brutish, if not necessarily short: and we may feel neither condemnation nor admiration, so much as pity.

POLICE VIRTUES

We argued in our book on police leadership (2003) that good police leaders needed to be trustworthy, open, honest, fair and compassionate, and to shine by their integrity, genuineness and warmth. We linked their moral virtues to those elucidated by Frankena (1973) and agreed the need for a sentimental education in their development (Rorty, 1992).

Aristotle pointed out that any virtue, if carried to excess, becomes a vice, and that the proper site of any virtue is the 'golden mean' between excess and deficiency. Thus courage is the golden mean between recklessness and cowardice; generosity is the golden mean between meanness and extravagance; and so on.

Similarly, we should argue that the cardinal virtues of policing need to be cited on a golden mean—whether those virtues be associated with an individual police officer or the occupation of policing itself. Thus, discretion fits between the extremes of rigid automatism—all laws must be enforced on all occasions, an impossible and indeed self-contradictory ambition—and dereliction of duty on the part of the police officer. Similarly, virtues such as loyalty, solidarity, diligence and obedience are all admirable, if placed within the golden mean. If carried to excess, they transmute into vices. Thus the cardinal virtue becomes the proper cultivation and use of judgement. This in its turn requires professional knowledge, independence of mind and confidence in oneself, practice in the exercise of discretion, and the capacity for sympathetic imagination into the minds and motives of others to which we have already referred under Frankena. It also requires that the state should regard the achievement of proper policing as a long-term investment, requiring the cultivation of disinterested virtue. In practical terms, this means that the police officer must not be under the immediate direction of the state and its functionaries, but have a certain degree of independence—although in the United States, at least, this has been able to be reconciled with the tradition of local democracy under which the local chief of police is elected.

POLICING AND HUMAN RIGHTS

Francesca Marotta (2000), an international human rights specialist in the Office of the UN High Commissioner for Human Rights, comments on human rights training for police as follows,[5] as a result of a 1992 UN review:

This review revealed a number of flaws in traditional human rights training for the police, which can be summarised as follows:

- An excessively theoretical approach, both in style and content—due to the use mainly of academics to deliver the training, and the exclusive use of lectures as a pedagogical technique;
- An emphasis on the negative rather than the positive—for example, by admonishing that police shall not use torture, or police shall not use excessive force, without providing information on professional police investigation, interrogation, crowd control or other techniques that can assist police in performing their duties without resorting to violative practices;
- A lack of emphasis on the practical implications of human rights norms for police duties and functions—deriving from the focus of the training on only general notions of human rights, and resulting in the failure to reveal to police trainees the relevance of human rights to their work;
- Distance and cultural and professional barriers between trainers and trainees—an inevitable result of the above elements.

Marotta continues:

> One of the first issues that the (UN Commission) had to deal with was the need to demystify the concept of human rights and to address the perception that human rights is something antithetical to effective police practice for law enforcement ... Human rights norms include the concepts of legality, accountability and the establishment of relations of confidence with the community—all implicit in the notion of modern and professional police forces.

Experience in consulting with the leading police officers from all over the world who have beaten a path to the door of Bramshill Police Staff College, leads us to agree whole-heartedly with the message expressed above. Since the United Kingdom incorporated the Human Rights Act into UK national law in 2000, the editors of this text have talked to, trained or consulted with senior police and government officials from: Mexico; Indonesia; Spain; Rwanda; Pakistan; Sri Lanka; Sierra Leone; the former Soviet Union and the Baltic States—to say nothing of the global compass of police officers attending the long-established International Commanders' Programme. From all sides, the message is the same. Police officers want usable advice and guidance, rather than high-flown rhetoric: although it may sometimes be necessary to raise the strategic level by referring to the wider consequences of unexamined patterns of behaviour and traditionalistic methods of command and control.

Dorothy Bracey, formerly a professor at the John Jay College of Criminal Justice, New York, argues in a perceptive if perhaps self-consciously optimistic article (2003), that the police could and should play a more active role in the area of human rights:

> Police can take an active part in the ongoing debates and procedures that formulate the definition of human rights in the particular time and place in which they serve. In many societies, police have avoided or even been barred from taking part in the political process. Removing the enforcers of the law from the process of making the law they enforce is often seen as a protection of human rights. But asking police to

participate in the conversation is not necessarily the same as asking them to lobby the legislature. It is asking them to place their particular knowledge and expertise at the service of those who struggle to balance competing interests with competing definitions of human rights.

Police are the interface between the bodies that make laws and the people upon whom they are enforced and it is their actions which turn legal statements into events that influence the well being and even the lives of members of the community. Consequently, it is the police who are often the first to be condemned if their actions ... are perceived to deny certain individuals their human rights. For this reason, police have the right and the responsibility to make themselves heard as the laws are being composed.

THE PUBLIC SAFETY MODELAND ITS MERITS

The public safety model of policing has three outstanding characteristics:

- an emphasis on the safety of people through risk reduction, including crime prevention;
- increased reliance on technology for routine policing; and
- increased co-operative relationships between police, other agencies and the public.

In our view, this contrasts with the ethos of the intelligence-led model of policing which although currently in official vogue in police circles has not attracted universal support. The official whose primary concern is for public safety does not set out to trap offenders, once an offence has been committed. Still less does that official set out to engineer a situation in which a suspected offender is offered an enhanced opportunity to commit an offence, so the bait is taken and the fish caught. The public safety concern is to prevent crime from occurring in the first place.

Public safety and the open society

Policing in public safety style is, we would assume, more easily pursued on private space than on public land. Contrast a busy high street with a purpose-built shopping mall: clearly, the latter is easier to police. (Indeed, we could easily argue that it does not need the permanent presence of a public police service at all, no matter how efficient and highly trained.) In the mall boundaries are secure; access is controlled; rules may be relatively easily enforced; evidence (from CCTV systems, for example) is usually available, and the concomitant invasion of privacy necessitated by surveillance causes relatively little public concern, in the United Kingdom at any rate. Moreover, the mall may eject tramps, beggars and drug addicts, or other citizens or non-citizens of whom the more respectable members of society would not approve, and whose company, in even the most remote sense, they would prefer not to share.

But a shopping mall is not a microcosm for an open society, and ease of achievement in the promotion of public safety is not the only criterion for the establishment of a just and tolerant community. An open society is not an exercise in conformity and deference to professional judgement: nor can it substitute the development of technology for moral choice. In an open society the police must be able to argue their case and demonstrate their virtue in the marketplace, in order to achieve a position of policing by informed consent. Indeed, under some circumstances we might imagine the police officers themselves putting the case for inclusivity rather than exclusivity, in regard to fostering the development of a living community.

CONCLUSION

In *Chapter 3* Edwin Delattre argues that the police service necessarily imposes exceptional demands upon those who choose to accept its discipline. He refers to:

> The tradition that calls upon all who bear positions of public trust to live up to higher intellectual and moral standards than are required of other citizens and residents ... In giving authority and powers that the rest of us do not have to public servants, we gain a reciprocal right to hold them accountable to fulfil their duties wisely, competently, and honourably.

Professor Delattre is a realist, and does not suppose that every citizen is predisposed to virtue. To the contrary, he states:

> Every jurisdiction of any size contains people of shockingly different and conflicting values, from devoted parents and law-abiding citizens to shrewd, manipulative, and violent predators; from benign and altruistic adults to practising paedophiles and rapists; from the fair-minded and responsibly respectful and tolerant to the remorselessly bigoted and cowardly; and from those who want to cooperate with and rely on police to those who would prefer, for reasons of self-interest, to corrupt them. Police have to deal with many people who are as vociferous in asserting their rights as they are in denying their duties ... Popular opinion, human passions, factional interests, and fashionable values can be and frequently are fickle, unwise, unjust, and unreasonable, and sometimes perverse and cruel.

These truths are worth stating, for it would be foolish indeed to devise a blueprint for a safe, just and tolerant society which took no cognisance of human nature. But such a view of human nature need not inspire a Hobbesian pessimism:

> Police should through sustained engagement in their communities aspire to live up to the high standards of judgement, duty, and conduct that follow from the Constitutional and legal foundations of their own authority. In practice, the most effective forms of policing ... are matters of leading, not merely following or reacting; and they succeed when police earn and come to possess, by their exemplary conduct and by the consistency of their words, policies, and deeds with the rule of law and the ideals of integrity, service, and concern for public safety, the trust and co-operation of a significant portion of the public.
>
> Often, police need to teach citizens and other residents how to work together to improve social conditions and how to co-operate with police to solve persistent problems. In so doing, police can sometimes lead and also reinforce the public in creating and implementing informal social controls that prevent disorder, limit intolerable behaviour, and reduce vulnerability to crime. Many achievements in modern policing confirm these facts, although even the best and most thorough efforts on the part of police do not always succeed ...
>
> Sometimes succeeding against all odds, police draw law-abiding residents into the arts of self-governance and self-reliance; they enable the public to engage in and

understand participatory democracy by acquiring a voice that goes beyond voting and serving on juries; they encourage both youths and adults to respect the rule of law and decent public behaviour; they help to illuminate and bring the values of civility to life in and for the public; and by patient teaching and listening, they help residents to overcome the grinding fear that attaches to ignorance and helplessness.

Policing has been described as a Sisyphean task. It is easy to see why the analogy is of appeal, but it is a misleading one. Sisyphus pushed the same boulder up the same hill, only for it repeatedly to roll down again. In the struggle of humankind against the intractable forces of nature, nature will always win. In the struggle of the community against the forces of criminal oppression, injustice and intolerance, transformation is always possible.

REFERENCES for *Chapter 15*

Adlam R and Villiers P (2003), *Police Leadership in the Twenty-first Century*, Winchester: Waterside Press.

Benn, S I and Peters, R S (1959), *Social Principles and the Democratic State*, London: Allen and Unwin,

Bracey, D. (2002), 'A Cross-cultural Consideration of the Police and Human Rights', *Police Quarterly*, Vol 5, No. 1, March, pp.113-122.

Bronowski, J (1983) ,*'The Ascent of Man'*, London: BBC Publications.

Frankena, W (1973), *Ethics*, Englewood Cliffs, NJ: Prentice Hall Inc.

Magee, B (1973), *Popper*, London: Fontana.

Newman, Sir K. and Laugharne, A. (1985), *The Principles of Policing and Guidance for Professional Behaviour*, London: Metropolitan Police.

Popper, K (2002), *The Open Society and its Enemies*, London: Routledge.

Richards, N. (2003), 'Policing's Noble Cause', *Merengue*, October, National Police Library, Bramshill House, Hook, Hampshire, UK.

Rorty, R (1997), 'Human Rights, Rationality and Sentimentality' in Ishmay, M (ed.), *The Human Rights Reader*, London: Routledge.

Warnock, G. (1971), *The Object of Morality*, London: Methuen.

---

1 In Popperian terms, the desire for an open society is not a utopianistic ideal, but a means to articulate how to set about preventing its opposite. As Karl Popper argued, utopianistic social engineering tends to fail, since we cannot predict the future and all actions must have unintended consequences. But this does not mean that governments (and police services) must abandon positive intent. Rather than promote virtue, then, it might be argued that the best way forward is to attack vice, on which there may be a greater agreement as to both ends and means. The motto of the Home Office as addressed in this spirit might then be to reduce insecurity, rather than to promote safety; to rectify injustices, rather than to promote justice; and to reduce intolerance, rather than to promote tolerance. The rectification of glaring and generally recognised injustices is less likely to lead to unintended consequences than utopianistic engineering, whether socialist or otherwise. However, a negative slogan has less impact, and we suspect that the Home Office motto will survive.

2 The relationship between reasonableness and proportionality is not something of which we should wish to offer a complete definition in a sentence. Let us simply say here that reasonableness is a broader category than proportionality, and that the human rights emphasis on the principle of proportionality does not render reasonableness otiose. Indeed, a jury might decide that under certain circumstances, it would be unreasonable to expect the potential victim of a crime of violence to have kept the principle of proportionality uppermost in mind.

3 This case, already discussed in *Chapter 13*, continues to arouse interest: see www.tonymartinsupportgroup.org

4 We might point out that some at least of the examples of frontier violence as dramatised by Hollywood concern the use of force by law enforcement officials in dire circumstances, rather than by the private citizen—although he or she may have become a member of the *posse commitatus* for the occasion.

5 Marotta, F. (2000) , in *Peace Building and Police Reform*, T. Holm and E. Eide of the Norwegian Institute of International Affairs (eds.), London: Frank Cass.

Index

Covert Policing
An Introduction to Surveillance Law
Denis Clark

Covert policing allows law enforcement agencies to obtain evidence and information without the cooperation of the suspects. This age-old practice has burgeoned in recent years, driven by modern developments in policing. The technique is now principally governed by the Regulation of Investigatory Powers Act 2000. This book is both a guide to the 2000 Act and to the use of surveillance - human and technical. It covers the interception of telephone and internet communications and the monitoring of financial or computerised transactions plus controversial data protection and exchange provisions and genetic monitoring.

ISBN 1 904380 12 3. Scheduled for 2004
172pp (approx) Waterside Press direct mail price £18

Principled Policing
Protecting the Public with Integrity
John Alderson

'John Alderson has the credibility to develop a cohesive philosophy of policing which he does with such distinction in this highly readable text. Aspiring senior police officers should find his work to be an inspiration': *Police Journal.*

1998 ISBN 1 872870 71 6. 192pp Waterside Press direct mail price £18

The Criminal Jury Old and New
John Arthur Hostettler

An absorbing account of the jury from its origins to the present day. This book deals with all the great political, social and legal landmarks and shows how the jury has evolved - and survived to become a key democratic institution resisting attacks, pressure, interference, controls, legal imperatives and on occasion plain law or compelling evidence. Linking the past and present, **John Hostettler** conveys the unique nature of the jury, its central role in the administration of justice and also its importance as a barrier to manipulation and the abuse of power.

ISBN 1 904380 11 5
Scheduled for 2004. 150pp (approx) Waterside Press direct mail price £16.50